MANAGEMENT OF DESIGN ALLIANCES

MANAGEMENT OF DESIGN ALLIANCES
Sustaining Competitive Advantage

Edited by

Margaret Bruce
UMIST

and

Birgit H. Jevnaker
Foundation for Research in Economics and Business Administration, (SNF), Bergen

JOHN WILEY & SONS
Chichester · New York · Weinheim · Brisbane · Toronto · Singapore

Copyright © 1998 by John Wiley & Sons, Ltd.
Baffins Lane, Chichester,
West Sussex PO19 1UD, England

National 01243 779777
International (+44) 1243 779777
e-mail (for orders and customer service enquiries): cs-books@wiley.co.uk
Visit our Home Page on http://www.wiley.co.uk
or http://www.wiley.com

Other Wiley Editorial Offices

John Wiley & Sons, Inc., 605 Third Avenue,
New York, NY 10158-0012, USA

Wiley-VCH Verlag GmbH, Pappelallee 3,
D-69469 Weinheim, Germany

Jacaranda Wiley Ltd, 33 Park Road, Milton,
Queensland 4064, Australia

John Wiley & Sons (Asia) Pte Ltd, Clementi Loop #02-01,
Jin Xing Distripark, Singapore 129809

John Wiley & Sons (Canada) Ltd, 22 Worcester Road,
Rexdale, Ontario M9W 1L1, Canada

Library of Congress Cataloging-in-Publication Data
Management of design alliances / edited by Margaret Bruce and Birgit
Helene Jevnaker.
    p. cm.
    Includes bibliographical references and index.
    ISBN 0-471-97476-5 (cloth)
    1. Product management. 2. Design, Industrial. I. Bruce,
Margaret. II. Jevnaker, Birgit.
HF5415.15.M2697 1997
658.5'752 – dc21   97–12957
                                                              CIP

British Library Cataloguing in Publication Data
A catalogue record for this book is available from the British Library

ISBN 0-471-97476-5

Typeset in 10/12pt Times from authors' disks by Dobbie Typesetting Limited, Tavistock, Devon
Printed and bound in Great Britain by Biddles Ltd, Guildford and King's Lynn
This book is printed on acid-free paper responsibly manufactured from sustainable forestation, for which at least two trees are planted for each one used for paper production

CONTENTS

ABOUT THE EDITORS

Professor Margaret Bruce
Professor Margaret Bruce is a Professor in Design Management and Marketing in the Textiles Department, UMIST. Over the past ten years, she has carried out major research programmes in the area of design management, all of which have been independently funded by the Economic and Social Research Council (ESRC). Three books arising from the research are *Winning by Design* (co-authored with Vivien Walsh, Robin Roy and Stephen Potter, Basil Blackwell: 1992; *Product Development* (co-edited with Wim Biemans, John Wiley: 1995); and *Design: Making Marketing Strategy Visible* (co-authored with Rachel Cooper, Thomson International: 1997).

Margaret Bruce has developed a Design Management course for marketing students and practitioners at UMIST and this has provided a model for University courses in Hong Kong and the US. She has been a Senior Visiting Research Fellow at the Design Management Institute and Harvard Business School.

Birgit H. Jevnaker
Birgit H. Jevnaker is, from 1998, an Associate Professor of Business Development in the Strategy, Language and History Department at the Norwegian School of Management, Sandvika. At present she is a senior Research Fellow at SNF, Bergen (Foundation for Research in Economics and Business Administration, co-founded by the Norwegian School of Economics and Business Administration, NHH) and also a Senior Lecturer in Market Strategic Design at the Department for Industrial Design, Oslo School of Architecture. Jevnaker has an Economics Degree, Sivilökonom (MScBUS) and has pursued doctoral studies in Administration at the NHH based on previous studies in Psychology and Public Administration & Organisation at the University of Bergen. From 1977 to 1991, she was a Research Fellow at the

institute of Industrial Economics, where she conducted several research programmes in various fields typically linked to competency, entrepreneurship, human resources and industrial economics. Her research has been grounded in close contact with industry and organisations and she has served as a consultant (e.g. for the Development Corporation between Norway and the Government of India, 1983–88). Most of her current research concentrates on the relationships between internationally working companies and design expertise as an example of the new knowledge-based competition. In 1995–96, Jevnaker completed a study on this in collaboration with the Norwegian Design Council and an official report (initiated by the Ministry of Industry and Energy) underlining industrial design as competitor factor for industry has arisen from this research. She is currently investigating design contributions in an information-strategic environment financed by the Research Council of Norway. Jevnaker also teaches a set of courses specially developed to relate design to business (e.g. design management, strategy and organisation, marketing and culture). Her articles are published in international journals, conference proceedings and books. Jevnaker is also a member of the international Executive Committee of the European Academy of Design (EAD).

CONTRIBUTORS

Dr Karen Freeze
Dr Karen J. Freeze is currently Visiting Lecturer in Design Management and Product Development in the Faculty of Economics and Business at the Technical University of Liberec, Czech Republic, where she taught as a Fulbright Lecturer in TUL's Engineering Faculty in 1995–96. Dr Freeze is a Research Fellow of the Design Management Institute in Boston, where she served for five years as its first Director of Research. Having learned the craft of case study development in the 1980s at the Harvard Business School, she has since written case studies on design management in both the US and Europe. Since the establishment of the International Forum on Design Management Research and Education in 1990, Dr Freeze has been active in the design management education community in Europe. Dr Freeze came to design and technology management from East European history, and finds that the recent trend towards cross-disciplinary thinking and teaching suits her well.

Professor Kiyonori Sakakibara
Kiyonori Sakakibara has recently been an Associate Professor of New Product Development at London Business School where he also researched design issues. He was previously Professor at Hitotsubashi University in Japan and is currently at the Keio R&D. Sakakibara has also contributed to valuable comparative research on design trajectories in Europe and Japan, and on product design-based competition in emerging markets for high-tec products such as for the personal data Assistant. He is the author of several books and co-authored the well-known US Japan comparison of strategy and organisation "Strategic vs Evolutionary Management" with Kagano, Nonaka and Okumura.

Dr Antti Ainamo
Antti Ainamo is a lecturer at the Department of Management, at Helsinki School of Economics and Business Administration. He has recently finished his

doctorate on industrial design and business performance including the longitudinal empirical case investigation of a Finnish fashion firm, Marimekko. His research centres on the complexities and linkages between design investments and business performance, and brings nuance and explorative investigation to the promotional premise that 'design' breeds 'success'. Part of his research work was done while he was visiting London Business School Centre for Design Management. In addition to fashion design, Dr Ainamo has also, in collaboration with Finnish and Japanese colleagues, published on product development strategies in the emergent product market of Personal Data Assistance.

Barny Morris

Barny Morris is currently working as a Design Counsellor for Business Link, a government funded network of one-stop shops for business advice. His role involves giving business advice on design and innovation related issues to small and medium-sized companies, raising design awareness and providing a focal point for the local design community. In a previous role he was a Research Associate for the Manchester School of Management, UMIST. During his time there, he graduated with an MSc in Marketing and contributed to the development of design management theory and research. Before this he worked as a product designer.

Dr Lisbeth Svengren

Lisbeth Svengren wrote her dissertation about the integration of design as a strategic resource. She participated as Case Researcher in the Triad Design Project, a global design management research project, initiated and managed by the Design Management Institute in Boston. She is now consulting on design management and has a position as lecturer at Stockholm School of Business, Stockholm University, where she teaches marketing and design management. She leads the development of 'Design and Culture' as a division within the Marketing department. She is also Head of Research and Education at the Swedish Industrial Design Foundation which includes the editing of a magazine, *Design Journal*, published biannually.

Dr Tore Kristensen

Dr Tore Kristensen is an Associate Professor of Product Development in the Marketing Department at Copenhagen Business School. In addition, he teaches design management-related topics at Denmark's Design School where he has initiated, and is the director of, a centre for design and business development to facilitate research and interdisciplinary learning among design, business and engineering students. Kristensen also now runs the process of change laboratory at Copenhagen Business School, a 'child' of the laboratory established in 1989 at Stanford University by its founding director and well-known designer Sara Little Turnbull. Kristensen's main research interests and publications encompass a broad field of economics, marketing, strategy, design and innovation; his current focus is design and quality in addition to the process of change.

Dr Brigitte Borja de Mozota

Dr Brigitte Borja de Mozota teaches Marketing and Design Management at the Université Paris 5 René Descartes and at the École Superérieure de Design Industrial in Paris, France. As a researcher, she specialises in design management. In 1994, Borja de Mozota was the 'Maitre de Conférences' of the Sixth International Forum on Design Management Education and Research in Paris, organised by the Design Management Institute, Boston, with Groupe ESCP, Paris School of Management, the Université René Descartes and La Chambre de Commerce et d'Industrie de Paris.

PREFACE

This book has arisen out of highly successful collaboration over the past few years between most of the authors, all of whom met through the Design Management Institute in the US. A workshop was held in Norway, hosted by SNF and organised by Birgit Jevnaker, and financed by the NOS-S Joint Committee of the Nordic Social Science Research Council with additional support from the Norwegian Design Council. From this workshop, the contributions to this book have been made. The theme of the book is the role of design in business. It provides theoretical and empirical work undertaken by European scholars to explore the relationships between design and business.

Margaret Bruce
Birgit H. Jevnaker

ACKNOWLEDGEMENTS

The editors wish to express our gratitude for the support and contribution of all the authors; the help and interest shown by the people in the companies and by the design consultants; and by the continued encouragement of friends and colleagues, in particular Professor Rachel Cooper, University of Salford and Dr Lisbeth Svengren, Svensk Industridesign, Dr Tore Kristensen, Copenhagen Business School, Louise Birkeland, Bergen College, Professor Eirik Vatne, SNF/Norwegian School of Economics, Per Hynne, Geelmuyden. Kiese and Professor Per Farstad, Department of Industrial Design/AHO. Financial support was forthcoming from the ESRC, the British Council of Norway, the NOS-S Joint Committee of the Nordic Social Science Research Councils, the Norwegian Research Foundation and the Norwegian Design Council. Mrs Julie McClearn in the Textiles Department, UMIST, prepared the manuscript and her input was invaluable. Thanks must go to our families for coping with late nights and editing "homework": Stephen Glennon, Ivan and Joyce Bruce, Jörund and Erlend J. Straand, Ingjerd and Torbjörg Straand Jevnaker and Torbjörg Jevnaker.

INTRODUCTION

Birgit Helene Jevnaker

Products are the lifeblood of companies, but products become outdated and obsolete. Consequently, firms need to innovate, not just once, but repeatedly, to keep their competitive edge. This book is not about well-designed products as such, but the management of the design expertise needed to develop profitable and user-friendly products. The ability to nurture and protect the advantages created through design alliances is a major theme of this book. Design is acknowledged as a critical source of value and competitiveness of companies. However, the use of design from a business perspective has been neglected. Through extensive cases and examples, the book attempts to provide insights into the strategic management of design.

WHAT IS A DESIGN ALLIANCE?

A design alliance, or design partnership, as it is used in the book, is a collaborative and interactive business relationship between a company and its design resource. The parties to the alliance are mutually dependent in terms of inputs, co-production and rewards (but usually not in terms of ownership). The alliance can represent a knowledge-based alliance of potential strategic importance, if this is recognised as valuable for the firm, and accordingly for the design consultant. The various design talents are considered in relation to the firm's particular business need. In fact, the diverse sources of design expertise and multiple design tools make this a major challenge for firms that want to explore design in relation to their particular business problems.

Management of Design Alliances. Edited by M. Bruce and B. H. Jevnaker.
© 1998 John Wiley & Sons Ltd.

WHAT MAY DESIGN ALLIANCES BRING TO THE FIRM?

The reasons for making design alliances the focus, rather than design in firms, or design companies, are manifold:

Closer access to design expertise. Unique or improved products that differentiate the firm can come out of design alliances. Since design knowledge resides in human experts – it is not fully codified nor easily transferable – firms need to nurture this competence over time. Only a few firms have access to advanced design expertise in-house, and tailor-made design skills are not easily bought, nor quickly developed. One way to building a sustainable design competence is to develop an alliance with design experts.

Managing uncertainty. In general, alliances or other collaborative relationships are seen as beneficial from an economic viewpoint when neither "buy" (classical contracts) nor "make" (through internal resources) are considered to be feasible and efficient. This applies especially to situations in which it is difficult to specify à priori the problem, the procedures and tools needed and the kind of solutions sought. Through collaboration in the design process, the parties may learn to cope with this uncertainty and ambiguity in ways that are fruitful for both. Over time and with more than one project, the firm and its management may be better able to create a productive climate for both parties.

Visualisation and product decisions. Design is a key asset in the era of new knowledge-based competition – that is, where the critical resources are no longer money, buildings or raw materials. In this context, the particular bundle of "invisible assets", or competence resources, as embodied in products and in people (managers, experts, users, dealers etc.) are seen as core sources of competitive advantage. Often this implies critical trade-offs, in terms of design focus. Interestingly, design expertise is an invisible as well as a visible resource and it is a specialised development activity. In addition to creating the meaningful "X-factor" (the character or personality of products) and the suitable interface with the user, design also can co-ordinate other fundamental and complementary resources (technical features, materials, components, marketing attributes, packaging etc.). This is achieved via preliminary outputs, such as product drawings, computer animation and prototypes, that may be seen, discussed, inspected and tested. This potential linking of core aspects of design and its management makes design a powerful competence to possess.

Design – "first mover" advantage. A distinctive design approach in a business setting was a fairly new item on the business agenda in the early 1990s. However, in the current competitive environment of product affluence, globalisation, customer sophistication and new technology opportunities, design is becoming essential in some industries. A design partner may be a possible route to attaining "first mover" advantage.

Access to a flexible but familiar design resource. If firms use professional design infrequently, or do not need design experts in-house, or need an outside creative input, then an alliance with a design consultant may be especially beneficial. A variety of collaborative approaches are feasible and depend on the firms' need for design solutions that are tailor-made or the ease of access to an external design supplier. Long-term relationships with design partners have some advantages (e.g. familiar with client's needs, possess appropriate skills and so on).

Strengthen name and reputation. By investing in design, the firm may strengthen its market position through, for example, brand building and projecting a quality image. This can be a highly valuable asset when recognised and preferred by the customer, dealer etc. Moreover, benefits may accrue from using a highly reputable design company.

Achieving a comprehensive visual image. Design can be co-ordinated so as to encompass products, communications and the overall corporate environment. Using design strategically can bring commercial benefits and serve to motivate and differentiate the company by creating a coherent corporate identity. Building a long-term relationship with the design company may be appropriate where a tailor-made solution and flexibility are required. External designers can help to stimulate new ideas and proffer creative solutions. Over time, the long-term design alliance may be acknowledged as a strategic asset.

DESIGN – A HIDDEN TREASURE

Up to the present time, the contribution of design expertise to business is not well documented. Although some authors trace the historical roots of industrial design back to the birth of the industrial revolution, it is associated mostly with product development in the twentieth century, in particular from the late 1920s. Since then, many products have been created by industrial designers making "everyday" products, in particular in the car industry (e.g. Ford Taurus) and technical appliances for the home and the consumer (e.g. Kenwood's food processors, Braun's and Gillette's razors). "Designed" objects are not necessarily luxury or expensive products (such as Ikea furniture), and their creation may be rooted in a human and democratic dimension (cf. the 50s and 60s vogue for "Scandinavian Design"). Design tends to be more associated with consumer products than with professional tools and machines. Managing design is concerned with diverse knowledge-based specialists that may work, both intuitively and analytically, to create new product qualities and communications. How do company leaders approach and foster creative design work and desirable solutions? What are the ingredients of a successful "design alliance"? How can creativity and novelty, originality, taste or uniqueness be "managed" successfully? Yet some companies compete precisely on their ability to create and market attractive products which serve the users well, not just once, but repeatedly, and co-ordination of design expertise is a crucial factor in their success.

MANAGING DESIGN ALLIANCES

Design is often overlooked in theory and practice as a source of innovation and increased profitability in business settings. Although poorly designed objects as well as "objects of desire" are all around us, few examples exist of design and its management in different types and sizes of companies and in different industries. This book provides both theory and practical examples and guidance about design and business. Based on company cases from different industries and countries, the book focuses on the combined efforts of firms and designers to create new products that have a range of "added values" (e.g. easy to use, aesthetically pleasing, fulfil their functionality, etc.) that may lead to competitive advantages for firms. This focus is, not surprisingly, related to fundamental changes in most firms' competitive environment. The unremitting take-up of new technology and globalisation of markets have changed the dynamics of competition and have brought new challenges for firms that want to take the lead. This book is concerned with one of these challenges: the design of products and communications.

BUILDING UP ORGANISATIONAL CAPABILITIES IN DESIGN

Harnessing the know-how of the external design expertise is a major concern in this book. The notion of the "lone inventor" or "lone designer" is not purported – rather, industrial design is treated as a combination of teams and individual expertise. Part One is concerned with issues about the interfaces between the design consultancy and the firm's own competencies.

Referring to recent literature in product development, strategy and design management, competing through design and development capabilities (rather than resources or products *per se*) is emphasised. A "capability" may be understood as the way resources, talents and processes are combined and used – in this book, the aptitude to foster design as value-creating activities. It is important to identify what this organising capability in design and its management consists of.

Some of the core questions raised in the book are:

- How are design-based advantages created through relationships with designers?
- How do firms even start using designers?
- How may firms organise their new design development to combine knowledge-based efforts, in practice?
- How do some firms design and develop products with the "right" qualities for the market, not just once, but repeatedly?
- How do management, designers and co-developers interact and govern design?
- What is the management's role, and what are the roles of design allies?
- How is work through design partnerships co-ordinated with strategy?
- Do design alliances play an innovative role in the firm?
- How are the new design processes and competencies generated via design alliance sustained?

All chapters in the book bring into focus various aspects and components in managing and co-ordinating design. In Part Two, six cases highlight different issues and show how companies have various capabilities for organising design, although practical examples are discussed in the more conceptual chapters as well.

Designing industrial products is an increasingly challenging task since consumers/users are more sophisticated than ever before and typically have a number of alternative choices. In order to make well-designed and feasible solutions for a successful production and commercialisation, one of the main problems is that of how to discover innovative ideas and to exploit fully the knowledge that resides in the firm's competencies and networks. Typically the firm is expected to brief and assist the designer as well as to mobilise its core development teams and networks in the joint design development.

Contact with design partners often go beyond particular projects. Yet product design and development projects may be the primary engine to build new capabilities in a firm, and it is within this development context that the book explores how design alliances and competencies are managed. Needless to say, the designed products also need to be profitable for the investing business firms, as well as suitable to market and handle for its distributors.

Some firms manage their "design dimension" well, such as the German Erco Leuchten, the Japanese Sony or the Danish Lego. These companies have transformed their product design processes into capabilities that repeatedly provide superior value to customers (although failures also may be visible,

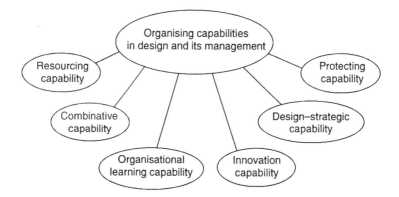

Figure I.I   Organising capabilities in design and its management
Source: Adapted with permission from Jevnaker in *Design Management Journal,* **6**(3), 1995

such as the limited range of Lego toys for girls). Is there a link between the approaches to creativity and management of design in these firms? What can be learnt from these exemplary stories about the organisational and managerial capabilities in design? The nature of these abilities for product creation needs to be identified and Part One of the book provides a conceptual and analytical framework.

In Chapter 1, it is suggested that a firm's design capabilities consist of six component capabilities. These focus on how the firm may source and combine competencies, as well as interact with design expertise to renew its products and communications in a manner that also protects its design-based advantages. The six capabilities are shown in Figure I.1.

DESIGN INTEGRATION: IN-HOUSE, OUTSOURCED OR A MIXED APPROACH TO DESIGN

As design is increasingly outsourced – as part of the wider trend to downsizing and delayering and the creation of "virtual" organisations – the integration of design within the company's strategy and its interfaces with other functions, notably marketing and production becomes critical. Three different approaches to the location of design – in-house, outsourced and a mixture of the two – are discussed in Chapter 2, and the main implications for the management and integration of design are delineated. Examples of each type of design location are provided. Though there is no clear view, it is suggested that design alliances are of particular use in situations with high strategic importance and where a flexible and innovative approach may be called for. Note that design alliances may be highly valuable even when the firm is "design-competent" and its management already has access to internal design resources. For instance, in the dynamic and intensely competitive computer industry, firms combine their in-house design with external sources because they need a creative and entrepreneurial approach to be able to expand, and indeed, survive.

DESIGN CAPABILITY IN GLOBAL NEW PRODUCT DEVELOPMENT

Part Two examines how firms may be capable of designing and developing profitable products with new or improved qualities attractive to buyers and end users in target markets. In all cases, the focus is on the design and business alliance and its ability to harness design. Design expertise emerges as a more or less integral part of the product and business development processes. More interesting is how particular managers, design experts and teams have learned to work together constructively to create a competitive edge.

Six Critical Components of the Firm's Sustained Design Capability

The cases underline the nature of a business firm's design capabilities, i.e. the ability to source design talent, to combine the designers' skills with the firms' core competencies and interact in creative ways with user groups, product engineers and marketers to create profitable products and longer-term competitive advantages. As illustrated by a selected group of business firms and their design alliances from Europe, Japan or the US, this case material-based section provides insights into design as part of the business process. The company cases range from large global corporations (Ingersoll-Rand and IBM) to smaller businesses and design firms in Scandinavia (HAG and Marimekko) to design professionals in the UK. In all cases, the customers' demands are tough and serve as cogent forces on the companies' capabilities to generate more user-oriented products more quickly than previously. One of the main themes is that of creating value through design on a long-term basis. Table I.1 gives an overview of the cases and their capabilities in design management.

CREATIVE CO-ORDINATION OF DESIGN AND BUSINESS PERSPECTIVES

Part Three examines and reflects on the roles of design and business expertise. Firstly, by revisiting the views of industrial design pioneer, Henry Dreyfuss, and his long-standing partnerships with American companies such as Deere,

Table I.I   Overview of component capabilities in organising design and its management

Component capabilities*	Case illustrations
1. Resourcing capability	Sourcing design expertise: Ingersoll-Rand (Chapter 3)
2. Combinative capability	Combining competencies in global new product development: The case of IBM Notebook Computers (Chapter 4)
3. Organisational learning capability	Absorbing or creating design ability: HAG, HAMAX and TOMRA (Chapter 5)
4. Innovation capability	Novo Nordisk AS: Innovative designing for diabetics (Chapter 6)
5. Design-strategic capability	Integrating design as a strategic resource: The case of Ericsson Mobile Communications (Chapter 7)
6. Protecting capability of design-based advantages	Design and sustained competitive advantage: The case of Marimekko Oy, a Finnish fashion firm (Chapter 8)

Source: Jevnaker (1994). From the Outside In: Building Organizational Capabilities in Product Design, SNF Working Paper No. 17/94, SNF, Bergen.

Coca Cola, etc. Secondly, the contribution of design to business is analysed from the competence-based perspective, which is rooted in new economic theories of the firm. Thirdly, two contrasting paradigms of design and business are delineated and discussed with reference to the need for an expanded knowledge building a "science of design". Finally, a survey is described that compares the status and current patterns of design and business relationships in Britain, Denmark and Sweden.

The conclusion in Part Four suggests that simple recipes for the management and creation of design-based advantages do not exist. Client–design relationships are always unique and typically design solutions need to be tailor-made. This is crucial from a competitive viewpoint as the design factors otherwise could be copied or imitated. Design partners are critical to generating value and it is finding a way to harness design know-how in the alliance that is the new challenge for business.

PART ONE

ACQUISITION OF DESIGN EXPERTISE

INTRODUCTION

Margaret Bruce

Investment in design for new products and services, as well as for corporate communications (e.g. brochures, packs, etc.) has a positive impact on business performance. However, building up a design competence that facilitates long-term business success is not an easy task. Companies that are well-known for design and have a sustained competitive advantage, such as Sony, Braun, Novo Nordisk and British Airways are atypical. With the current trend towards downsizing, delayering and outsourcing, design is usually outsourced. It is not common for an organisation to have full in-house design skills, consequently, design management entails outsourcing of design. Different practices exist, ranging from establishing close relationships with preferred design suppliers to treating design as a commodity that can be bought in and integrated into the business processes as and when required. Managing the relationship with design suppliers is about buying in personalised knowledge and utilising this to produce creative solutions to business problems. And so, design relationships entail personal and social factors as well as business factors such as price, working practices, etc. Therefore, the design–client relationship is sensitive and one that needs to be carefully managed.

In larger British organisations, a rosta of approved design suppliers are drawn up that have been sourced according to specified criteria. The design firms on the rosta will be used for different tasks, depending on their appropriate skills. This approach makes the choice of designers formal and on a professional basis and leaves the judgement of the appropriate nature of the design skills to design buyers. For smaller companies, the choice of design suppliers is much more *ad hoc* and left to chance, for example, through

Management of Design Alliances. Edited by M. Bruce and B. H. Jevnaker.

reference to the telephone book, friends or by working through government agencies who may not themselves have the appropriate expertise to facilitate effective sourcing.

Sourcing is not the only concern for the effective use of design. The integration of design in business processes is another. This refers to the level of design competence in the company to understand the interface of design with other activities in order to harness its full potential. Design can be used in an *ad hoc* manner or it may be so well integrated that it has become "silent", i.e., an inherent part of the culture and business activities of the organisation.

Chapters 1 and 2 address these issues of design location and design integration. In Chapter 1, Jevnaker asks why do some firms design and develop products with the right qualities for the market, not just once, but repeatedly? According to recent literature in product development, strategy and design management, competing through design and development capabilities rather than resources or products *per se*, are given greater emphasis. Although for the most part a neglected element of competitiveness, some firms such as Erco Leuchten (Germany), Sony (Japan) and Lego (Denmark) evidently have transformed their product design processes into capabilities that repeatedly provide superior value to customers. Is there a link between the approaches to creativity and management of design in these firms? The missing link could be the organisational and managerial capabilities in design, and we need to explore what these abilities for product creation consist of. The aim of this chapter is to provide a conceptual and analytical framework as a lens for the subsequent case presentations so as to enhance the empirical insights.

The issue of design location is the focus of the contribution by Bruce and Morris in Chapter 2. They note that as design is increasingly outsourced within the wider context of the restructuring of companies away from monolithic firms to virtual organisations, the integration of design within the company's strategy and its interfaces with other functions, notably marketing and production, becomes critical. Three different approaches to the location of design – in-house, outsourced and a mixture of the two – are discussed in this chapter and the main implications for the management and integration of design are delineated. Examples of each type of design location are provided.

CHAPTER ONE

BUILDING UP ORGANIZATIONAL CAPABILITIES IN DESIGN

Birgit H. Jevnaker

INTRODUCTION

In this chapter, the focus is on the nature of a business firm's design capabilities, looking "back stage" into how design-based advantages are developed and sustained. Designed objects have been an integral part of attractive shops (like the Bodyshop), have shaped public spaces like museums (e.g. the Louvre), or "good design" has been admired in more industrial environments as in shipyards (e.g. steering consoles) or in computerized offices (Apple, Olivetti etc.). And yet, very little is known about *how* firms actually explore and exploit design to create prosperous advantages in various business environments.

From research on innovation and technology, it is necessary to innovate not just once, but continually. Moreover, businesses need to be able to commercialize the new designs to generate a profit for the firm as well as new benefits for their customers. There is ample evidence to show that this does not happen overnight – the credibility of products, brands and favourable attributes and identities of firms and their services may take years to develop. Hence, to explore design more broadly in a business context, a longer time perspective – *beyond* individual products or projects – seems crucial in order to capture any

---

Management of Design Alliances. Edited by M. Bruce and B. H. Jevnaker.

sustainable competitive advantages. Moreover, a qualified design approach is closely related to human skills and talents in imaginative concept development and in converting ideas and concepts into the material world of models, prototypes, real products or other visual artefacts and services. Industrial designers often see themselves as problem-solvers and creators. Bernstein (1988) underlines that design is *more* than problem-solving and points to its value-creating possibilities.

This chapter therefore concentrates on exploring two related problems: First, how to *organize, direct* and *nurture* design resources in a business setting in order to create value and a competitive advantage. The emphasis here is on the human design expertise, although it is acknowledged that rapid tooling and other facilities are increasingly of great value. Second, how to *sustain* a created design-based advantage, i.e. over time and in various product markets?

It is argued that both questions are related to building up a *dynamic organizing capability* in, or around, firms taking the human competence and its dynamics as a point of departure. Furthermore, the organizing capability *needs to link* the use of design resources to dynamic value-creating activities, as design resources *per se* may not yield long-term advantages. Up to the present time, no actual theories specify or predict what would be effective ways of organizing and managing design resources, although certain insights are beginning to emerge from practice and from detailed studies of design management in firms. Grounded in these carefully described experiences, it is time to identify and analyse what this organizing capability may consist of in various contexts.

The contribution of this chapter is therefore to delineate a set of *components of capabilities* that may be useful for further knowledge development and practice. Although no quick fix exists in design management, knowing how to go about it is essential for managers who want to benefit by working with designers. In particular, the capabilities will be used to clarify and understand six company cases, presented in Part Two of this book, which explore how these businesses, in various industrial contexts, actually do relate to, and exploit, advanced design resources embodied in industrial design experts.

OVERVIEW

The chapter is organized as follows: first, the managerial challenge of exploiting and directing appropriate design resources is introduced. Second, it is argued that a long-term capability approach is favourable, and six component capabilities are presented. Finally, the dynamics of working with design expertise is introduced.

CALLING ON DESIGN EXPERTISE

Designers are often called upon to solve acute problems in projects or are wanted for "styling" already planned products adding the "creative flair" (Porter 1985). Not surprisingly, designers are demanded when managers have had negative feedback from the market or otherwise are in a "push" situation:

> "90% of my clients have come when they have discovered it for them-selves...that they are 'ill' in some area; they have met it in the market, they have met it at competitors, they have met it some place or the other and felt it personally that their products miss something compared to competitors."
> (industrial designer E.Wingerei; in Jevnaker 1996, p. 252).

From the organizational change literature, it is known that new approaches often are not implemented before the issues at stake have reached critical proportions. This cognitive avoidance has recently been labelled the "Donald Duck" syndrome (Sörhaug 1996). In the design field it may be even worse, since managers do not seem to see or realize that their problems have anything to do with 'design'. Hence, this *design neglect* is a mental as well as a practical problem: *connections* are seldom made between design, business development and strategic market issues.

Not surprisingly, then, design problems are treated in more or less random ways (Mollerup 1987, Olins 1987). Currently, very few managers use design and designers as a strategic or even systematic resource (Walsh 1992, Svengren 1995, Jevnaker 1996). To date only a few surveys and comparative case studies to measure professional design use have been conducted (see Walsh et al 1992, Potter et al 1991, Finiw 1992, Bruce and Morris 1995). Nevertheless, in-depth descriptions and evidence from practitioners, from design councils and from research all point in the same direction: a qualified design approach in business is an *exception* more than a rule, and yet, exceptional firms highlight the usefulness of design in various settings ranging from a tea-cup to the design of aeroplanes (Lucie-Smith 1983, see also reviews in, for example, Walsh et al 1992, Svengren 1995).

Despite the *value-creating potential* of design in contributing new perspectives and skilled approaches to business, there is ample evidence to suggest that only a few firms have built a design-based competitive advantage.

Some examples are the German electrical appliances company Braun, the Japanese electronic giant Sony, the Danish toy company Lego, the Italian Alessi and the US computer giants, e.g. the renowned Apple Computer, Inc. ("Apple"); all of these firms have exploited the value-creation possibilities linked to design-improved products and communication material (Lorenz 1990, Svengren 1995, Parsey 1995).

This book gives new additional and research-based illustrations from more traditionally technology-driven industry and smaller manufacturing firms and their efforts to exploit design expertise effectively in their particular businesses. Understanding the business context is essential, as design typically is a tailor-made effort to improve a firm's products or other visual artefacts. How design resources may help a firm to find and capture profitable opportunities is highlighted in different settings, ranging from the giant American–British toolmakers Ingersoll-Rand to Novo Nordisk, the Danish innovator in insulin delivery systems, as well as to smaller innovative furniture-makers like the Norwegian companies HAG and Stokke who both focus on making chairs better adapted for the human body, making the world a better place to sit in. Before investigating the details of these practical cases, it is worth reflecting on why it is necessary to organize and manage design at all. Is not design enough, by itself? Why is the *management* of design expertise important?

THE MANAGERIAL CHALLENGE

Many firms face great difficulties in exploiting design resources effectively. This is not surprising, as most countries' school systems[1] do not seem to give their citizens a good introduction to design subjects such as aesthetics, ergonomics and semiotics. Moreover, the designers represent a highly *personalized* profession and *heterogeneous* competence. Although certain design values, standard methods and solution types may be shared, the designers are generally seen as having heterogeneous skills which need to be tailored to each *unique* design situation (Schön 1987, 1988). However, the rather individualistic and even heroic perspective of seeing designers as "stars", has often dominated the literature (Walker 1989, Dumas 1993), thus not bringing forward the social and path-dependent dynamics which seem to be essential between designers and their clients; how they met, how they started to work together, what kind of support and management that framed the design work etc.

These particular attributes of the supply and demand side as well as the mostly hidden contextual features may be beneficial from a competitive perspective as a value-creating (rare and complex) resource may generate a sustained competitive advantage relative to other firms. Nevertheless, in order to understand and learn from these unique cases, a need to explore the organizing dynamics behind a sustained design-based advantage is required (cf. Barney 1991).

NEW TRENDS IN ORGANIZING DESIGN POTENTIALS

Industrial design expertise is accepted to be a necessary, and potentially critical, resource in developing competitive products in more and more internationalized markets, as encapsulated by the term "winning by design" (Walsh et al 1992). Even though the conditions for using design resources profitably are not yet known, a *qualified* industrial design approach is already a must in developing computer products, according to Apple's design manager (Parsey 1995).

Moreover, the rare but complete in-house self-sufficient design supply, or complete outsourced transaction, seems to be bypassed by "new" trends of more *collaborative industrial design approaches* such as are practised by the British–American IDEO and Samsung. The latter, a Korean electronic firm, has recently chosen to *co-locate* itself with a design firm just across the street of its main studio in Palo Alto. This shows the value of rich, intensive interaction in current product design. The international design consultancy Fitch works through *close partnerships*, and invites their major clients to so-called "war rooms", that is dedicated space for genuine interdisciplinary collaboration on their "design farm" in Columbus, Ohio. These mixed hybrid approaches may combine, tailor and stretch external creativity in design with internal people and skills, bringing in the critical interfaces with other functions such as marketing, technology and strategic management. Indeed, it may be difficult to sort out where ideas actually come from as knowledge and concepts are created and refined across previous borders. Not surprisingly, the outside designers may emerge partly as "insiders", as identified by Kicherer (1990) when exploring the Italian design management scene, and Olivetti in particular.

However, the above trends have evolved as unique capabilities in particular firms only. Most firms do not exploit design effectively, nor do they explore it as a strategic resource (Svengren 1995). Robert Hayes and his colleagues at the Harvard Business School, have for some time pointed to design as "the missing link" in the new global competitive environment, but he puts design in a realistic perspective when he states, "it will not be an easy one for companies to master" (Hayes 1990, p. 9).

As noted by Robert Blaich (1995), Philips's as well as Herbert Miller's former design manager,[2] the management of design by the business corporation is *"unfinished business"*. This seems to be linked to both supply and demand side factors: as design expertise is an external and mostly *unfamiliar competence* for the client users, interacting with designers is expected to be posing particular challenges to the business firms, and vice versa.

WHY ARE DESIGN RESOURCES DIFFICULT TO MANAGE?

As seen from a business perspective, the company may want to control and govern design resources and relationships, as management is used to govern *material* resources. However, managing design resources is different, as the most critical design resources are embodied as human expertise, i.e., a combination of design-related talents, skills and knowledge in a broad sense, and at a very high competence level differentiating the expert from the novice, from the craft-based skilled practitioner and even the competent problem solver. According to Dreyfus and Dreyfus (1990), this means that the expert has achieved more rapid and complex abilities to respond, with interpretation and diagnosis, to familiar problem situations in immediate and even intuitive ways, analogous to an advanced chess player being able to "read" their partner's strategy and to draw on a repertoire of permutations and solutions. We know that such analogies and prototypes are taken as models in design, even though each design situation is to be seen as unique. In most designers' studios, for instance, design journals and magazines on new materials, new cars or other product categories are used for inspiration. Schön (1988) calls these reference models "types" to be drawn on for the design and architecture professions.

In general, skilled and knowledgeable people are difficult to "control" – they are resources but not controllable assets in the traditional economic sense (Nordhaug 1993). Furthermore, how to control experts that move in and out of the firm and in so doing may take the most important resources with them (Löwendahl 1992)?

Most design firms are located *outside* the boundaries of the business organization, although their expertise is offered as some kind of *mixed* market and organizational transaction or *collaborative arrangement* as demonstrated above (see also Bruce and Morris 1995, Chapter 3). In short, these hybrid structural arrangements pose particular problems as well as opportunities in exploiting design for value-creating purposes.

MANAGING THE NEW "HYBRIDS"

As outlined elsewhere, a mixture of governance strategies is used in design management, embracing price mechanisms, authority mechanisms and relational mechanisms (often coined "trust mechanisms"). Based on a theoretical relational perspective, we may be able to capture why design relationships are valuable. Three features of the design situation may call for a collaborative approach, also known as "relational contracting" (Macneil 1980); that is:

1. difficulties in specifying the problem beforehand
2. difficulties in specifying the suitable work processes beforehand
3. difficulties in specifying the solution criteria beforehand.

In such situations, the partners need each other to work towards both suitable problem definitions (finding and formulating the problem in the briefing and task research-like activities), suitable work processes, and also finding and selecting perspectives or criteria to test and evaluate solution concepts and models. Not surprisingly, both partners' competencies, as well as their networks, may be of great value in order to create and realize effective solutions. This often seems to be the case in more complex design development, although not always implemented as more short-term competitive (price) mechanisms may leave too little room for genuine collaboration over time (see Bruce & Morris, Chapter 3). In particular, in more innovative solutions, the parties may need to mobilize resources and combine forces to be able to commercialize successfully, as many new products fail (Urban et al 1987). From internal corporate venturing, it is known that harnessing both market and technology, as well as long-term managerial and strategic support, may be critical (Burgelman and Sayles 1986).

How, then, to combine the internal and external design and business expertise to stretch the company profitably for current and future problem-solving? A key to this challenge may be to develop *organizational capabilities* in design that bridges the input, output and, in particular, the *throughput* factors in using design effectively: i.e., from sourcing design expertise to combining this expertise creatively with the core competences linked to the firm, as well as its customer base and end users (current and future customers/users).

A DYNAMIC CAPABILITY-BASED APPROACH

As yet, very little is known about how firms create leading-edge products and communications by a qualified design approach not just once, but repeatedly. In accordance with the new resource-based perspective in strategic management, it is suggested that behind these competitive performances is a set of *dynamic capabilities* in designing products and its communications to the customers. Based on insights into firms that have an established reputation in design (Braun, Olivetti, Bang & Olufsen to mention just a few), creating new designs seems to be more about nurturing and motivating and combining competencies and expertise, than just administration and control of the assets. Hence, a more *fluid* image, of competent players and activities, comes to mind, rather than a schedule or plan (those are often necessary but do not capture always the rich stories of design developments). Even though these abilities seem to be mostly embedded and hidden in the design-competent firm, they need to be identified – as we need to uncover what the firm's overall core competence[3] consists of.

As already noted, a "capability" is associated with a complex interaction of material and immaterial resources in a firm, conceived of as an interaction in which managers, as well as other competent parties, have a role to play. This capability concept of the firm has been defined in various ways as core or distinctive competencies; i.e. relative to the competitors, as collective learning, as a set of business processes strategically understood or as the glue in the organization which makes things happen for example in design. We need to move beyond these diffuse or abstract categories to capture how the designer and the firm actually collaborate.

COMPONENTS AND LOCATION OF CAPABILITIES

"What, how and where" questions may be useful to try to identity capabilities behind, and *in*, the skilled processes moving the firm towards improved design. Some core dimensions have been suggested by Leonard-Barton (1995), e.g. skills and knowledge, managerial systems and cultural values. These indicate, in a multi-faceted way, where the competences are *located* – in the people, in the management systems, and in the corporate culture (or sub-culture) – but do not fully conceptualize what they may consist of. From research-based insights in both graphic/information design and industrial product design, it seems to be certain repeatable components in design management practices that may be emergent, as well as consciously developed or combined in various ways (Jevnaker 1994). These may therefore be coined "component capabilities" in the management and organizing of design.

THE CONCEPTUALIZATION OF COMPONENT CAPABILITIES

Based on research and relevant theory, six keys to a design-based advantage are identified. As can be seen from Table 1.1 these capabilities may bridge the

Table 1.1 Component capabilities in organizing design and its management

Component capabilities	Core abilities
1. Resourcing capability	Ability to acquire and manage potentially profitable design resources
2. Combinative capability	Ability to configure design resources Ability to tap firm-specific or otherwise distinctive resources
	Ability to create interaction of design resources and competences
3. Organizational learning capability	Ability to absorb and recreate design competences on the organizational level
4. Innovation capability	Ability to create something new and valuable which may be commercialized
5. Design-strategic capability	Ability to integrate design in strategy or otherwise make design strategic
6. Protecting capability of design-based advantages	Ability to protect design-based advantages

Source: Jevnaker (1994). From the Outside In: Building Organizational Capabilities in Product Design, SNF Working Paper

firm's value-creation to its *chain of competence* (Nordhaug 1993); that is its way of acquiring expertise, combining it with core and complimentary assets and making value-adding interactions among the firm's relevant resources in order to make a visible distinctive difference in its products and services.

RESOURCING CAPABILITY

The ability to acquire and manage potentially profitable design resources is a basic capability in exploiting a more qualified design approach. Attractive design resources are mainly the appropriate human capital resources embedded in *design expertise*, but who knows who is appropriate for whom?

As both parties may not know the other party beforehand (mutual information asymmetry), there often is an *information gap*. Part of this gap tends to be solved through networks; for example through:

1. *"The jungle telegraph"* (friends, neighbours, colleagues, contacts, partners, suppliers, trade associations etc.);
2. various *brokers* such as design councils, design consultants, managerial consultants;
3. *other firms* that may be sought as credible advisors;
4. More *random* connections are also observed.

It is worth noting that all of these connections may be transformed into conscious and long-term *design alliances* – that is, experts who contribute and commit their personal value-creating ability over time to the benefit of a particular firm (Jevnaker 1994).

What, then, is a good match or appropriate design expertise to be allied to the firm? "Appropriate" means fit for a task and business environment, e.g. products designed for a target market and being manufacturable by the firm or the firm's sub-contractors. This "fit" is important and is related to the conceptualization of competencies (Nordhaug 1993). It should, however, be understood in a dynamic, not in a bureaucratic or static sense. A complete "match" may not provide any new perspectives to move beyond the present competitive level.

Not surprisingly, experienced design users often emphasize the benefits of working openly with a designer (Jevnaker 1995b). However, there is more to it than appreciating any new perspectives. As in other fields of knowledge-based consultancy, the client's participation, and indeed co-production, is necessary to produce the tailor-made and unique service (Löwendahl 1992). In line with a business network's perspective (Hedberg et al 1994), this competence acquiring for resourcing can be differentiated from both outsourcing and in-house design expertise, as suggested by the so-called transaction cost economics theory. The transactional approach does not include this solution of resourcing more *creative*[4] competencies (cf. Williamson 1985, p. 244), and combining the specific assets of the client with the generalist-specialism of the expert designer.

A somewhat *detached creative design contribution* may be wanted, although a certain familiarity[5] with the problems of the firm or the industry also is demanded to reduce risks and enhance profitable commercialization. But where can firms search for such design resources which may not market themselves effectively? Indeed, industrial firms face the dilemma of buying something *unknown*, partly unknown or known only through reputation. Not surprisingly, the ability to resource appropriate design expertise may be a critical design management component.

At the Danish company Bang & Olufsen, which is famous for its hi-fi design, finding and dealing with the "right" designer talent is therefore regarded as crucial in product design. (Palshöj 1990). This statement means that the *material abilities* of the designer are reviewed through his/her previous or current work (via portfolio presentations, pre-qualification efforts and design group competitions), indicating that visible presentation skills and the portfolio are seen as reflecting the expertise which can only be observed indirectly.

The conscious search for suitable designers is illustrated in this book. Notably, some of the successful smaller companies using industrial designers, such as the high-tech firm Tomra (return automates for drinking beverage) and the high-touch office furniture-maker HAG, both searched for "the best designers" through their networks of professional designers. In this setting, the most important source was the national design council (based in Oslo) and its knowledgeable individuals who were familiar with the local design networks (see Jevnaker, Chapter 5).

More generally, only a few firms seem to follow a conscious resourcing strategy in design areas. This may be due to not knowing the value of relating to design expertise more closely so as to transform design costs into a sustainable competitive advantage. However, it is worth noticing that particular *designers* may in fact follow a proactive resourcing strategy, since some designers actually are searching for, finding and selecting "appropriate firms", that is, appropriate for their skills and long-term interests.

In the case of Ingersoll-Rand, the new design relationship did emerge through the initiative and good timing of the design experts making themselves accessible for the "local industry" (see Bruce & Morris, Chapter 3). Indeed, this also happened in the Stokke case: designer Peter Opsvik literally knocked on this firm's door (Jevnaker 1995a), and in the Sandvik Bacho case where the Ergonomi Design Group took the first initiative (Svengren 1995a).

As revealed through a recent interview with design expert Deane Richardson from Fitch and Richardson Smith, this is not entirely a new practice: He and his initial partner Dave Smith, after setting up their design business in the early 1960s and after gaining some experience to have something to offer, proactively searched for clients with some design potential. As they stated:

> "We projected ourselves to new 'plateaux' by finding new and interesting clients: e.g. by going to fairs and other meeting places sourcing interesting firms, and even drove around their premises to see if they really cared ... From these sources we made a list to 'eliminate from'. Afterwards, we identified 6 strategically interesting 'future industries', and then, in each sector, selected one prospect firm to pay a personal visit."

(interview with Jevnaker 2.9.96)

Not surprisingly, this design consultancy grew to be highly profitable and soon had clients all over the US and eventually in three continents.

COMBINATIVE CAPABILITY

The combinative capability consists of at least these three components:

1. the ability to configure design resources;
2. the ability to tap firm-specific or otherwise distinctive resources;
3. the ability to create interaction of design resources and the firm's core competent people.

CONFIGURING ABILITY

In addition to resourcing and dealing with design experts, the "configuration" of design and design management resources, that is the *composition* and *location* of these resources, are essential to a technical and organizational effectiveness in design. For instance in product design, the designers may be located:

- inside product development department;
- within the research and development staff;
- linked to the marketing and sales departments;
- located more directly as a resource under the top management staff; or
- the design consultant may be working within a cross-functional team set up by the client.

Research suggests that design competencies tend to be incorporated within existing corporate structures in informal ways, and are organised by more or less *silent* design management practices in the business firm. This silent practice may not always be productive, as pinpointed by Dumas and Whitfield (1989), who state: "Do not expect a design policy to be effective if the structure does not exist to implement it."

This informal approach may lead not only to random or tradition-based designs as outputs, but also to unquestioned product design and development practices as described by Henderson (1991). An unquestioned practice may be unproductive, for instance when the task environment changes. Indeed, bringing in new product designs without co-ordination may at one extreme lead to no or only minor impact or, at the other extreme, may even bring about a radical and unwanted departure from the firm's production or marketing capabilities.

A minor impact of this practice is suggested in the LM Ericsson case (Svengren, see Chapter 7): Designers were linked to product development projects in which the engineering people were the dominant group. Although marketing managers were eager to integrate the designers on a more strategic, user-oriented level, the practices of the product development projects made design a stop-go process. Design developments were influenced by managerial shifts and a somewhat half-hearted design collaboration. In this early period, design never really got off the ground.

This partly unsuccessful integration process of design in a high-tech and very successful firm, is not surprising. Historically, the configuration and integration of the design expertise with the core competencies of the firm, have rarely been dealt with carefully enough by manufacturers (see Sparke 1983, 1986). Fairly recently, "concurrent design" and "concurrent engineering" have emerged as major topics due to the rate of change, instability and complexity in technology as well as markets. Not surprisingly, the composition of multidisciplined teams and "integrated" organizing of product developments are often referred to in recent literature (Wheelright and Clark 1992, Bowen et al 1994). Scrage, an American writer on new technology proclaimed in his book "No More Teams!" to draw the attention not to teams as such, but to the *problem of constructive collaboration* among skilled personnel (Scrage 1995).

It is not only high-tech firms and engineers that have problems with relating to design as such, or to design expertise. In many countries, even apparently "design-conscious" firms such as in the furniture industry have not yet explored and exploited design fully.[6] From this background, it is worth noting that the Scandinavian furniture-maker HAG, for example, *reconfigures* design expertise consciously in *each* development project according to the individual design expert's potential contributions and ways of operating, as well as the firm's need to ensure the right quality and manufacturability of the refined design solutions. Moreover, this company has been transformed from a traditional manufacturer to a kind of three-wave firm[7] exploiting both visual and verbal rhetoric to reach and seduce the customer (Jevnaker, see Chapter 5). An integrated approach to product development is managed by project leaders with multiple skills, a certain rotation is practised in the product development department and a physiotherapist serves as project manager. Eight to ten design expert groups are exploited and there are many links and contact points among the designers and the core group of the firm.

Although this social architecture of design teams seems crucial, design and development resources may also be located at different corners of the world, and still be able to interact efficiently, as illustrated by the design teams creating the new IBM Notebook (Sakakibara, see Chapter 4). The tendency to cross-national (and cross-cultural) borders in product and communication design, should be seen also in the perspective of tapping the best expertise and design milieus wherever these are located, be it in Milan, in Singapore, in Palo Alto, in London, or in Scandinavia. However, this international approach raises the challenge of communicating across borders, while still being able to tailor-make design solutions for the client.

FINDING CORE EXPERTISE

The more integrated design and development approach improves the possibilities to *tap the firm-specific and industry-specific resources* in technology, manufacturing and marketing. Looking more closely at the Scandinavian furniture-maker HAG, this firm's most "independently" working designer is exposed to, for instance the needs of the sub-suppliers and of the assembling factory. This is stimulated by a series of meetings combined with visits to the local sub-suppliers and the factory, the latter being located in a rural district (Röros) in the mountains of Eastern Norway. To be in direct interaction on site is an important factor in appreciating the multiple needs and requirements in complex product development, as also demonstrated in the LM Ericsson case and in the development of Novo's insulin pens (see Chapters 6 and 7).

According to a resource-based economic perspective on growth,[8] the ability to tap into, that is to be in touch with and exploit, the firm's unique resources, is crucial from a competitive viewpoint. The reason is that the potential benefits of making things differently with a *distinctive* and *worthwhile quality*, are better, relative to competitors. The strategist is attempting to make his company stand apart from its competitors (Porter 1980). Based on the resource-based theory in strategic management, the critical information is not similarities, but *differences and particularities* among firms (Teece et al 1990, Barney 1991). If successfully developed, design may provide a visually attractive difference. This means an ability to create and configure idiosyncratic, or otherwise different and better qualities, and making these visible in an attractive and distinctive way, as for instance in the corporate identity of the Lillehammer Winter Olympic Games 1994: innovative pictograms inspired from a 4,000-year-old rock carving from the North of Norway (Schwartz 1994, Jevnaker 1995c). Another illustration is

Marimekko's competence in tapping the distinctive textile cultures of Finnish producers, transforming them into modern expressions (see Ainamo, Chapter 8).

INTERACTIVE ABILITY

Moreover, the ability to create a constructive *interaction of design-related resources* is crucial in order to avoid failures and costly iterations (Wheelright and Clark 1992).

Studies of product design and development teams in some dynamic Japanese firms, such as Matsushita, illustrate the importance of constructive group dynamics. In these types of firms, collaborative creative efforts evolve from the "middle-up-down", i.e. from the middle managers and development teams up to the top and down again for further knowledge-creation and refinement (Nonaka 1991). This is an evolutionary approach that may be neglected by American and other Western firms, which focus more on top-down generated development projects (Kagano et al 1985). As illustrated in the NOVO Nordisk insulin-pen development, interaction between the development team members was indeed crucial to enable the design of a user-friendly *Novo pen* (injection of insulin) suitable for diabetic users (Freeze, Chapter 6).

ORGANIZATIONAL LEARNING CAPABILITY

In order to sustain, and further develop, the ability to create leading-edge designs in products and communications, the ability to "absorb" or take in and sustain the design competencies seems to be crucial, but is often neglected. Design may emerge (or be discontinued) by the turnover of knowledgeable persons or through the potential fragility of relationships with individual managers, for instance as experienced in a telecommunication firm in Scandinavia.[9] When a particular person was in charge of marketing, conscious investments and a distinctive profile were achieved in corporate identity design. However, when this manager later left the firm and was replaced by a new manager, the relationship with the outside design consultancy faded away. The firm's design development seemed to be disrupted. This story is not unique; many designers are dependent on a few design-committed managers on whom the firm's qualified design development depends.

After reviewing the design management literature and investigating four firms in-depth, Svengren (1995) found that the conceptual integration of design in the business firms is the most critical component of making industrial design a "strategic resource". In line with Jevnaker (1993), the learning processes among designers, managers, distributors, dealers and so on are seen as crucial in order to genuinely value the particular design development and grasp some of its intricacies in practice. However, projects tend to operate within short-term goals and temporary task forces or teams. Often, there are few incentives to accumulate experiences in a systematic way *beyond* the project levels. And yet, learning may occur on a more collective level when good (and bad) design is demonstrated, explained and practised in a manner visible to the firm's core groups and networks. If this is done repeatedly *over time* within the corporate structure as well as in its networks and core relationships, then the chances for learning on the corporate level seem greater.

The embodiment, embeddedness and distributive aspects of design expertise may make this difficult but not impossible. *Embodiment* refers to design as a personal expertise as well as a tangible product. *Embeddedness* refers to design competence being an intrinsic part of a culture, or something only visible through action or as part of relations and networks. *Distributive* aspects of design competence means that design knowledge may be presented in notes and sketches, or found in a variety of contacts with modelmakers and suppliers etc. These aspects are not entirely codified or codifiable and may also be taken for granted, making it more difficult for a novice design user to understand fully.

And still, novice design users among business firms may learn. Design may be both incorporated in people; in the firm's philosophy and cultural values; as well as inscribed in the various routines and strategies of the firm. Interestingly, the collaboration with a design expert may not only improve the quality of products and communications; the experiences may also represent a common ground for emotional and social involvement and reflection. What is typical for design experience is that "everyone" has an opinion which often is expressed (Brochmann 1987). To capture design reflections to initiate, or inaugurate, the other parties in the conceptual seems to be crucial, especially when the designer or manager demonstrates the design development by examples and storytelling. In the Scandinavian furniture firms HAG and Stokke, a fascinating sort of "inaugurative learning" was practised by both designers and managers (Jevnaker 1993): indeed, telling others what you still need to grasp yourself may be very insightful (Raaheim and Wankowski 1991).

INNOVATION CAPABILITY

The ability to create something new and valuable (i.e. creative) on the product or process level for the market is a crucial element of product design capability.

At a product design level, this consists of problem-finding, framing problems/ needs and developing solution concepts, as well as generating two- and three-dimensional designs followed up with instructions and suggestions. At an organizational level, this includes design management abilities to stimulate, direct and nurture, follow up and facilitate direct communications with other areas. This activity is important for organizing innovative efforts (cf. Burns and Stalker 1961).

This does not mean that innovative efforts are unsystematic or necessarily chaotic. An illustration of a systematic innovative approach is the Swedish Ergonomi Design Group as they apply analytical methods in exploring the user situations. In, for instance, Sandvik Bacho's ergonomically designed tools for professional users, both good design and commercial results are visible. Their findings were applied to new designs for screwdrivers and other tools (Svengren 1995).

In the case of Novo Nordisk, an innovative approach to product design resulted in the user-friendly Novo Pens for diabetics. This case is further illuminated by Karen Freeze, Chapter 6.

DESIGN-STRATEGIC CAPABILITY

In the product development literature, product design and development projects have traditionally been regarded as isolated from the development of the firm (Leonard-Barton 1992). The excellent study of Burgelman and Sayles (1986) highlights the need to view these phenomena as a dynamic relationship. New product designs, in particular the innovative and unconventional solutions, may lead to changes in other areas such as marketing and production.

Hence design can become an integral part of the business strategy. Whether that means changes in the design strategy to fit the firm's business strategy, or the firm's competitive strategies are adapted to design needs, is an empirical question. In line with what Itami and Numagami (1992) suggest for technology and business strategy, dynamic interplay between design and corporate strategy are manifold.

In the case of LM Ericsson, design was not successfully integrated in the firm's competitive strategies during the time period investigated, although certain efforts were made, such as the development of mobile phones to make design a strategic part of the technologically advanced products (see Svengren, Chapter 7). In contrast, the new product design direction transformed the competitive strategies and even changed the overall business philosophy of the furniture-makers HAG and Stokke. These innovative designs were adopted and expanded due to management's collaborative relationship with the designer Peter Opsvik, acknowledging his contribution to the new ergonomically-based design concepts as well as appreciating the visible commercial results (see Jevnaker, Chapter 5).

PROTECTING CAPABILITY OF DESIGN-BASED ADVANTAGES

This component is defined as the ability to protect the commercial design results; for instance making imitation difficult by applying patents or otherwise developing barriers for "copy cats" of the firm's designs. Rumelt (1987) stresses this ability to create "isolating mechanisms" is necessary for the firm to achieve and sustain its profitability.

Many product design cases underpin the importance of design protection, such as the Norwegian *Balans* products based on an innovative and alternative seating concept, which exploited its heterogeneous design expertise and manufacturing assets as well as ensuring patent rights. Although at first very successfully received by the customers, the product designs were not sufficiently protected to sustain a competitive advantage in the US market, and a range of imitations was soon launched in the US, but made in Far Eastern factories. The reduced quality of the rival products led to "customer confusion". Consequently, the Scandinavian furniture maker withdrew from the US market and focused on developing a more careful step-by-step marketing strategy in Europe (Jevnaker 1995a). Later, a unique distribution network, including highly committed distributors and dealers in Germany and the Netherlands, was developed (Berg 1994).

THE DYNAMICS OF DESIGN CAPABILITIES

The products of designers can be seen everywhere, but who or what determines the outcomes? Bucciarelli (1994) studied "design engineers" and found that at a superficial level they appeared to be highly objective in their approach to design. However, by probing more deeply, Bucciarelli found that even engineering design is a social process that involves constant negotiation among *many parties*, not just engineers but marketers, research scientists, accountants, and customers. Designing, he concluded was as much about agreeing on definitions as about producing "hard" artefacts.

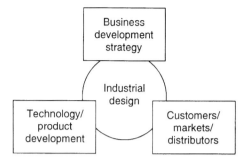

Figure 1.1   Industrial design as in-between process between technology, customers and business development/strategy etc.
Source: Jevnaker (1996b)

Following the Japanese professors Nonaka and Takeuchi (1995), this process is akin to a dynamic knowledge-creation and knowledge-conversion process. The parties seldom have ready-made definitions to negotiate in the process, although some initial criteria, such as technical or market-specs may be contained in the design brief. However, product designing is an evolutionary process with creation and refinement occurring through many iterative cycles. These cycles entail the exploration of needs and wants, as well as development and experimentation of preliminary ideas to prototypes (see also Kristensen, Chapter 10). Figure 1.1 illustrates the many interested parties in product design.

Hence, this partly social, partly economic and partly technical process, may be expected to change dynamically and according to the spectrum of *interested parties* involved. How can the most essential dynamics be captured? In this book, the focus is on the *relationship* between the firm and its "design alliance" as a core part of the design process. And so, the dynamics in these relationships have to be considered. A classification of the different managerial capabilities in design may be helpful (see Table 1.2).

Applying a *strategic fit* (Itami 1987) implies that partners for design alliances are consciously sought for strategic long-term reasons (Nordhaug 1993). This perspective allows for change and adaptation between the firm and its external design resources, and so creative tensions in the collaboration are expected and are not a threat to the survival of the relationship. It is interesting to note that creative tension and dialectics actually were indicated in a recent study of five firms' relationships with designers (Jevnaker 1995b) and are referred to in some of the cases in this book. Indeed, the sourcing and use of external design

Table 1.2   Managing design collaboration according to the business firm's design capabilities in relation to the designer's expertise

The designer's expertise	The business firm's design capabilities		
	Low	Medium	High
Low	Will not survive? Solution-driven (CAD)?	Driven by the firm's competences	
Medium			
High	Relationship-driven, designer's strategies essential	Relationship-driven, potential of developing the client	Dynamic advanced, dialectics between the parties

experts may be one of the few opportunities to introduce constructive tensions, heterogeneity and fresh development efforts, which may be beneficial for the survival or growth of the firm (Itami 1987).

The design allies need to develop social aspects, not only its technical ones. Using the word "art" hints at the expressive human dimensions which are evident when managers and designers work constructively together, even when budgets are tight. This is not to ignore the different competitive environments that design allies are operating in and the various opportunities there may be to generate value.

CONCLUSIONS

Many different situations exist in which a strong design approach may be significant for firms and beneficial for its customers and other stakeholders. Overall, there is evidence to support the case that a capability for *continued* innovation and quality performance can lead to improvements over time. Nevertheless, only a few firms have developed a systematic approach to design management. The core capabilities presented in Table 1.2 indicate the activities and skills required. Moreover, visual experts are seldom consulted when top managers discuss how they may achieve a competitive advantage (see, for example, Blaich and Blaich 1993, Svengren 1995b). This suggests that design should be regarded as a strategic resource because design-based competencies (such as those embedded in design-client relationships) may be rare and hard to imitate (cf. Barney 1991).

NOTES

1. For Britain, see Gorb (1988, 1990); for Norway, see Grunnskoleraadet/ Kulturraadet (1991).
2. In addition to being the former design manager of Philips at its headquarters in the Dutch city of Einhoven, Robert Blaich has experience also from the American furnituremaker Herbert Miller, as well as insights into many other design business settings (see Blaich and Blaich 1993).
3. The core competence concept as introduced by Hamel and Prahalad (1990) is highly diffuse and seems to have remained so – see a critic in Nordhaug (1993).
4. Oliver Williamson informs, in a note to one of his books, that he has not included the influence from variation in creativity; he thus treats creativity as a "constant" in his model (see Williamson 1985, p. 244).
5. See a discussion on familiarity knowledge (Johannessen 1988) in Jevnaker, Chapter 5.
6. See e.g. Sparke (1986), Lahti (1990), Jevnaker (1993), and Svengren (1995).
7. The term third-wave companies was coined by Alvin Toffler (1980).
8. The resource-based perspective on economic growth originates in Penrose (1959, 1968), but has recently gained much more attention as a cornerstone of competitive advantage (see Peteraf 1993).
9. Source: own interview with the design consultancy in the early 1990s.

REFERENCES

Ainamo, A. (1996). Industrial Design and Business Performance. A Case Study of a Finnish Fashion Firm. Thesis, Helsinki School of Economics and Business Administration.

Arbeidsgruppen om industridesign (1995). Industridesign som konkurransefaktor for norsk næringsliv (Industrial Design as a Competitive Factor for the Norwegian Business. In Norwegian), Nærings-og energidepartementet (the Ministry of Industry and Energy with Norwegian Design Council), Oslo.

Bae, B. (1992) Acknowledging Children's Experiences – Focus on the Quality of the Teacher–Child Relationship. Paper presented at the ETEN-Conference, Viborg College, Denmark, 3–5 May 1992, College of Early Childhood Education, Oslo/ Norway.

Barney, J. (1991). Firm Resources and Sustained Competitive Advantage, *Strategic Management Journal*, **17**(1), 99–120.

Berg, H. (1994). A comparative analysis to explore critical success factors linked to establishment of a sales and distributional company in a foreign market (in Norwegian). Confidential student report, Norwegian School of Economics and Business Administration, Bergen.

Bernstein, D. (1988). The Design Mind, in Gorb, P. (ed.) with Schneider, E. *Design Talks!*, London Business School Design Management Seminars, The Design Council, London, 202–216.

Blaich, R. with Blaich, J. (1993). *Product Design and Corporate Strategy: Managing the Connection for Competitive Advantage*, McGraw-Hill, New York.

Blaich, R. (1995). Design Management: Unfinished Business for this Millennium. Speech and Abstract presented at the Challenge of Complexity, 3rd International Conference on Design Management, 21–22 August, University of Art and Design Helsinki (UIAH), Helsinki.

Bowen, H.K. et al (eds) (1994). *The Perpetual Enterprise Machine. Seven Keys to Corporate Renewal Through Successful Product and Process Development*, Oxford University Press, New York.

Brochmann (1987). *Om stygt og pent* (*On Ugly and Beautiful*. In Norwegian.) 3rd edition, Cappelen, Oslo.

Bruce, M. and Biemans, W.G. (eds) (1995). *Product Development Meeting the Challenge of the Design Marketing Interface*. John Wiley, Chichester.

Bruce, M. and Docherty, C. (1993). It's all in a relationship: a comparative study of client–design consultant relationships, *Design Studies*, **14**(4), 402–422.

Bruce, M. and Morris, B. with Svengren, L. and Kristensen, T. (1995). Strategic Management of Design Consultancy: Comparisons from Sweden, Denmark and Britain, School of Management, UMIST, Manchester.

Burgelman, R. and Sayles, L.R. (1986). *Inside Corporate Innovation*, The Free Press, N.Y. & London.

Burns, T. and Stalker, G.M. (1961/1994). *The Management of Innovation*, Tavistock, London.

Design Management Journal (1993). 'Design and National Policy', **4**(3), The Design Management Institute, Boston.

Bucciarelli, L. (1994). *Designing Engineers*, MIT Press, London/Cambridge Mass.

Dierickx, I. and Cool, C. (1989). Asset Stock Accumulation and Sustainability of Competitive Advantage, *Management Science*, **35**(12), December, 1504–1513.

Dreyfus, H. and Dreyfus, S. (1990). What is morality? A phenomenological account of the development of ethical expertise, in Rasmussen, D. (ed.) Universalism versus Communitarism: Contemporary Debates in Ethics, MIT Press, Cambridge, 237–264.

Dumas, A. (1993). The Effect of Management Structure and Organisational Process on Decisions in Industrial Design. London Business School, Ph.D. London.

Dumas, A. and Whitfield, A. (1989). Why design is difficult to manage: A survey of attitudes and practices in British industry, *European Management Journal*, **7**(1), 50–56.

Farstad, P. (1994b). Styring av markedsrettet produktdesign i produktutvikling. Paper 28.9.94, Institute for Industrial Design, SHKS, Oslo. (IFID was later reorganized into AFID at the Oslo School of Architecture).

Finiw, M. (1992). Analytical Framework for Design Management and Comparative Analysis of Design Management Institute Case Studies, Special Report, Design Management Institute Press, Boston.

Freeze, K. with Powell, E. (1991). Design management lessons from the past: Henry Dreyfuss and American Business. Article, Design Management Institute (DMI), Boston.

Gorb, P. (ed.) with Schneider, E. (1988). *Design Talks!*, London Business School Design Management Seminars, The Design Council, London.

Gorb, P. (ed.) (1990). Design Management. Papers from the London Business School (LBS), Architecture Design and Technology Press, London.

Grunnskoleraadet Norsk Kulturraad (1991). Inntrykk Uttrykk Avtrykk. Handlingsplan for styrking av de estetiske fagene i skolen. (Action plan for the primary school to improve the aesthetic subjects. In Norwegian).

Hart, S. (1995). Where we've been and where we're going in new product development research, in Bruce, M. & Biemans, W.G. (eds), *Product Development Meeting the Challenge of the Design–Marketing Interface*, John Wiley, Chichester, 15–42.

Hayes, R. (1990). Design: Putting Class into "World Class", *Design Management Journal*, **1**(2), 8–14.

Hedberg, B. et al. (1994). *Imaginära Organisationer* (in Swedish), Liber-Hermods, Malmö.

Hedlund, G. and Nonaka, I. (1993). Models of Knowledge Management in the West and Japan, in Lorange, P. et al (eds), *Implementing Strategic Processes: Change, Learning and Co-operation*, Blackwell, Oxford and Cambridge, MA.

Henderson, R. (1991). Architectural innovation as a source of competitive advantage, *Design Management Journal*, **2**(3), 43–47.

Hollins, B. and Pugh, S. (1990). *Successful Product Design*, Butterworth, London.

Itami, H. with Roehl, T.W. (1987). *Mobilizing Invisible Assets*, Harvard University Press, Cambridge MA and London.

Itami, H. and Numagami, T. (1992). Dynamic Interaction Between Strategy and Technology, *Strategic Management Journal*, **13**, 119–135.

Jeppesen, B. et al (1994). *Dansk design – fra kirke til kafé*, Systime, Herning.

Jevnaker, B.H. (1993). Inaugurative learning: adapting a new design approach, *Design Studies* **14**(4), October, Butterworth-Heinemann Ltd., Oxford, 379–401. SNF-reprint No. 39/1993.

Jevnaker, B.H. (1994). From the Outside In: Building Organizational Capabilities in Product Design, SNF Working paper No. 17/94, SNF, Bergen.

Jevnaker, B.H. (1995a). Developing capabilities for innovative product designs: A case study of the Scandinavian furniture industry, in Bruce, M. & W.G. Biemans (eds), *Product development: meeting the challenge of the design–marketing interface*, John Wiley & Sons, Chichester, UK.

Jevnaker, B.H. (1995b). Den skjulte formuen. Industridesign som kreativ konkurranse-faktor (in Norwegian). SNF-report 36/95, SNF, Bergen. A summary in English is to be found in Jevnaker, B.H. (1995). The Hidden Treasure – Competitive Advantage through Design Alliances, SNF-Working paper No. 58/95.

Jevnaker, B.H. (1995c). Designing an Olympic Games in the Face of Chaos: The Case of Lillehammer, *Design Management Journal*, **6**(3), The Design Management Institute, Boston. 41–49.

Jevnaker, B.H. (1996). Industridesign som kreativ konkurransefaktor: En forstudie (in Norwegian), SNF-report 54/96, Bergen.

Johannessen, K.E. (1988). Tankar om tyst kunskap (Thoughts on Tacit Knowledge. In Swedish), *Dialoger* (6), 13–28.

Kagano, T. et al (1985). *Strategic vs. Evolutionary Management, A US–Japan Comparison of Strategy and Organization*, North Holland, Amsterdam.

Kicherer, S. (1990). *Olivetti: A Study of the Corporate Management of Design*, Trefoil Publishers, London.

Kotler, P. and G.A. (1984). Design: a powerful but neglected strategic tool, *Journal of Business Strategy*, **5**(2), 16–21.

Kristensen, T. (1995). The Contribution of Design to Business: A Competence-Based Perspective, Process of Change Laboratory, Stanford University and Copenhagen Business School. Proceedings from the 1st European Academy of Design, *Design Interfaces.* 11/13 April 1995, **4**, Design Management, University College of Salford.

Lahti, A. (1990). The Competitive Position of the Scandinavian Furniture Industry, Report for the Furniture Excellence Club & Basprojektet, Helsinki: Inrikesminis-teriet (Ministry of Internal Affairs).

Lauvaas, P. and Handal, G. (1990). *Veiledning og praktisk yrkesteori* (Supervision and Practical Theory of Professions, in Norwegian), Cappelen, Oslo.

Leonard-Barton, D. (1992). Core capabilities and core rigidities: a paradox in managing new product development, *Strategic Management Journal*, **13**, 111–125.

Leonard-Barton, D. (1995). *Wellsprings of Knowledge, Building and Sustaining the Sources of Innovation*, HBS, Boston.

Lorenz, C. (1986). *The Design Dimension*, Basil Blackwell, Oxford (New revised ed. 1990).

Lucie-Smith, E. (1983). *A History of Industrial Design*, Phaidon, Oxford.

Lövlie Schibbye, A.L. (1996). Anerkjennelse. En terapeutisk intervensjon? (Recognition: A Therapeutic Intervention? in Norwegian), *Tidsskrift for Norsk Psykologforening*.

Löwendahl, B.R. (1992). Global Strategies for Professional Business Service Firms. Dissertation in Management, University of Pennsylvania.

Löwendahl, B.R. (1994). När strategiske ressurser har både egne meninger og ben å gå på (in Norwegian), *Praktisk økonomi og ledelse*, (3/94), 83–92.

Macneil, I.R. (1980). *The New Social Contract: An Inquiry Into Modern Contractual Relations*, Yale University Press, New Haven, Conn.

Mancini, E. (1993). The Company as a Cultural Operator – Design and Management of the New Qualities, *Management '92 Qualities of Success*, University of Industrial Arts, Helsinki.

Mollerup, P. (1987). Organisasjonens designprogram (The Design Programme of the Organization; in Norwegian). Norwegian Design Council (original ed. Danish Design Center), Oslo.

Nonaka, I. (1991). The Knowledge-Creating Company, *Harvard Business Review*, November–December.

Nonaka, I. and Takeuchi, H. (1995). *The Knowledge-Creating Company. How Japanese Companies Create the Dynamics of Innovation*, Oxford University Press, New York/Oxford.

Nordhaug, O. (1993). *Human Capital in Organizations*, Scandinavian University Press & Oxford University Press, Oslo/Oxford.

Norwegian Design Council (1993). Design i norske bedrifter 1993 (in Norwegian). Internal report by Scanfact, based on survey by telephone February/March 1993 (N = 347 bedrifter), Oslo.

Nyrnes, A. (1990). Omvegen om språket. Eit essay i og om kunnskapsdebatten (in Norwegian), *Norsk Pedagogisk Tidsskrift*, (6), 328–336.

Øijord, A. (1992). *Analytisk esterikk – eller jakten på skjonnheten (Analytical Aesthetics – or Hunting after Beauty*, in Norwegian), Teil forlag, Asker.

Olins, W. (1987). Mysteries of design management revealed, in: Bernsen, J. (ed.) *Design management in practice*, European/EEC Design Editions, Copenhagen/Barcelona: Danish Design Council & Foundación BCD.

Olins, W. (1989). *Corporate Identity. Making Business Strategy Visible through Design*, Thames & Hudson, UK.

Palshoj, J. (1990). Design Management at Bang and Olufsen, in: Oakley, M. (ed.), *Design Managment: a Handbook of Issues and Methods*, Blackwell, Oxford, 37–42.

Parsey, T. (1995). Design as Strategy. Speech and abstract from The Challenge of Complexity, 3rd International Conference on Design Management, UIAH, Helsinki. (Tim Parsey is industrial design manager in Apple Industrial Design group, Cupertino, CA.)

Paust-Andersen, C. and Henni, C.K. (1990). Balans – alternative seating. Paper in Design History, Department of Furniture and Interior Architecture, National College of Art and Design, Oslo.

Peteraf, M.A. (1993). The Cornerstones of Competitive Advantage: A Resource-Based View, *Strategic Management Journal*, **14**, 179–191.

Polenyi, M. (1958). *Personal Knowledge*, Routledge & Kegan Paul, London.

Porter, M.E. (1980). *Competitive Strategy*, The Free Press, New York.

Porter, M.E. (1985). *Competitive Advantage*, The Free Press, New York.

Potter, S. et al (1991). The Benefits and Costs of Investments in Design: Using professional design expertise in product, engineering and graphics projects. Report DIG-03, Design Innovation Group, Open University and UMIST, Milton Keynes/Manchester.

Prahalad, C.K. and Hamel, G. (1990). The Core Competences of the Corporation, *Harvard Business Review*, May–June, 79–91.

Raaheim, K. and Wankowski, J. (1991). *One is Learning as Long as One has Pupils* (in Norwegian), Sigma Forlag, Bergen.

Rumelt, R.P. (1987). Theory, Strategy and Entrepreneurship, in Teece, D. (ed.), *The Competitive Challenge: Strategies for Industrial Innovation and Renewal*, Ballinger, Cambridge/MA. 137–157.

Schön, D.A. (1987). *Educating the Reflective Practitioner*, Jossey-Bass, San Francisco.

Schön, D.A. (1988). Designing: Rules, types and worlds, *Design Studies*, **9**(3), 181–190, Butterworth, Oxford.

Schwartz, L. (1994). Bruken av olympisk design i CBS' sendinger fra Lillehammer-OL. (On the use of the olympic design elements in CBS' broadcast from the Lillehammer Olympic Games, in Norwegian), in Moshus, P. et al (1994). Designprogrammet for OL. Report on the design program for the XVII Olympic Winter Games, Lillehammer. Kulturdepartementet og Norsk Form, Oslo.

Scrage, M. (1995). *No More Teams! Mastering the Dynamics of Creative Collaboration*, Doubleday, New York.

Sparke, P. (1983). *Consultant Design: The History and Practice of the Designer in Industry*, Pembridge Press, London.

Sparke, P. (1986). *An Introduction to Design & Culture in the Twentieth Century*, Routledge, London.

Starbuck, W.H. and Hedberg, B.I.T. (1977). Saving an Organization from a Stagnating Environment, in Thorelli, H.B. (ed.), *Strategy + Structure = Performance*, Indiana University Press, Bloomington.

Svengren, L. (1995a). *Industriell design som strategisk ressurs* (in Swedish). Ph.D., Lund University Press, Lund.

Svengren, L. (1995b). Industriel Design as a Strategic Resource. Proceedings from the 1st European Academy of Design, Design Interfaces, 11–13 April 1995, **4**, Design Management, University College of Salford.

Sörhaug, T. (1996). *Om ledelse* (On leadership, in Norwegian.) Scandinavian University Press, Oslo.

Teece, D., Pisano, G., and Shuen, A. (1990). Firm Capabilities. Resources, and The Concept of Strategy, Economic Analysis and Policy. Working Paper. EAP-38, University of California, Berkeley.

Toffler, A. (1980). *The Third Wave*, USA.

Urban, G.L., Hauser, J.R. and Dholakia, N. (1987). *Essentials of New Product Management*, Prentice-Hall, New Jersey.

Walker, J.A. (1989). *Design History and the History of Design*, Pluto Press, London.

Walsh, V. (1992). *Winning by Design. Technology, Product Design and International Competitiveness*, Blackwell Business, Oxford.

Wheelright, S. and Clark, K. (1992). *Revolutionizing Product Development. Quantum Leaps in Speed, Efficiency and Quality*, The Free Press, New York.

Wickman, K. (1996). Drømmen om Scandinavian Design lever endnu. (The Dream of Scandinavian Design is Still Alive, in Danish), *Louisiana Revy* Nr. 2/96, 18–23.

Wildhagen, F. (1988). *Norge i Form. Kunsthåndverk og Design under inudstrikulturen* (*Norway in Form . . .* in Norwegian), Stenersen, Oslo.

Williams, J.R. (1992). How Sustainable Is Your Competitive Advantage? *California Management Review*, **34**(3), 1–23 (special reprint).

Williamson, O.E. (1985). *The Economic Institutions of Capitalism*, The Free Press, New York.

CHAPTER TWO

IN-HOUSE, OUTSOURCED OR A MIXED APPROACH TO DESIGN

Margaret Bruce and Barny Morris

INTRODUCTION

Attention has been placed on the management of design, as a core competence, within the boundaries of the firm. This assumes that a design competence within the company is a prerequisite for developing successful products. However, the delayering and downsizing of organisations has meant that outsourcing of design is occurring, which raises several questions concerning the management of design activities. At a strategic level, how can innovating companies develop and nurture a design competence utilising an external design consultancy? At a tactical level, skills in the acquisition and management of external design consultancy need to be found.

Just as the interface between "in-house" design and other functions within the firm have been shown to be critical (Cooper and Jones 1995), the nature of the relationship with the external design supplier also has to be considered. Are there advantages to long-term, close relationships between client and design consultant or should an arms-length, more distanced relationship be adopted? What is "best practice"?

Management of Design Alliances. Edited by M. Bruce and B. H. Jevnaker.
© 1998 John Wiley & Sons Ltd.

This chapter addresses some of the key issues raised by the outsourcing of design expertise. A taxonomy of the different ways of organising the design function is outlined, covering solely in-house, solely outsourcing and a mixture of the two. A model is outlined to help design managers to "get the most out of" their design relationships.

OUTSOURCING OF DESIGN EXPERTISE

Over the past ten years, changes have occurred in the organisation of the design function. Design activities are being displaced from the firm and increasingly are being outsourced. (Bruce and Morris 1994) A number of factors have contributed to this trend:

1. The increasing complexity of products and their shorter life-cycles demand expertise from a range of different sources.
2. The use of technology in the design process has facilitated a change in practice. As Francis and Winstanley (1987) note:

   "Firms are now facing a high degree of competition and as the nature of the design process is changing (with the greater use of computers and technical expertise) then the opportunities for changing organisational forms are increasing and the pressures for switching to forms perceived as more effective are intensifying."

3. Design expertise is being availed by service organisations, which are moving away from more traditional in-house design practices towards buying in design expertise. To manage this effectively, service organisations like the Royal Mail and the British Airports Authority (BAA) have dedicated design managers to source, brief and liaise with external design firms. They recognise that management of their design resource is an asset and so reflect Mahoney and Panadian's (1992) statement that:

   "Successful firms in most industries possess one or more types of intangible assets – technological know-how, patented process of design, ... and marketing assets ... even if the firm can market its intangible assets effectively, it could not disentangle them from the skills and knowledge of the managerial team."

4. The development of the "virtual organisation" or "network organisation" or "value-added organisation" means that companies utilise a network of suppliers to carry out value-added functions. For the network organisation to sustain a competitive position, the management of the supplier-manufacturer relationships is critical (Lamming 1993).

DESIGN COMPETENCIES

Another effect of the outsourcing of design expertise is the emergence of design management as a distinct management function. The tasks, responsibilities and skills required by design managers include:

■ the selection and commissioning of design expertise
■ preparation of design briefs
■ evaluation of design work
■ project management skills.

A major survey of UK companies found that those companies that are effective at design management have a sustained competitive advantage (Potter et al 1991). But what constitutes this capability?

Whilst there may be formally an identifiable and distinct design management function, the design management skills may not be located in one place. The formal and informal machinations of different functions (such as design, marketing and engineering in product development) necessitate a certain degree of skill sharing, i.e. marketing and engineering may jointly evaluate design work, project manage design projects, prepare design briefs and make other major design decisions jointly. Therefore an externally based design capability may evolve into a design competence that resides both partly within the boundaries of the firm and also outside (see Jevnaker, Chapters 1 and 5).

From this perspective of design as a competence (rather than simply a "pool" of skills that can be tapped into, or switched on and off when required) (Prahalad and Hamel 1991), the totality of the interfirm linkages between an external design capability and client firm need to be considered. Over time, the design knowledge and its management in the interfirm alliances can become a source of distinctive competence and so become difficult to replicate or substitute (Mahoney and Panadian 1992). Thus interfirm linkages become a source for sustainable design-based competitive advantage.

Long-term relationships with external design consultancies are one approach to the building of a design competence. In Chapter 5 Jevnaker describes a Norwegian furniture company which utilised a design consultant and where the collaboration led to the innovative design, the "Stokke chair". Over time, both companies "learnt by doing" in terms of how to work together effectively to produce a stream of innovations. Through the development of a long-term relationship, the external design resource became recognised as a core competence by the furniture company.

Anecdotal evidence suggests that some firms appear to be more successful at utilising design capabilities than others (Pilditch 1987). Merely having design skills is not enough, so it appears, to ensure sustainable design-based competitive advantage. What enables some firms to use design as a strategic tool, whilst others struggle? In order to investigate this area, a taxonomy of approaches to organising design has been put forward (Bruce and Morris 1995) to compare and contrast the different combinations of design capabilities with a company's own internal resources:

1. in-house design capability
2. external design capability
3. a mixture of in-house and external design capabilities.

A description of each type of capability is given as follows:

In-House. Design capabilities lie within the firm and can be located in a design department, or be dispersed through R&D, production or marketing. As well as full-time design staff, other personnel, such as the technical director may be counted as additional design resource.

External. Design capabilities lie outside the firm and design professionals are selected and commissioned to carry out the design activities required by the firm. Design managers (or those with the responsibility for design) source, commission, liaise and evaluate the design skills.

Mixture. The Design capability comprises a mixture of in-house and external design skills. The external design professional is brought in maybe to interject additional resources, to ensure that the project is completed on time, or to input fresh ideas, or to provide a specific technological expertise.

COMPARING CAPABILITIES

A review of the design literature reveals certain benefits and disbenefits of each type. For instance, the strength of an in-house approach to design is that the designers are integrated into the overall design team and aware of company practices. However, the danger is that they may become complacent and fail to provide innovative ideas.

In contrast, external design professionals can make fresh inputs and not be hampered by the politics and culture of the firm, or other rigidities of previous product development practices. Yet, because of this lack of familiarity with a company, they may make mistakes in moving from the concept to development stages. Fear of leakage of proprietary knowledge is one problem: how much information should the external designer have?

A blend of in-house and external design expertise appears to overcome the problems and build on the positive aspects of each situation. However, the integration of the in-house and external professionals has to be managed carefully to ensure that they are truly working together. The tension between fear of giving away commercially sensitive information and the need to build up an open and trusting relationship is particularly acute.

DESIGN INTERFACES

Whatever the approach adopted, the interface between the design capability and other functions has to be managed and the nature of this interface considered, planned and integrated within the firm. Despite these different approaches to the location and organisation of design (in-house to outsourcing), the product development literature is biased towards the management of in-house expertise. A critical success factor for new product development is that of effective management of the different functions involved in this process. Souder (1988) argues that a positive outcome is likely to arise from "... openness, good cross-functional co-operation and communication, and mutual respect and trust". In terms of the organisational structure, Bentley (1990) suggests that:

> "Flat, or decentralised, systems of control... (coupled with)... integrative mechanisms, good communication systems and individuals who can take broad perspectives, solve problems and cope with risks... are the best performers."

These "rules of best practice" refer to a situation where the design capability resides inside the firm. But how do they relate to a situation of outsourcing? Mutual respect and trust, which eventually lead to openness and co-operation, take time to build and may not be required when an external designer is engaged to work on a "one-off" project. Can "shared values and mutual goal commitments" be achieved with an external design function? Using an external design professional often leads to a formalised *modus operandi* to try to ensure that proprietary information is not "leaked" and to tighten up control of the process. This in itself may undermine the feeling of openness and may constrain the free flow of ideas across the boundaries of the client and design firms involved in product development.

A strong theme in the product development literature is that of multi-disciplinary teams that work together from inception to completion of the process (Craig and Hart 1992). When using an external design consultant, to what extent is their design expertise openly involved in the team? Can the external design professional truly be regarded and treated as a full team member? At what stages in the process can the external designer be actively involved? Which members of the team should have responsibility for liaison with the external design professional?

THE INTERFACE BETWEEN CLIENT AND DESIGNER

As mentioned earlier the interface(s) or linkage(s) between the design capability and the firm need to be considered. Research on the nature of the client–design relationship has focused on the use of external design consultancy. It suggests that the social aspects, rather than the economic aspects, of the relationship are particularly acute in this situation and directly influences the likelihood of establishing a long-term relationship between the two parties.

To illustrate the major categories of relationship found between client and designer a relationship matrix can be created (Figure 2.1). Different characteristics can be found to be prevalent for each type. For instance, from the design professional's perspective, Bruce and Morris (1994) have argued that long-term relationships are desirable because they allow "... the design firm to gain a better insight into the needs of the client and thereby produce better quality solutions".

The degree of empathy or compatibility established between the client and design professional is dependent upon such "social" elements as personal chemistry, the ability to speak the same language (that is, to mix commercial concerns with the visual interpretation of these needs) and mutual trust (Bruce and Doherty 1993). With a long-term relationship, it is expected that a degree of trust will be attained, thus enabling a greater sense of openness and fluidity

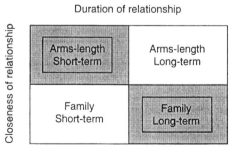

Figure 2.1   Relationship matrix

of information exchange. The dilemma between the fear of losing proprietary knowledge and wishing for an open and trusting relationship is handled by investment in long-term relationships between client and design professional. Achieving, and then sustaining, a balance between control of the external designer and providing sufficient scope for the designer to give vent to his/her creativity is difficult. With long-term relationships, the understanding cultivated between the client and designer may help to attain this balance.

For the client, it is vital that the design professional captures and is able to express the company's spirit and identity. Good personal chemistry allows the designer to understand, at a deep level, the problem from the client's perspective. Factual information is not enough: the designer has to become absorbed and imbued with the values of the organisation as well as the project objectives. In other words both client and designer experience a learning curve as they work with each other during a design project (see Jevnaker Chapter 5).

The evidence seems to suggest that long-term relationships engender certain critical factors, mentioned above, that are enablers for effective design to take place. This supports the competency-based perspective that design is more than a set of design skills; in addition it entails integration and utilisation by the firm. In order for a dynamic and sustainable design-based competency to emerge, investment of resoures by both the firm and the consultancy have to occur over and above the economics of the transaction (i.e paid expertise) and that once established the linkage can be a source of competitive advantage.

METHODOLOGY

The research design was chosen to explore design management practice and to provide insight into design issues associated with the outsourcing of design expertise. Eight manufacturers based in the UK were involved in the research.

Data was collected using a semi-structured questionnaire administered by a tape-recorded personal interview with those responsible for design and product development, for example, Marketing, Design and R&D. In addition, secondary company information was gathered either at source, or by follow-up telephone conversations. Tape recordings and interview notes were transcribed, and these were combined with secondary sources of information to create interview reports. The interview material was analysed by categorising the data and looking for "patterns" that corresponded from one company to another. Where there was data deficiency, follow up telephone interviews with the original interviewee were undertaken. The initial draft of the interview report was returned to the interviewee for approval to cross-check for accuracy.

COMPANY SUMMARIES

Of the eight companies interviewed three summaries are presented below. Company A represents the "in-house" model, Company B is indicative of the "out-of-house" model, and Company C illustrates the "mixture" model.

COMPANY A: IN-HOUSE

Company A designs and manufactures mostly "white goods" for the consumer market using an in-house design department. It is a member of a group of companies where each company retains their own in-house design unit giving the products their particular style of appearance. Thus, the industrial design manager at Company A describes the design department's role as "appearance designing", with the result that the "nuts and bolts" of products for each group company are similar, if not the same, whilst the appearances have been designed differently. Product development projects are achieved in a team atmosphere at Company A, consisting of a project engineer and product co-ordinator, with marketing and design personnel. Marketing has a dominant role in the team, particularly in the initial stages of product development, by generating effective marketing research from which ideas for products are created. Whilst the design department would like to have more authority and involvement in this initial stage of product development, more often than not, Design is brought in by Marketing in the latter stages of product development. Thus, design skills at Company A are used when most of the major design and development decisions have been made by other functions in the company.

A large proportion of new product development is undertaken by R&D who create the "bare bones" of the product. Around this skeleton the designers wrap an outer skin based on a tightly-defined specification created by Marketing. Different appearances are evaluated in a presentation to Marketing where the designs are compared in terms of the "bottom line cost versus appearance" compromise. Good rapport with Marketing is critical as this leads to generation of appropriate solutions by Design first time round.

The marketing department at Company A is perceived to be in a more influential position than design. Marketing at Company A is very strong, they hold the "purse strings" and perceive Design as subservient. However, the design manager is trying to change this situation by raising the status of Design within the company. Tension between Marketing and Design at Company A is rare, however when there are differences it is due mainly to the different department "time horizons", as the designers work to a two- to four-year time horizon compared to a twelve-month time horizon in marketing. This creates two problems:

1. "Prostitution" of a product occurs, i.e. the modification of a product to meet different market needs after product launch, usually triggered by Marketing. This causes technical problems that could have been avoided earlier in the product development process.
2. "Marketing change the goal posts", where the specification of the product changes during the development stages of a product (unlike "prostitution" that is post-product launch). This lengthens the development time of the product and causes Design to generate inappropriate workloads.

The design manager at Company A believes that in order to reduce the lengthy development times of products, Design needs more resources to become proactive in product development. Company A is perceived by the participants in the study as bureaucratic. Despite this the in-house design team have a free rein within the company, particularly if sidestepping bureaucracy is seen to save time. In this respect they are described as a "breed unto themselves".

Relationships with Consultants

Company A uses external design consultants to supplement their in-house team to relieve heavy workloads. The design manager thinks that in-house designers have a level of familiarity with the company that puts any external designer at a disadvantage. When external design consultants are used, they have slowed down the design process and for this reason the use of external designers is not considered a serious option for the foreseeable future. The design manager admits that in-house design departments can become "stagnant", leading to lower work rates and less creativity when compared to out-of-house designers, but sees a number of advantages:

- cost (e.g. a "hidden" fixed overhead)
- familiarity in terms of production, marketing and corporate culture contexts
- stability
- appropriateness of work (because of familiarity)
- control of the resource (to produce appropriate and creative work)
- proprietariness of the work guaranteed.

The relationship with external consultants has in the past been at an "arms-length" basis where the contact between the consultant and other personnel at Company A was tightly controlled. Controlling the work of consultants is considered a major "headache" because the fact that they are external makes it difficult for a client to monitor their work. Because of the lack of familiarity that each individual external designer has with the client organisation, he or she cannot exercise "self control", moulding his/her work according to his perception of what a "Company A" product should be. The design manager perceives the need to allow the designers to be creative, but at the same time, making sure their work is appropriate.

COMPANY B: EXTERNAL DESIGN

Company B is a subsidiary of a large Swedish electrical company. Marketing and design at the company are taken very seriously. The marketing director believes that only by "developing relationships" with his customers has the company managed to produce products that match market requirements closely. Marketing strategy stems from working with a core sample of customers (such as banks and high street retailers), who are used to predicting market trends and growth opportunities. The marketing director believes that the only way to maintain growth is to "keep developing and changing the product, the only way to stay in front is to keep doing this, and not get complacent or lose the initiative". Within this process, customers are encouraged to take a more participative role in product development. As the company becomes closer to the customer, the marketing director sees design as more of a critical issue, since "value" is in terms of the "brand proposition" rather than "added value" in manufacturing terms. He views design as a concept rather than a department, and thus believes good design is everyone's responsibility.

Relationship with Consultants

Since the launch of the company, external design expertise has been utilised to design products. Whilst having an in-house engineering expertise for the other two business areas, the pedestrian barrier system required the use of industrial design input for the first time. This product established a lead in the market around which a whole business has grown. The marketing director now has a strong relationship with one particular consultant and associations with several smaller ones. Designers are used as specialist expertise to solve certain problem areas and form part of an integral part time development team. This team consists of sales, marketing, production, engineering and quality personnel. Suppliers are considered as development partners.

The team decide on a three- to five-year development strategy from which short-term tactical product development plans are created, which are then explained to the design consultant. Once the customer has outlined the type of product required, the external designer is brought in to be briefed informally, and to take part in "brainstorming" exercises with the development team. The brief is viewed as evolutionary until a product specification is mutually agreed in the team. Whilst generating concepts is seen as the consultant's responsibility, evaluation of the consultant's work is undertaken by the whole team. Throughout the development process re-evaluation of the product is continual to check its relevancy with market requirements that may also be changing simultaneously.

The marketing director believes consultants should be viewed as "extensions of your own expertise. If you don't know anything about a subject and you hire an outside consultant, it may not help you because you don't know what you're talking about. You have to have a knowledge base to start with". The trigger for using the design consultant stems from the lack of confidence by the company to deal with a particular task itself.

When "buying-in" design the marketing director sees the altruistic characteristics of the consultant as the most important considerations since other tangible aspects (reputation, quality work) are to be expected as a minimum. He goes on to describe how he met the design consultant at a presentation, where "I listened to what he had to say and I thought I could understand what this guy's talking about", thus mutual language is seen as an important factor. Trust is another important ingredient in the partnership. Trust is about communication, e.g. *talking about the same issues in the same way*.

The marketing director believes that mutual language and trust enhanced by good communication leads to better quality solutions, and that irrelevance is the hardest factor to control. Design management is seen, therefore, as managing the link between customer needs and the design input. Whilst controlling the resource is important the marketing director also suggests that creativity requires freedom:

"I think you have to give them the freedom to let them do it. You have got to choose the right person otherwise you won't trust them to do some free thinking. Quality of input is down to the consultant used."

Thus, design managers should be dogmatic and open minded, i.e., keep pulling designers back to the brief but also have an open enough mind to listen to some lateral thinking. Whilst design is viewed strategically, the internal development team drives the implementation of design, not the external design consultant.

COMPANY C: MIXTURE

Company C began life as a supplier of spectacles to the patients of ophthalmologists in 1917, and is now a subsidiary of a large optical group. The company has won many awards for technological achievement and design. The company researches, develops, designs and manufactures a wide range of instruments for hospitals, doctors and dentists. The market is very conservative, thus 75% of product development tends to be modifications or upgrades of existing products. Many of the products made by Company C last a lifetime, so customers are not looking for radical changes. This also means that production volumes for these products are fairly low.

Generation of new product ideas is confined to the marketing domain since traditionally many new ideas are driven by customer feedback. However, this situation is changing as, to be innovative nowadays, ideas have to be technologically driven. This requires substantial investment in R&D.

When ideas are developed by R&D, full-scale models are made to present to Marketing for evaluation. Solutions are presented within the bounds of "what is thought to be acceptable", however it is suggested by the project engineer that "we are on a hiding to nothing at the end of the day whatever we do, since some people don't know what they want until it is put in front of them." The project engineer sees his role as looking at the practicalities of the Marketing "wish list", and communicating the impact of this in terms of resource allocation required for R&D purposes. The project engineer feels that Marketing do not appreciate either the complexity of the products or the timescale of R&D projects. Design is viewed by Marketing as a service to the company rather than as a strategic resource.

Relationship with Consultants

External and internal design expertise has been used at Company C for at least the last 10 years, with external consultants accounting for approximately 20% of all design work undertaken. External expertise is mainly used if there is a problem that cannot be resolved internally or because of excessive internal work loads, and in this respect consultants tend to be used as and when required. The design consultant has little input in formulating the product specification; this is an internal undertaking between R&D and Marketing only. Consultants are criticised because: "they tend to be full of bright ideas, but when it actually comes to the crunch they don't actually deliver: their ideas just aren't practical."

Whilst the external designer is needed for his/her design skills, the project engineer perceives that in-house designers have more advantages, such as:

- *accessibility*: with an in-house department problems are sorted out immediately;
- *familiarity*: in-house designers know the history of the product better because of the amount of upgrading and modification work that is required;
- *commitment*: in-house staff seem more committed to meeting deadlines;
- *briefing*: is a problem with out-of-house consultants, for instance "we will say we want so and so, and when we get it back its nothing like what we asked for. Consultants don't know what you really want or what the product really does, they don't listen to you properly."

Company C have "been through more external design consultants than hot dinners", with only 30% of their relationships with consultants deemed successful. Whilst one or two good designers have had repeat business from the company, these are the exceptions to the rule.

USING DESIGN EXPERTISE

All of the three companies regarded design as a central resource that added value to the product or service. The main benefits cited were:

- It built the customer's perception of a brand.
- It maintained and improved the product in the face of competition.
- It reduced manufacturing costs.

The use of design in product development was triggered initially by a "need to change". In all three companies, being close to the customer was a priority and when customer circumstances changed then this was considered to be the main trigger to redesign products. The translation of customer and company requirements into design requirements that allowed the company to plan their design input was a critical aspect of design management in product development. In this sense, the design resource interacted with Marketing. If building a design competence was considered a strategic source of competitive advantage in chosen markets, then Design was integrated at a higher level into the overall business plan (for instance, resources would be allocated to Design in the business plan).

DESIGN MANAGEMENT ISSUES

It was evident from the cases above that choice of design supplier was influenced by a number of factors. These are discussed below.

MATCHING THE DESIGN CAPABILITY TO THE DESIGN PROJECT

The "character" of the design solution required, and the temperament and reputation of the designer was matched so that radical "new to the world" product development, for instance, was generated by designers used to handling "clean sheet of paper" situations. In one of the companies in the sample, the marketing controller wanted the external designer to "give me ideas I haven't thought of." In contrast, the managing director of another company found creativity a "pain" and suggested that "... radical design has its place when you're starting out in the marketplace because you have nothing to lose, and you need to make a mark to get a good market share."

MATCHING INTER-FIRM TECHNOLOGIES

All companies were concerned that the consultancy had the expertise to follow through design concept proposals with detailed designs that could be made using the most cost-effective manufacturing methods. One client only considered consultancies where the concept chosen utilised a technology that they were already *au fait* with and that the consultant could demonstrate experience of using before. In this sense a *specialist* expert was preferred who could be innovative within a particular technological field. Another company preferred using *generalists* because, whilst the consultancy may not have expert experience in any one field, their diverse experience enabled them to span accross technological areas and thus innovate through cross-fertilisation of ideas.

The research suggests that companies involved with regulated high-technology products in mature markets required external *specialised* designers on a short-term basis. Products in these markets changed rarely in terms of their core technology, but when changes did occur they required individuals with a thorough working knowledge of the product and its production process. In contrast the evidence also suggests that companies which dealt in low technology products and which have a more liberal customer base require more *generalist* help on a long-term basis.

Another technological issue was related to the data interface between client and design consultancy and between design consultancy and other stakeholders in the development process. For instance, some companies felt that it was important that consultancies could speak to their preferred suppliers in similiar CAD and CAM language, or were linked via IT to facilitate communication.

The research suggests that most technologically sophisticated companies have to "know what they are doing" to begin with (e.g. have in-house design know-how) in order to be able to fully exploit the specialist expertise. Good "matching" was seen as critical in some companies as it led to more acceptable integration of the design capability with the client company.

MATCHING CUSTOMER EXPERIENCE WITH THE CONSULTANCY'S OWN INSIGHT

It was felt to be important by all companies that the consultant was able to understand the world of the client's customers. For instance, customer preferences, behaviour, lifestyles, competitive activity in the marketplace etc., not just the core functionality of the product. In this sense, particularly where Marketing were involved with consultancy liaison, it was felt that the designers had to "speak the same language" as their marketing counterparts in the client firms.

ACTIVE VERSUS PASSIVE EXPERTISE

It was apparent that clients were treating their designers (both in-house and out-of-house) in two ways. Firstly, some companies were using the designer as a "partner" in product development, where the designer took an active part in the decision making in the development of the product, such that the designer worked *with* other departments on an equal footing. For instance, one company used their consultant as a "sounding board" for marketing/product ideas because "the product designer's opinion was important".

Particularly in the case of the external design capability, it was apparent that some consultancies assumed a passive role despite the efforts of the client to involve the designers proactively. For instance, in one company, the "industrial designer was uncomfortable with the level of involvement" they were looking for. They had an "aloof attitude, e.g. the consultants didn't want to work *with* us but were happy to work *for* us." This may be explained by the consultant's anxiety that the "involvement" could escalate and become difficult to charge the client for on a quantitative basis.

DEPENDENCE, PROPRIETARY INFORMATION, TRUST AND CONTROL

These three issues were particularly prevalent in the external design capability situation. Certain clients were reluctant, in the first instance, to give the designer "the full story" – this was motivated by their lack of trust in an "outsider". As trust in the relationship developed, clients became more open with revealing the "nuts and bolts" of their core technologies. Where a design competence developed it became apparent that clients began to become dependent upon the input of the consultancy. For instance, in the case of the medical products company (Company C), the client had to use the same consultant when changes or modifications were required because only that consultancy had the skill and depth of knowledge of the product to carry out these changes. This raised the issue of power and control in the relationship.

Whilst employing an external consultancy in some ways suggested that the client required "help", the client was anxious in all respects to maintain control particularly where major design decisions needed to be taken, notwithstanding the client's possible lack of understanding or experience of design. Company A believes that out-of-house designers are difficult to control, particularly their creativity, whereas Company B suggests lack of control of external consultants is due to weak project management skills by the client company. Regular contact to ensure that the external designer is "along the right lines" is important.

Some companies were anxious about the way in which some consultancies exercised confidentiality, particularly when the consultancy was known to provide expertise for other competitors.

COST ISSUES

How did companies gauge the cost of design expertise? Several companies had problems with assessing the cost and "value for money" both before, during and after purchase of the design expertise. However, the companies in the study considered external designers as a variable cost (i.e. able to be switched on and off) and as a result, more cost efficient when considered over a full financial year in comparison with an internal designer.

There were also some indirect costs which some companies identified, in particular that of familiarity. Familiarity was described as the "learning curve" that both partners (client and the designer, whether in-house or out-of-house) pass through, as they become more and more knowledgeable of each others' working styles, personalities, the design constraints (customer and company requirements) and (from the designer's viewpoint) the client's corporate culture or company "ethos". Company A believed that consultants could never be as familiar with their situation to the same extent as an in-house designer and hence could never produce wholly effective design solutions. Where companies used external design consultancy, familiarity was a barrier to both purchasing design consultancy and to switching to other design suppliers. Familiarity from the designer's point of view was a source of competitive advantage – it "added value" to their service.

In-house designers were more familiar with the company's past products, manufacturing processes, materials and market requirements. However, familiarity was viewed as a "factor of communication" remedied by good project and relationship management, rather than an inherent disadvantage of external designer consultants. Long-term relationships ensured that familiarity was developed over time and facilitated the building up of trust, respect and understanding that are important in producing effective design solutions.

If familiarity is as important as this research suggests, the cost of losing or replacing the level of "familiarity" (for instance when an in-house design department is downsized or removed, or a new consultant is used) is another important indirect cost of the move towards outsourcing.

MANAGING IN-HOUSE DESIGN VERSUS AN EXTERNAL DESIGN CAPABILITY

The literature assumes that the management process with in-house design is the same as the process of managing outsourced design. The management of the client-designer relationship is significantly more critical than for the in-house situation, because of the assumption, by clients in particular, of communication and control "difficulties". These difficulties may lead to the following management activities:

1. *Work evaluation*: evaluation of the designers' work was more acute in the out-of-house situation (perhaps driven by anxiety over a perceived loss of control, resulting in inappropriate work).
2. *Relationship "honeymoon"*: intense level of contact (enforced familiarisation) in the initial stages of the relationship in the out-of-house situation.

3. *Purchasing criteria*: choosing the external designer was a more critical and analytical procedure than when initially employing an in-house designer.
4. *The brief*: this was an evolutionary document in the in-house situation as opposed to a "nailed down" document in the external consultancy case. The in-house brief was more of a loose and exploratory document, whereas the brief in the external situation had additional contractual constraints that put more clearly defined financial constraints on the scope of work.
5. *Financial constraints*: In-house departments tended to have political spokespersons who were able to argue for acquisition of extra resources if required within the organisation. External design consultancies had an agreed budget within the confines of a contractual arrangement. However, the extent to which the budget was strictly adhered tended to lessen as the relationship between client and consultant developed.

These points are summarised in Table 2.1.

RELATIONSHIP CHARACTERISTICS

The *compatibility* of intrinsic partner characteristics were significant in successful relationships. Commitment and enthusiasm to the project was important and enhanced by the client "selling" the product to the consultant to get him/her on their side. A sense of urgency, meeting deadlines, professionalism and understanding of commercial realities was also significant. Whilst the ability to both work together and work independently was highlighted, the most important characteristic was to have confidence, from both partners, in each other's abilities, resulting in respect and trust. Understanding the demarcations of authority in terms of accountability and responsibility were also important, particularly if there was a dispute.

Dimensions of *compatibility* relate to the personal characteristics of the individuals involved in the relationship, the type of expertise required and offered by the client and design professional and the respective company cultures and *modus operandi* (See Table 2.2).

Repeat purchase of design from the same design supplier suggests that the relationship is compatible between the partners involved. Long-term relationships were typical for the companies participating in the research, because such relationships were perceived as having benefits (such as stability), understanding the client's needs and markets, and loyalty and trust, which can help the client to relax and give consultants more creative freedom (Bruce and Docherty 1993). There was also the recognition that where design was

Table 2.1 Comparison between design management approaches

	In-house	Out-of-house	Mixture
Purposes	Accessible	Solve short-term problems	Flexibility
	Integrated within company practices and product development team	Relieve workloads	
		Access new ideas	
	Cost efficient	Access specialist expertise	
		Easier to abort unsuccessful projects	
		Cost efficient	
Management characteristics	Encouraging creativity	Evaluation of work more intense during the design process	Creation of design team complex
	Less anxiety over control factors		
		Level of contact higher in the initial relationship stage	
		Choosing the designer is critical	
		Communication factors uppermost	
		Fear of leakage of proprietary information	

(Reproduced by permission of Elsevier Science)

perceived as a strategic tool, any linkages between client and design company were perceived to be very significant.

RELATIONSHIP LIFECYCLE MODEL

Design management at a strategic level entails making a decision about the location of design expertise, particularly whether this should lie inside or outside the firm. The trend towards outsourcing is driven partly by cost considerations and a belief that this may be cheaper than having design in-house. Keeping design in-house is driven partly by control factors, as well as by fear of leaking proprietary information and loss of expertise. The client's

Table 2.2   "Pros" and "Cons" of short-term versus long-term relationships

Short-term advantages	Long-term advantages
1. *Comparison purposes* Having a relationship with more than one consultant enabled the client to compare quality and efficiency factors between consultants	1. *Familiarity* This improved the effectiveness of the design input from project to project
2. *Cost* Relationships were open to market forces	2. *Stability* Once a project had been completed successfully with a consultant, management anxiety and uncertainty about the relationship and product development in general reduced
3. *Access to different expertise* Gave the client more choice in the type of expertise required	
4. *Time* Consultants were used to relieve short-term in-house design workloads	3. *Continuity* Retaining the same consultant ensured that the brand proposition within and, if required, across product ranges remained the same. It also made the initial stages of each new project much easier because the "process" of using the same consultant remained consistent
5. *Compatibility* By maintaining a short-term relationship with a consultant, if the relationship is "difficult" it gives the client the freedom to choose a more compatible designer parter	

Source: Bruce and Morris (1994), reproduced by permission of Elsevier Science

previous experience and the individual external design manager's personal preferences have a role to play in the decision about the location of design expertise, so a wide range of design management practices exist.

At a tactical level, design management, where an external design consultancy is used, entails the procurement, commissioning and project management of the design capability. Compatibility is an aspect influencing the selection of design company. A major facet of the management process is that of fostering close and long-term relationships, or arms-length and short-term relationships. Long-term relationships may have certain perceived benefits in attaining security, trust and understanding (Bruce and Docherty 1993). A comparison of the relative merits of long- and short-term relationships is shown in Table 2.2. By investing in an in-house design capability, then accessibility, familiarity and control are more likely to be perceived as being ensured. However, complacency coupled with the rigidities imposed by the firm's current and past product development practices can be seen as a barrier to innovation and may be perceived as a major cost of relying solely on in-house design expertise.

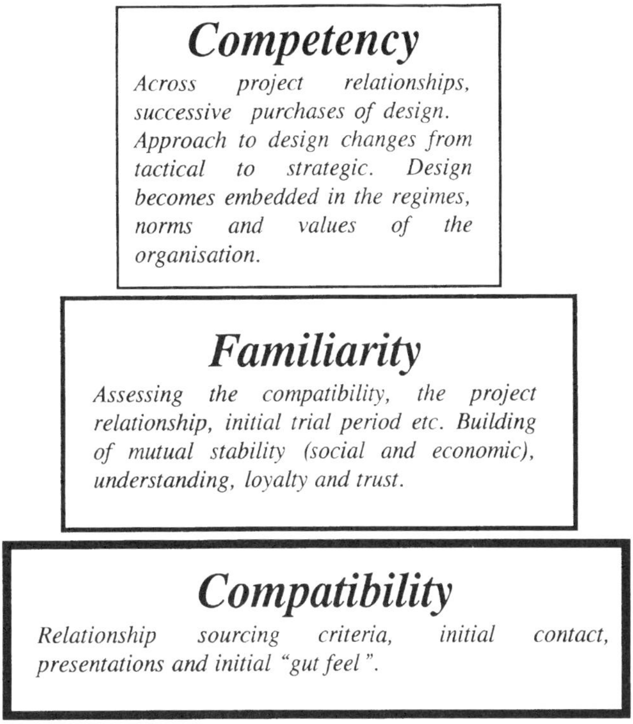

Competency

Across project relationships, successive purchases of design. Approach to design changes from tactical to strategic. Design becomes embedded in the regimes, norms and values of the organisation.

Familiarity

Assessing the compatibility, the project relationship, initial trial period etc. Building of mutual stability (social and economic), understanding, loyalty and trust.

Compatibility

Relationship sourcing criteria, initial contact, presentations and initial "gut feel".

Figure 2.2   Relationship lifecycle mode

The stages in the life cycle of a client–design relationship are outlined in Figure 2.2.

The model sets out the stages in the client–design relationship, whether long or short term, and serves to formalise the types of decisions required at different stages. There is a need for design managers to acquire, preserve and use experience of relationship management for the future. Each client relationship entails a set of stages, from initial contact, to appraisal of client-design compatibility, to the project and its completion. Once a project has ended, then ongoing contact is required between parties to ensure that the client-design relationship is continued, if there is a potential to establish a longer term relationship. Moving from a one-off project to an ongoing relationship takes time and commitment in building up a personal relationship. Compatibility between client and design firms also entails a resonance of operating procedures and the design company's ability to understand the client's business, in order to devise effective design solutions. Good design, a positive personal relationship and company compatibility all have to dovetail to facilitate a longer term relationship.

From the perspective of design as a competency, the design relationship lifecycle model depicts the nurturing and growth of a design capability into a full design competency. Initial projects with design consultancies are akin to tapping a "pool" of resources. Emerging from further repeat purchases, if client/design/compatibility dovetail, then the linkages between consultancy and client company may become stronger, represented by both familiarity aspects and possibly the triggering of personal relationships. These familiarity aspects become embedded in the culture (values and beliefs) of the firm and thus may not be obvious but hidden as a design competency. In this sense the design relationship lifecycle evolves from pure compatibility issues at initial purchase, to familiarity issues through successive purchases, to a recognisable competency after an appropriate period of time. Eventually this process can provide a sustainable design-based competitive advantage.

CONCLUSIONS

The trend towards outsourcing has been identified in the product development process and the product development literature for management practice has been shown to focus on design as an in-house capability. Three different approaches to the management of design expertise have been identified: an in-house capability, an external capability and a mixture of the two, coupled with two main approaches towards client–design relationships – short-term and long-term.

The challenge to design managers is to recognise that design as a competence serves as a strategy, i.e. resource that can positively benefit competitiveness, and to strive to manage interfirm design linkages in such a way as to help foster a design competence in the longer term.

ACKNOWLEDGEMENTS

The authors would like to thank Elsevier Science for their permission to reproduce some of the figures and tables in this chapter.

REFERENCES

Bentley, K. (1990). A discussion of the link between one organisation's style and structure and its connections with its market, *Journal of Product Innovation Management*, 7, 19–34.

Bruce, M. and Docherty, C. (1993). It's All in a Relationship: A Comparative Study of Client–Design Consultant Relationships, *Design Studies*, **14**(4), 402–422.

Bruce, M. and Morris, B. (1994). *Strategic Management of UK Design Consultants: Policy and Practice*, Manchester School of Management, UMIST, Manchester.

Bruce, M. and Morris, B. (1995). Approaches to Design Management in the Product Development Process, in Bruce, M. and Biemans, M., *Product Development*, John Wiley, Chichester.

Cooper, R. and Jones, T. (1995). The interfaces between design and other key functions in product development, in Bruce, M. and Biemens, W., *Product Development*, John Wiley, Chichester, 81–99.

Craig, A. and Hart, S. (1992). Where to now in new product development research? *European Journal of Marketing*, **26**(11), 2–49.

Francis, A. and Winstanley, P. (1987). Organising Professional Work: The Case of Designers in the Engineering Industry in Britain, in Pettigrew, A. (ed.) Procs. of British Academy of Management Conference, Blackwell, Oxford.

Lamming, R. (1993). *Beyond Partnership: Strategies for Innovation and Lean Supply*, Prentice Hall, UK Ltd.

Mahoney, J.T. and Panadian, J.R. (1992). The Resource-based view within the conversion of strategic management, *Strategic Management Journal*, **13**, 363–380.

Pildlitch, J. (1987). *Winning Ways*, Harper and Row, London.

Potter, S. et al (1991). The benefits and costs of investments in design: *Using professional design expertise in product, engineering and graphics projects*, report DIG-03, Design Innovation Group, Open University and UMIST, Milton Keynes/Manchester.

Prahalad, C.K. and Hamel, C.T. (1990). The Role of the Core Competencies in the Corporation, *Harvard Business Review*, May–June, 81–92.

Souder, W.E. (1988). Managing Relations between R&D and Marketing in New Product Development Projects, *Journal of Product Innovation Management*, **5**(1), 6–19.

PART TWO

CAPABILITIES IN GLOBAL NEW PRODUCT DEVELOPMENT

INTRODUCTION

Birgit Helene Jevnaker

Based on real-life business cases, this section examines in more detail how firms may be capable of designing products with new or improved qualities to be attractive for buyers and end users in target markets. Being capable and repeatedly innovative is often a must in today's competitive business worlds. Being competitive with a visible "character" intact seems to be particularly necessary for firms aspiring for a leading edge. But how to do all this *in practice*? Although established firms may have access to valuable development competence, very few have a qualified industrial design staff or allied expertise, with some notable exceptions such as Sony and Philips, Alessi and Brown – to name some of the more famous well-known ones. Interestingly, some of these design-conscious firms started working with design through a designer relationship (see Chapter 1). Hence, a priority for most firms who want to improve their design is to find (or meet) designers that may be valuable contributors for the company and its customers. But who knows what is "right" for whom, where and when? How do you buy unknown expertise "off the shelf"? Corporate borders and organisational charts may not give much advice as to the best sources of expertise, nor do company files inform managers about how to deal with this type of increasingly knowledge-based supplier. Nevertheless, access to value-creating sources is just one important factor: just as essential is organising the value-creation. As a heterogeneous often neglected multi-disciplined expertise, product design/industrial design is a particularly interesting aspect of this new and more general competitive challenge.

Management of Design Alliances. Edited by M. Bruce and B. H. Jevnaker.
© 1998 John Wiley & Sons Ltd.

Moreover, design expertise varies with context, time and space, and is often located outside the corporate walls, but even when located inside seems to be not well understood nor fully exploited (Blaich 1993). In general, 'people and processes' are the most neglected themes in the product development literature (Hart 1995). Although new products typically are seen as the "life-blood" of the differentiated manufacturing firm, and the need for up to date information and integrating knowledge is painstaking, the leadership of design and development people and processes may be messy. This is alarming since industrial designers need to be extremely well informed of the firm's needs and wants (as well as its customers, distributor chain needs etc.), in order to envision and tailor-make new and profitable product concepts.

This book's perspective, therefore, is that we need to focus on the nature of business firms' organising *design capabilities*, i.e. the firms' abilities to source trained and talented designers, to combine the designers' skills with the firms' core competences and otherwise foster interaction with user groups, product engineers and marketers in order to convert skills to profitable and sustainable advantages. Part Two contains six papers describing and analysing these important aspects of business firms' competence in managing design alliances. Each chapter tells a unique story, nevertheless each contributes to a better insight into certain core component and common themes in managing design relationships. The section is structured in accordance with the book's conceptual framework encompassing a (dynamic) set of organising capabilities in new product development.

RESOURCING CAPABILITY

A new approach to the design and development of products for professional use, is discussed by Bruce and Morris in Chapter 3. This draws on recent product design development in the British part of the American company Ingersoll-Rand, famous for its construction tools. Ingersoll-Rand's redesign effort to launch a new generation of hand-held construction tools was developed through a leading Manchester-based industrial design consultancy. One of the main issues for Ingersoll-Rand was that of finding and selecting appropriate design expertise. After trying another external design input, a more long-term multidisciplinary and close interactive approach was sourced. The new design relationship actually emerged through the initiative and good timing of the design experts making themselves accessible for the "local" industry. Lengthy practical industrial experience on both sides, as well as the personal rapport between client and designer, helped to accelerate the time to market resulting in a successful launch of the more user-friendly products.

These were targeted to meet the market gap created by new health and safety legislation, especially in the German market.

COMBINATIVE CAPABILITY

The focus of Chapter 4 is on how a large and mature high-tech firm may combine its best sources of design ideas and expertise in products targeted for global competitiveness. Kiyonori Sakakibara tells the story of IBM's ThinkPad Series. ThinkPad is the trade name for the company's portable computers, which have been developed through global collaboration across the United States, Japan and Europe. The use of and collaboration with design expertise was nothing new in itself as IBM has a long tradition in exploiting both internal design resources and external design consultants. Co-ordinating corporate design is not new either among the company's 15 design centres. Yet new design opportunities were a major challenge when IBM, in the late 1980s, started development of portable computers within a new product market strategy. This particular product development focused more on product differentiation and unique features of individual products to be sold in world-wide markets. Industrial designers played an especially critical role in the whole development process in order to give a competitive edge. According to Sakakibara, the way IBM combined its design resources helped its breakthrough in the sector of personal computers.

ORGANISATIONAL LEARNING CAPABILITY

In Chapter 5, Birgit Helene Jevnaker describes how five Scandinavian small and medium-sized firms (SME) have explored industrial design to create a competitive advantage. Working with mostly external design experts, the organisational knowledge dimension emerged as critical to sustain and further enhance the design-based advantages of the firm, both in product development itself (so as not to start from scratch in next PD-project) and in a wider corporate context: How are the firms taking in, "absorbing" and recreating design knowledge from their design allies? The article explores this knowledge-related capability with special reference to three of the five design relationships in various SME: an office furniture company (HAG), an information technology-based firm (Tomra) and a firm manufacturer of plastic products for leisure purposes (Hamax). The design allies in these settings are both long-term and medium-term, allowing for potential investments in knowledge creation and improved absorptive capacity. Differences are also visible, such as in the location and relationship with the designer allies. In these design relationships, two factors coined mutual "acknowledgement" and "entrepreneurial mobilisation" are emphasised together with particular hidden routines which also seem essential for the firms' sustained innovation in product design and communications.

INNOVATION CAPABILITY

The Novo Nordisk case by Karen Freeze (Chapter 6) provides further insights into innovative designing for particular user groups such as designing for diabetics in the pharmaceutical sector. Novo Nordisk has its headquarters in Copenhagen and a North American organisation, but competes in global markets with its specialised products. The Novo Pen was conceived in new ways to enhance ease of use for modern multi-injection insulin therapy. This case reveals several levels for managing design in a business company: from the horizontal contribution of designers in multi-disciplined team processes to the corporate, more hierarchical decision-making to foster and implement new innovative strategies. In this firm, design decisions are raised also in relation to corporate and brand consistency and cost-effectiveness in information design. The author points to certain challenges for organising the future design directions related to diversity in user groups. Furthermore, the personalised management of design with support and enthusiasm at the very top of Novo, a style that earlier provided a creative but consistent environment for design, is concurrently replaced with more decentralised and competitive measures raising new challenges for the integration of innovative resources over time and space.

DESIGN-STRATEGIC CAPABILITY

In Chapter 7, Lisbeth Svengren describes the slow and somewhat difficult integration of a modern industrial design approach for a division of Ericsson which manufactures mobile telephones. Ericsson is at the forefront of the technology, but how to develop a design management strategy and co-ordinative system is a different matter. Since technological problems are being resolved and the competition shifts to new combinations of (price and) user-friendliness, product integrity/personality, or other user-communicative factors enhancing the technological facilities, then the design concepts and ergonomic issues become more significant. Ericsson is working on the transition towards smaller and inexpensive consumer-oriented work/leisure and functional/status products to be able to keep up its share in global markets. In this increasingly fast-moving competitive context, product design embedded in brand-building and an improved technology-marketing interface have evoked new interests. Some of the trade-offs and difficult decisions behind launch and relaunch of the so-called HotLine or just "Ericsson" (mobile phone) are illuminated. Case descriptions also highlight the unfruitful disruptions when visionary managers leave – and the stop-go of searched-for collaborations with outside design consultants even when management perceives design as important.

PROTECTIVE CAPABILITY OF DESIGN-BASED ADVANTAGE

How may a firm both create and sustain a design-based competitive advantage? Antti Ainamo gives a detailed description of the management of design creativity in relation to commercial outcomes, in Chapter 8. This case explores and documents the making and evolution of the Finnish Textile and Clothing firm, Marimekko, which obtained a widespread reputation due to its visionary exploitation of unique craft-based techniques and design approaches for specific patterns and colours in fabrics. Later, the company entered a sustained period of decline combined with a rigid financial control and failure to create a climate for designers to produce innovative and marketable designs. Rejuvenation began when a new entrepreneurial manager took over Marimekko and renewed the spirit of its original owners. Yet the article documents that the critical relationship between industrial design and business performance is more intricate than that captured in slogans such as "design gives success".

The empirical evidence in the following six articles may provide the necessary substantial grounding for new insights and guidance as well as remind us of the reality of how design and business is developed through creative partnerships over time and space.

REFERENCES

Blaich, R. and Blaich, J. (1993). *Product Design and Corporate Strategy. Managing the Connection for Competitive Advantage*, McGraw-Hill, New York.

Bucciarelli, Louis L. (1994). *Designing Engineers*, MIT Press, London and Cambridge, Mass.

Hart, S. (1995). Where We've Been and Where We're Going in New Product Development Research, in Bruce, M. and Biemans, W.G. (eds), *Product Development: Meeting the Challenge of the Design–Marketing Interface*, J. Wiley and Sons, Chichester–NY–Brisbane–Toronto–Singapore, 15–42.

CHAPTER THREE

SOURCING DESIGN COMPETENCIES: INGERSOLL-RAND
Margaret Bruce and Barny Morris

INTRODUCTION

A major product opportunity had arisen that would allow Ingersoll-Rand to dominate the Construction Powertool Market with the proviso that a product could be brought to market rapidly within 12 months. John Schofield was the international product marketing manager based at the UK headquarters of Ingersoll-Rand. The product he wanted was to be best in its class for power, vibration and ergonomics. These were important criteria considering the imminent introduction of rigorous work, health and safety regulations that were to put European working practice legislation two to three years ahead of their American counterparts.

Graham Dewhurst, the project engineer, believed that by exploiting the Vibra-Smooth, a vibration reducing device he had worked on for many months, would ensure their market leadership position for a number of years. He envisioned a tool that would position Ingersoll-Rand as a leader and innovator in the European Construction Tool Market and wanted his fellow colleagues to share his enthusiasm. But to fully exploit the Vibra-Smooth meant radical design changes for which they did not have the in-house

Management of Design Alliances. Edited by M. Bruce and B. H. Jevnaker.
© 1998 John Wiley & Sons Ltd.

Mr John H.L. Schofield (project leader), marketing manager. Started his career in the computer industry and joined IR in 1983.

Mr Graham Dewhurst, design engineer. Started as a mechanical apprentice in 1976, and joined IR in 1989 as a design engineer.

Mr Dave Hill, production/shopfloor.

Mr Bob Buxton, industrial design consultant. Senior founding partner of Buxton Wall McPeake Design Consultancy.

Figure 3.1   Irgo-Pic – the people involved

expertise and so would have to rely on an external design consultant's competence for the first time, which added to the project risks.

INGERSOLL-RAND

Ingersoll-Rand has manufacturing establishments in seventeen countries and world-wide sales and distribution. The company manufactures all types of process plant and portable air compressors, mining equipment, pumps, oilfield equipment, automated assembly systems, and a comprehensive range of air-powered construction tools. Its main markets span automotive, energy and construction. Ingersoll-Rand is a multinational company with a turnover of $4.2 billion in 1993 (when this case was prepared) and employs 35,000 people world-wide.

In 1993, the total world market for construction hand tools was estimated at 250,000 units approximately. This was reduced from a peak in 1990 of an estimated 328,000 units reflecting the world-wide recession in the interval. However, the construction industry was predicted to grow in 1994 between 1% and 4%. Mr Schofield believed that the demand for power tools would begin to show once pre-recession sales levels had been reached.

THE POWER TOOLS GROUP, UK

The UK company was established in 1921 in London and later that year a warehouse was acquired in Trafford Park, Manchester. Manufacturing commenced in Trafford Park in 1933 and the range of products produced was extensive. Post-war growth in production meant expansion was vital and the company now has their manufacturing establishments in the North of England. One of the UK plants is part of the International Power Tools Group of Ingersoll-Rand and forms an integral part within that group, alongside US sister plants in Athens, Pennsylvania and Roanoke, Virginia. The 300-strong workforce are concerned with the manufacture, sales and marketing of hand-held air-powered tools such as scalers, chippers, drills, impact tools and sand-rammers for use in all industries where air power is used. Design and development of all products has traditionally been the sole responsibility of the sister plant in Athens, Pennsylvania, until the Irgo-Pic project began at the UK plant.

STRATEGY

Ingersoll-Rand's strategy has been to broaden its customer base and to manufacture more of its products abroad. Europe was identified as a major emerging market, and in accordance with the company's long-term strategy, an application was made by the general manager for Europe, supported by the plant manager in the UK and authorised by the Divisional general manager in the US to set up a European Design Centre in the UK. Authorisation to access appropriate resources for the project took almost two years to process. Whilst this was happening, John Schofield took the initiative and started to lay the groundwork for the project. It was imperative for John Schofield to get an early start with the project in order to meet the market gap created by changes in health and safety legislation, especially in the German market.

EUROPEAN DESIGN CENTRE

The aim was to set up, as a long-term commitment, a European Design Centre for Ingersoll-Rand that was responsible for new products for Europe. Part of the initiative involved the employment of Graham Dewhurst as a design engineer. However, John Schofield needed a starting point for the project, as he explains:

> "We had nothing. We had no in-house experience of developing products from scratch. We had no supplier base. This has positive and negative benefits. Starting from fresh meant that we could do what we wanted, however the rest of management saw it as 'opening a can of worms' as they weren't sure how it was going to work."

John Schofield was highly motivated to become involved with setting up the design centre because he wanted to sell a product that had European equity, rather than American. It was decided to base the organisation of the project along similar lines to Project Lightning (an air powered grinder) which ran in the US where product design teams, concurrent engineering, user groups and rapid prototyping were used to develop products quickly and effectively. As John Schofield comments during interviews with authors: "It was not so much a decision as an acceptance that if we were to collapse the time frame with a market-orientated product, there was no other way to be organised."

THE DESIGN TEAM

John Schofield had the responsibility for setting up a design and development team with the aim of bringing to market, within 12 months and within budget, a product in the 10 kg weight range that would be best in class for power, vibration and ergonomics. He decided that the team approach would be best used as a way of cutting down the development time from four years, as was typically the case for new product development in Ingersoll-Rand, to one year. However a number of questions were raised by top management:

- Could the company organise an efficient and effective design team?
- Who would be the members of the team?
- Would this team be able to manage the process, having little experience of new product development?
- Would they be able to source external design expertise successfully?
- Would the project be to schedule, meet all customer requirements and still be within budget?

After much discussion, John Schofield managed to gain support for his idea and a small full-time team was put together consisting of representatives from Marketing, Design, Engineering and Manufacturing from within the company (i.e. John Schofield, Graham Dewhurst, Dave Hill) and Product Design which was sourced externally. Dave Hill had been with Ingersoll-Rand on the "shopfloor" for almost 30 years, and so knew the capability of the UK manufacturing plant and what it could or could not make.

This core team was given sole responsibility for all the decisions made concerning the project, and reported to a steering committee made up of directors of different functions. John Schofield persuaded his peers that this was the only way to get real commitment:

"Unless you give the team the authority to do the job, they won't take any of the responsibility for it. It helps get the motivation. By getting everyone in the room together it meant that everyone knew what was going on. We all believe that everyone can contribute to the design of the product, not just the engineers, and not just the core team members either."

Each team member contributed on an equal footing. This meant that they bounced ideas between each other, giving different views on subjects that were not ordinarily within their traditional area of expertise. Normal traditional hierarchical forms of authority were also forgotten. Instead, project leader's duties were rotated amongst the group so that different people took command at different times.

Control was exercised through goal orientation, so that the team focused collectively on achieving tasks and the satisfaction accruing from solving problems together, rather than individual conformity to meeting a series of established milestones, or from subservience to an authority figure. The members of the team viewed their relationships with each other as being "akin to a marriage"; whilst there was bound to be conflict (since the free flow of opinions and ideas was encouraged) the members always made up afterwards!

THE STEERING COMMITTEE

The Steering Committee oversaw the team but, in fact, took no part in the team's decision-making process. The Committee could advise and guide the team, but not make any of the final decisions. Its responsibilities were:

1. to set and concur with the team vision for the project;
2. to review change in the scope of the project;
3. to review changes in time, budgets and key product features.
4. to project status and milestones;
4. to remove strategic barriers.

The Steering Committee consisted of top management from Finance, Quality, Purchasing, Manufacturing and the general manager. The core team and Steering Committee interacted closely together throughout the project.

MARKET ANALYSIS

The type of information and the means of generating and collating market information was carefully planned, in order that an appropriate marketing strategy could be put together. The main areas that the team had to consider were:

- Market research that would generate product specifications, e.g. user needs/ customer needs: industry regulation and legislation.
- Product positioning.
- Sales: past, present and predicted (and estimations of market size and value).
- Competitor information.

MARKET RESEARCH

Remaining close to the customer was an overriding concern of the product development team. Accordingly, the team worked closely with a core user-group which consisted of Ingersoll-Rand distributors, competitor's distributors, sales people (Ingersoll-Rand staff) and end-users.

The User Group Members (UGM) were compiled mainly from Europe, although support was also solicited from the US, Canada, South America, Asia and the Pacific Rim. The 50 to 60 members of the group were used to evaluate concepts and to verify that the product was "on the right track" in terms of the product specification's ability to satisfy market requirements. Most of the user information and specifications were compiled via close interaction with the UGM. Three approaches were used to talk to the UGM:

1. The UGM were asked for product feature preferences.
2. The UGM were then asked for direct requirements in order to create a "wish list" of product features.
3. Finally the UGM was asked what product features they disliked.

The team had difficulty in getting customers to articulate exact and precise needs in the abstract, so throughout the product development process, the UGM were shown a number of competitor tools (and in the final stages of the process, prototype tools) to elicit a better response. By having tools in front of them to criticise the team found that this tended to focus the UGM's attention on key issues.

John Schofield already knew that health and safety features of power tools were becoming important as purchase criteria of Ingersoll-Rand's customers. This demand was driven primarily by health and safety regulations that were laid down to protect the end-user. Whilst at the time there was no regulation in force that limited the use of tools with a high level of vibration, the pace of regulation in the industry, particularly in Europe, suggested that this would soon become an issue. John Schofield identified that the European market was ahead of the American market in terms of concern for health and safety legislation at work, and a concern for the ergonomics of the product. John Schofield explained that:

> "We have legislation two or three years in advance of the US market. We have an opportunity for designing products specifically for the European Market, which will not only benefit us in Europe, but give us a product advantage in the US market."

COMPETITION

Ingersoll-Rand and Atlas Copco were the only two world-wide suppliers in the construction tool market. However, each major geographical market had its own indigenous manufacturer, who challenged strongly in that area. Using competitive benchmarking, John Schofield categorised competitor products into a particular power/weight/vibration/cost ratio-low weight (in the 10 kg range), low vibration and low cost coupled with high power being the optimum for hand-held tools.

IRGO-PIC

John Schofield realised at a very early stage that lack of in-house skills meant that suitable expertise would have to be bought into three areas: business, engineering and design. The team lacked the necessary skills in managing design and development projects so enlisted the help of a local university's business services centre with the long-term aim of being able to manage future projects autonomously. Graham Dewhurst identified the need to be able to simulate the "power cycle" of the product on computer and used a local university's engineering facilities to do this also.

It was the first time the UK division had used a *local design consultancy* to model the power tool, and whilst this partnership was productive, it was not exactly the "long-term" relationship that the team were looking for. As Graham Dewhurst laments: "When it came down to actually solving our problems they didn't have the expertise to do it." Essentially the consultancy was a specialist in model making rather than offering a full design service such as detailing the design from concept models, therefore it was unable to provide the expertise the company was looking for. Whilst this was a setback to the team, they learnt the importance of sourcing the appropriate skills from design consultancy.

During an interview with the authors John Schofield explains his approach to using the design consultancy as follows:

> "We wanted someone who wanted to come to the party. He had to take on some of the responsibility, and put his own stake in as well. If we fell, then we all fell together. We had the objective of starting a product design facility in Europe that went beyond this initial project. We wanted someone who was part of the team."

This caused a rift to form between the team members. Should they stay with the consultant, or start afresh with another consultancy? This dilemma also coincided with the development of "Vibra-Smooth" – a vibration-reducing device that would give the product massive advantage over current competitor products. The inclusion of Vibra-Smooth would radically change the shape of the product, however, the detailed design of this device had still to be undertaken. Whilst in theory the idea was proven, it was unknown whether the device could work in practice or even be engineered into the product, along with a new body shell, within the allotted time.

This caused a second major dilemma within the team. The Vibra-Smooth device would meet the customer requirement of less vibration. Did they try to incorporate this device into the product at the risk of missing the deadline, losing their market opportunity and potentially their market leadership position? Alternatively, perhaps it would be less risky to go into production, and try and sell the product without the vibration requirement but to schedule?

After much discussion, the team took the decision to use an alternative design supplier to detail design. The company was approached by a local design company, Buxton Wall McPeake and John Schofield decided to employ the Manchester branch of this multi-disciplinary design consultancy. Buxton Wall McPeake had expertise in rapid prototyping and had in-house CAD facilities.

BUXTON WALL McPEAKE

Buxton Wall McPeake is a leading multi-disciplinary design consultancy in the North West of England. When the company was formed in 1979, the directors recognised the potential of bringing together the disciplines of product and graphic design to provide a comprehensive range of design services.

The consultancy aims to achieve the optimum design solution for the market, by working closely with client's marketing and production teams during a design project. The consultancy has the capability to manage projects from initial concepts through to production, dealing with many other design-related activities throughout the process.

Bob Buxton, a founding partner of the consultancy, believes that design and development is the key to strategic market positioning of all successful products. For a specific target sector, it is vital to have the appropriate blend of appearance, function, economic manufacture and presentation.

WORKING WITH CLIENTS

The senior partners try to establish with each client a framework at the beginning of a project which defines the degree of freedom the consultancy can work within. However, this framework has to be flexible to allow for change in a product's development, and for this reason communication with the client at all times is seen to be key to a successful project. Awareness of the market requirements and what the client desires is critical. Bob Buxton describes the process during an interview with the authors:

> "You have to tell the client everything, otherwise at the end of the project, the product is not acceptable. This takes a lot of time, and typically we have put more time in than we wanted to."

It was in December 1992 that the partners of the consultancy were cold-calling local businesses to drum up some business. Fortunately, Ingersoll-Rand was on their list. In mid-December of 1992 Alan Wall and Bob Buxton were soon on their way to Ingersoll-Rand for an initial interview with the core team. At this initial meeting John Schofield explained that they had already used a design consultancy firm and a prototype had been built. However, the vibration requirement had not been incorporated into the design and to date no decision had been taken to incorporate the device. The team welcomed the design consultant's views in this matter. With time pressing, the Ingersoll team needed a design consultancy that was flexible, highly committed and could work quickly to design the product to schedule. BWMc agreed to meet again in early January for a project briefing session.

DESIGN AND DEVELOPMENT PROCESS

The project between BWMc and Ingersoll-Rand was divided into four design and development stages:

1. Briefing
2. Feasibility study and detail design.
3. CAD development
4. Rapid prototyping and tooling up.

BRIEFING

The two companies met again in early January to discuss the details of the project. The briefing at this stage was very informal, as John Schofield explains:

> "What I'm looking for, gentlemen, is a new image for the product. I don't just want the product to be a market beater functionally, I want our customers to be able to look at a product, and know it instinctively to be made by Ingersoll-Rand."

The team was still undecided as to whether to incorporate the Vibra-Smooth Isolater. Whilst some members of the core team wanted to do some minor modification to the existing prototype, others wanted to make use of the Vibra-Smooth device. Time was running out and the possibility of starting a new design from scratch was not viewed with particular relish given the time pressures. Before making a final decision, they decided to invite some fresh input from Buxton Wall McPeake. While the team described their requirements, industrial designer Bob Buxton made small "thumb-nail" sketches. Graham Dewhurst, the design engineer, commented later to the rest of the team that he was particularly impressed with the way the consultant "put pencil to paper" and started sketching in this initial discussion. This briefing was critical for a number of reasons as the consultancy needed to know:

1. how the product was to be made;
2. the effect the additional Vibra-Smooth device would have on the internal geometry;
3. the type of material and process to be used for the moulding, and how it was to fit to the inner mechanisms;
4. about other existing Ingersoll-Rand products, and how this new product was to fit into, or be a departure from, the existing range;
5. the critical elements in the design as perceived by the end-user and customer;
6. project management procedures;
7. the number of units (as batches) to be produced in the first and second years;
8. the handle configurations.

Mid-December '92	Initial discussion between Ingersoll and Buxton Wall McPeake
6 January '93	BWMc project briefing at Ingersoll-Rand, and initial feasibility study by BWMc signifying the start of Stage I.
12 January	Presentation to Ingersoll-Rand Team. End of Stage I.
13 January	Debrief at BWMc.
4 February	Fax sent of breakdown of consultancy costs, and of the product costings (not including the design of the T-Handle). Ingersoll-Rand were very focused on completion of the job rather than the cost of the job.

Figure 3.2   Irgo-Pic – set-up schedule

As Bob Buxton walked around the Ingersoll-Rand factory and was shown the existing product range by the design engineer and the project leader, he soon realised that the product was going to be used in a fairly tough environment. Bob Buxton thought back to his student days. He had worked on a building site and on motorways during summer vacations and remembered the way the workmen had treated the tools, for example leaving them exposed to all weather conditions, never cleaned and handled roughly. Bob Buxton believed that, as a designer, these briefing situations were invaluable in absorbing "the approach, or the culture" of the company.

DESIGN CONSIDERATIONS

During the briefing process, Bob Buxton realised that the Vibra-Smooth device would give the product immense added value. If the Vibra-Smooth device was to be included in the product, it meant a new product image and a change in dimensions so that from an industrial design standpoint, they would have to start again. Bob Buxton's view was that the Vibra-Smooth device *should* be included and he saw this as an opportunity to do something very different. The designer's view was very strongly supported by the design engineer Graham Dewhurst, and eventually they managed to persuade John Schofield, the project leader, that despite the time limitations, a radical redesign would reap greater benefits than modifying the existing product.

With the team thus united, the Steering Committee were convinced that this was the way forward since their worry was that a "me too" product would be developed. It was decided that an initial feasibility study conducted by the design consultancy would allow other possibilities to be explored. John Schofield appreciated the idea of an initial trial period as this allowed him to evaluate the work of BWMc and the potential of the working relationship that was to ensue. Bob Buxton was enthusiastic not only at the prospect of redesigning the product from scratch, but also because he was entrusted with some freedom in this process by Ingersoll-Rand. Aware that time was short, John Schofield gave BWMc less than two weeks to come up with a conceptual design for the product.

Graham Dewhurst explained that the product had to be used in a variety of work situations. It needed to have interchangeable D-Handle and T-Handle components (i.e. shape of handles). Both tools were to be used with two hands and have triggers which could be "inside" or "outside" the handle. Bob soon realised that the "barrel" of the product, which tapered towards the pneumatic chisel, was the common component in each different variety of the product. Thus, the solution was to arrange a suitable universal fixing system between the different types of handle and the main barrel, which was durable enough to withstand the environment in which the product would be used.

In terms of the product styling, the original prototype model was short and stumpy. The new product was going to be longer, and the main problem would be hiding the fixings used to attach the handle to the barrel. This last problem ended up dictating the final styling of the product.

THE PRESENTATION

After the two-week period, Buxton Wall McPeake returned to Ingersoll-Rand with some conceptual sketches. Bob Buxton had been told of the project time constraints, and whilst normally in a Stage One project situation he would show a range of proposals to his client, he homed in on one proposal simply to save time. To illustrate his proposal, full-size two-dimensional representations were produced, along with a full-size cardboard cut-out of the product for the core team to evaluate. Back-up sketches were also brought (see Plates 1, 2 and 3).

When the colour illustrations were unveiled, the reaction to the concept from the core team was very positive. Bob Buxton's instincts were right about the proposal and the concept was considered for further development. What surprised the consultants was the reaction to the cardboard cut-out model.

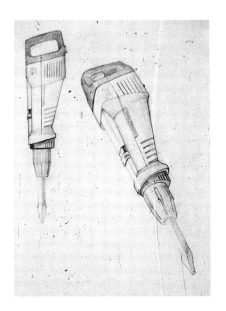

Plate 1 Drawings and models

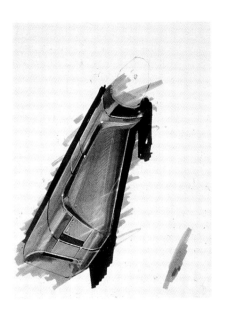

Plate 2 Drawings and models

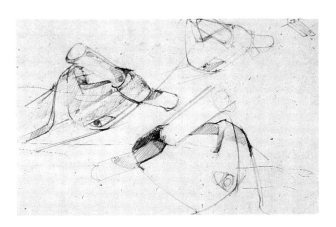

Plate 3 Drawings and models

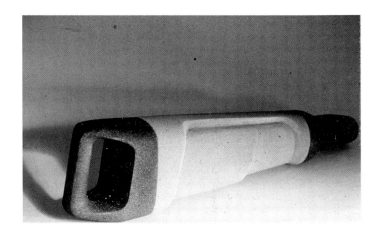

Plate 4 Foam model

Plate 5 The finished product

Graham Dewhurst remarked on how this gave a very clear indication of scale and the ergonomic problems involved.

The two companies discussed how to progress from concept stage to product development. Bob Buxton was asked to cost the components that made up the barrel housing and handles, and was given the name of the moulder and toolmaker, which had been previously sourced by Ingersoll-Rand.

John Schofield again reiterated the time pressures on the project. He felt that this could not be stressed too much. They had already spent over nine months of their allotted time, and had another nine months to go. This meant that the exterior of the product had to be designed, developed and manufactured well within that timescale. Bob Buxton voiced his worry about proceeding from development to manufacture without undertaking an appearance model:

> "How are we going to have time to produce an appearance model? It's important to realise that once we reach the tooling up stage, it's very difficult to change the design at that point and so it's far better to model the product now whilst the design is still on paper. Are you confident that the design will be exactly what you want?"

Bob Buxton had known other clients miss out this important stage in the development process and then regret it later on. However, John Schofield had already paid for a prototype from the previous consultancy, and felt that with time running out, it was best to proceed to full manufacture as quickly as possible. He also knew that the earlier the product was produced, the more advantage it had over its competitors, and the higher price premium the market would be prepared to pay for it. He believed that Bob Buxton was able to visualise the product well enough and so took the risk that Bob's expertise would avoid the need for another detailed replica appearance model. After much discussion it was decided to produce a quick appearance 'foam model' of the product (see Plate 4).

FEASIBILITY

While Buxton Wall McPeake started work on the external casing of the product, Graham Dewhurst was still, at this stage, completing details for the Vibra-Smooth device and testing the product, right up until the end of March. This affected the overall internal geometry, and in turn the external geometry of the product. Bob Buxton needed to stay in constant contact with Graham Dewhurst, should any significant developments occur. He noted that:

12 February	Bob Buxton visits Ingersoll-Rand to discuss engineering details with Graham Dewhurst.
13 February	Creation of a sculpted model from foam by BWMc. Bob Buxton gains John Schofield's approval to enlist the help of an ergonomics consultant Ergonomist is sent the original model made by the first design consultancy.
19 February	Received relevant ergonomic data on the product.
17 March	Visit to Gloucester to see Formation Engineering (an external 3-D CAD specialist) to explain detailed general arrangement drawings.
27 March	BWMc receive fax from Formation that the CAD model had been completed.
30 March	BWMc change the outside of the foam model to incorporate the fixing bolts for the handles, and the ergonomic specifications.
16 April	Ingersoll-Rand invoiced by BWMc for work completed in Stage Two.

Stage Two involved BWMc working very closely with Ingersoll-Rand, such that over 35 hours were spent in meetings between the two companies between early February and late March.

Figure 3.3   Stage Two

"We received sketch drawings with general sizes of components, and where they fitted internally. Elements were still changing such as the diameter of the isolator and the barrel, because these were still being developed, and this affected the appearance obviously. That's the frustrating stage where things keep changing. Everything's fluid, but again, you have to expect that. It's a normal part of development."

Bob Buxton now knew enough about the moulding to produce some preliminary detailed development drawings that would enable the toolmaker and moulder to put some more exact costs together. These General Arrangement (GA) drawings were done manually, but more detailed views had to be worked out using BWMc's CAD software. Whilst 2-dimensional CAD is a mechanisation of traditional manual drawing it is not necessarily quicker. As Bob Buxton explained, the advantage of CAD was that it was quicker to perform many iterations of drawings.

By the beginning of.April, the team knew that all of the components would fit together without any problems occurring. They knew how they were going to mount the internal components and the exhaust baffle had also been finalised. As Bob Buxton comments:

> "We spent quite a lot of time detailing the bosses (where the bolts attaching the handle to the casing located), and the rib sections that connected the bosses to the case, so a lot of the later development was to do with those sort of details. There was more work inside this moulding than there was outside."

CAD DEVELOPMENT

Buxton Wall McPeake was well-versed in the use of 2-D CAD. The process of moving from 2-D CAD drawing to a finished product was divided into five stages:

1. The design was developed to a detailed design stage using 2-D CAD.
2. The detailed development work was translated from a 2-D to a 3-D computer model using sophisticated CAD software by an external CAD company (Formation Engineering).
3. The CAD model was then loaded into a Stereo Lithographic (SL) machine which, through a chemical process, actually reproduced physically the shape designed on computer.
4. The resultant shape was finished off quickly by traditional model makers. This was used by the toolmaker to make several polyurethane castings to enable prototype products to be built for testing.
5. The feedback from product testing enabled the development of the 3-D CAD model file which was eventually used to make an injection moulding tool to enable full scale manufacture of the outer-casing.

RAPID PROTOTYPING AND TOOLING UP

Rapid prototyping was an expensive but effective and fast way of progressing from drawings on paper to prototype products. For instance, the normal price for a model made by a model maker in the traditional manner could cost between two and five thousand pounds. Rapid prototyping (RP) cost a

13 April	Meeting with Formation Engineering to approve pattern for "tooling up".
15 April	Meeting with toolmaker to progress the development of the injection moulding tool.
28 April	Preparation of final detailed General Arrangement. Remodelling of certain details required with the toolmaker.

After mid-April much of the liaison with the toolmakers and moulders was carried out by Graham Dewhurst, the design engineer, as Ingersoll-Rand had financial constraints concerning the commissioning of BWMc to do this.

Figure 3.4   CAD development progress

minimum of £10,000 but produced a pattern far more quickly. The Ingersoll team had not used rapid prototyping before because of the cost, but the project had to be on schedule, and the fortuitous sourcing of a competitively-priced RP supplier, Formation, meant that rapid prototyping was a realistic option. Normally BWMc would have been given the task to find a supplier, but because of the cost issue, this task was given to Ingersoll-Rand. Their experienced purchasing staff, and their company size, gave them more bargaining power compared with BWMc and in John Schofield's view, BWMc were being paid to design, not source suppliers.

Before the product design could be finalised and put on to CAD, the toolmakers, moulders and designers had to agree on the way the product was manufactured. Bob Buxton, Graham Dewhurst and John Schofield arranged to meet the CAD engineers from Formation and the more traditional toolmakers all together. The mix of manufacturing tradition (toolmakers) and manufacturing innovation (IR, BWMc and Formation) gave rise to a lively discussion. Bob Buxton commented:

> "If everyone sits around the table agreeing then you're not going to get progress. If there is this sort of argument, push, and determination to look along a certain route, then new things can happen. John's team were great because they wanted to be progressive."

The main argument was about how the product casing was to be moulded, as this affected the shape of the CAD model and ultimately the SL prototype. Whilst the tool maker was sure that a one-piece moulding was feasible, he took a little convincing that it was a practical route to follow. There was also a cost involved, as a one-piece moulding compared with a clam shell arrangement (e.g. a mould that came in two halves, similar to the construction of DIY hand drills) meant more expense. John Schofield was adamant:

> "Our customers want to see a continuous surface on the products they buy; any lines or cracks may indicate a weakness to them. I don't want to be able to see any split lines on the outside surface, so the casing must be moulded in one piece."

While John knew little about injection moulding he knew that the outside of the product had to look strong. He was especially aware that any "seams" apparent on the surface of the product would be perceived as a point of weakness by his customers. Whilst the moulder, toolmaker and Bob Buxton all suggested that a clam shell design would be easier and cheaper to mould, John Schofield wanted a one-piece moulding. This was a brave route to follow as it presented quite considerable moulding and tooling problems. Bob Buxton wanted to make sure that the translation of his drawings into a 3-dimensional shape were performed correctly. Despite Ingersoll-Rand not being able to pay him for this time, Bob decided it was good investment to make the effort to ensure that his design turned out right. Bob Buxton explains:

> "I think at that point John had hit some cost limitations so Graham took over, however we were still needed as we had to liaise closely with Formation Engineering because we were getting queries back from them. The product may look a fairly simple thing, but it's actually fairly tricky to model on computer because of some quite subtle blends and changes. For instance, if you look at the shape of the handle grip, you can draw it in two dimensions, but what's really happening? How do you define that?"

Formation Engineering actually quoted to do the work in four days, but it eventually took 10 days to complete the moulding. Bob Buxton lamented:

> "I could have done, really, with several visits down to Formation just to sit in. It's like in traditional model making, where you don't just give them the drawings and then go away, you would actually, if there were any problems, call in. You are having to rely on some else's interpretation otherwise. I did my best using the fax to check the drawings. The whole point is, of course, that you can change a model on CAD quickly and easily because its a virtual model."

The major part of BWMc consultancy work finished once their drawings had been translated into the 3-dimensional CAD model. BWMc's input from this point was to finish off some small details (such as the exhaust baffle plate) and generally to be accessible for advice by the Ingersoll-Rand core team should the need arise.

FROM DESIGN TO MANUFACTURE

It was not until July 1993 that most of the details of the product were completed. With Graham Dewhurst now overseeing the process from 3-dimensional CAD model to manufacture, Bob Buxton did not see the "real" design until the moulders were starting trial production runs (or "first-off" sampling).

It was at this point that Bob Buxton detected a small, almost unnoticeable flaw with the exterior of the product. Where the barrel body met and blended with the end nozzle section there was a slight ridge, caused purely by the CAD solid modelling process. When Formation had translated Bob Buxton's drawings, the model had been divided into two separate sections and then "joined" on screen. Because of the limitations of computer screen definition technology, the join looked perfect. However, once transformed into a "real" solid model, the ridge became evident. This was noticed by the designer and regarded as important aesthetically, but the client did not regard this as likely to affect customer sales.

19 May	BWMc still working on the T-Handle.
30 May	Preparation of component drawings. Sorting out the nose ring detail, exhaust baffle and moulding the D-Handle.
3 June	Logo label added to the moulding/casting.
6 June	IR polyurethane castings.
21 July	Ridge for nose ring completed.
	Toolmaker makes wooden "trial" version of carbon electrode prior to spark erosion of tool. Also polyproplene exhaust baffle snap fit finished.
3 November	Product launch for D-handle expected.

Figure 3.5   Final stages

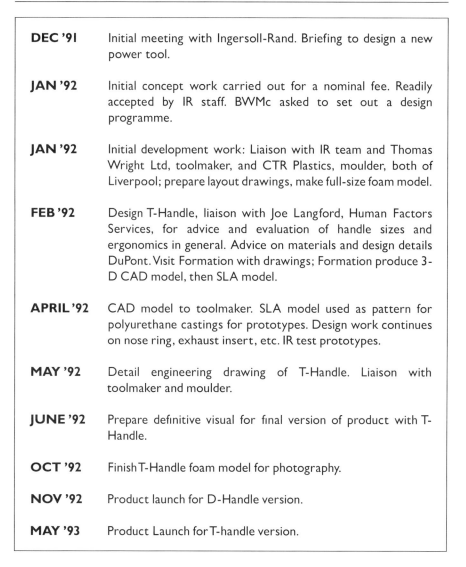

DEC '91	Initial meeting with Ingersoll-Rand. Briefing to design a new power tool.
JAN '92	Initial concept work carried out for a nominal fee. Readily accepted by IR staff. BWMc asked to set out a design programme.
JAN '92	Initial development work: Liaison with IR team and Thomas Wright Ltd, toolmaker, and CTR Plastics, moulder, both of Liverpool; prepare layout drawings, make full-size foam model.
FEB '92	Design T-Handle, liaison with Joe Langford, Human Factors Services, for advice and evaluation of handle sizes and ergonomics in general. Advice on materials and design details DuPont. Visit Formation with drawings; Formation produce 3-D CAD model, then SLA model.
APRIL '92	CAD model to toolmaker. SLA model used as pattern for polyurethane castings for prototypes. Design work continues on nose ring, exhaust insert, etc. IR test prototypes.
MAY '92	Detail engineering drawing of T-Handle. Liaison with toolmaker and moulder.
JUNE '92	Prepare definitive visual for final version of product with T-Handle.
OCT '92	Finish T-Handle foam model for photography.
NOV '92	Product launch for D-Handle version.
MAY '93	Product Launch for T-handle version.

Figure 3.6 Project history – summary

Bob Buxton was tempted to change the model to rectify the flaw, however, as he explains:

> "At the end of the day there was so much time pressure the ridge remained although it was feasible to have taken it out. When I went down to the toolmaker and saw the carbon electrode used to spark erode the tool, I really should have got some "wet and dry" (sandpaper) there and then, and removed the detail. I

think I would have been thrown out of the workshop if I had done that, because it was a fairly traditional workplace! I think this is a good illustration of the process and its pitfalls. It's essential to have the designer right the way through the process."

The Irgo-Pic was launched in the Autumn of 1993 and despite recession, the Irgo-Pic has proved to be a success. The power provided by Vibra-Smooth was immediately recognised as the main selling point, but with the increasing awareness of the damage caused by exposure to hand and arm vibration, the ergonomics of the tool have become an important feature too. In terms of the power to vibration ratio (e.g. the aim was more power, but less vibration), Irgo-Pic is a leader and is way ahead of the competition, such that in 1994, Ingersoll-Rand sold double the units of Irgo-Pic in Europe than those of the previous model in the previous year. The product also won two prestigious design awards for innovative design and use of materials. John Schofield commented:

"There are many things learned during the project, which besides being bought into the next project, will also be applied to Irgo-Pic – *continuous improvement* is the name of the game! *There is no doubt this facility will remain the Ingersoll-Rand Power Tool Design Centre for Europe* and for tools for world-wide sales. The Irgo-Pic is the start of the "right" product image for Ingersoll-Rand. The image of the future will be one of modern styling coupled with super-efficiency which will be instantly recognisable as Ingersoll-Rand's."

ACKNOWLEDGEMENTS

Thanks are due to John Schofield, marketing manager, Ingersoll-Rand; Bob Buxton, partner of Buxton, Wall, McPeake; ESRC for financial support; and to Ingersoll-Rand and Buxton, Wall, McPeake for permission to reproduce some of the figures.

CHAPTER FOUR

GLOBAL NEW PRODUCT DEVELOPMENT: THE CASE OF IBM NOTEBOOK COMPUTERS

Kiyonari Sakakibara

How may a large and mature high-tech firm combine its best sources of design ideas and expertise in products targeted for global competitiveness?

For years IBM has been failing to keep up with its nimbler and more stylish competitors in the personal computer market. In the notebook sector that has all been changed and one of the biggest factors in the change has been IBM's successful use of good design. In 1993 sales of the ThinkPad series were estimated at $1.4 billion worldwide, making it market leader in the notebook sector. According to a survey in the US, over one-third of purchasers in 1993 bought it because of its design.

This chapter describes the detailed development process of IBM's ThinkPad notebook computer, and how IBM harnessed design to help its breakthrough in the notebook computer market. The story is a model for companies in general.[1]

IBM'S NEW APPROACH TO PRODUCT INNOVATION

ThinkPad is the trade name for the company's portable computers, which have been developed through global collaboration across the United States, Japan and Europe.[2]

Management of Design Alliances. Edited by M. Bruce and B. H. Jevnaker.
© 1998 John Wiley & Sons Ltd.

" 'Speed, beauty, hard-nosed practicality and grace': such was one media description of IBM's ThinkPad 700C, launched in 1992. The language in *Business Week* verged on hyperbole. It called the 700C one of the best products of the year: 'The IBM ThinkPad 700C has pizzazz! The 10.4 inch diagonal active matrix screen is 50% larger than most other notebook screens and offers resolution as crisp and clear as some colour desktop computers. The 7.5 pound machine has a unique pointing device built into the keyboard: the TrackPoint looks like a pencil eraser but acts like a mouse, allowing the user to manipulate it while hands never leave the keyboard.' "[3]

The world personal computer market has been changing rapidly. Personal computers, once archetypal high-tech products, have become commodities in a market driven by price. One factor is the rise of manufacturers of IBM PC clones, including Compaq, Packard-Bell, AST, Dell and many others. IBM's reaction has been twofold: a strategy of low cost and product differentiation. The company has cut cost aggressively and now offers more price-competitive products than ever before. IBM has also pursued product differentiation by utilising its global resource. Notebook computers, or notebooks, have been a focal product for this strategy.

Two prominent figures behind IBM's new "differentiation" approach are the (now former) manager of the company's Design Program, Tom Hardy, and the corporate industrial design consultant Richard Sapper. The product innovation in notebooks described below illustrates their pioneering efforts in product differentiation at IBM.

Product differentiation was not undertaken as a matter of course at IBM until recently. Traditionally the company had pursued a system-oriented strategy, and emphasis had been placed on the consistency or integrity of office systems as a whole rather than the unique features of individual products. This was natural since the mainframe business was at the heart of the company. In short, product differentiation was relatively unimportant at IBM and products of marked individuality were not welcomed.

A CONFUSING START

In portable computers, IBM had started development of the differentiation strategy in the late 80s, but the old strategy was also sustained, resulting in two conflicting products: the PS/55 Note and PS/2 Laptop. It was not until autumn 1991 that the conflict was resolved (see the chronology in the table at the end of this chapter).

The company's first product with the new differentiation strategy was the PS/55 Note, which was introduced in Japan in April 1991. This was IBM's first

A4-size notebook with a black and white liquid-crystal display (LCD). Its simple rectangular form and black colour distinguished it from any other product that IBM was selling.

The PS/55 Note was a rapid success in Japan, and eventually became the base-model for developing a worldwide product series that was later named the ThinkPad. However, the model was originally marketed only in Japan, because Japan was the world's largest market for notebooks, and IBM Japan was under severe competitive pressure there from Japanese manufacturers, led by Toshiba. Another factor was the availability in Japan of many of the key technologies for manufacturing notebooks.

In fact, IBM depended heavily upon external capabilities in Japan to build the PS/55 Note. For example, Ricoh Co. Ltd. performed the final assembly of the product, including the most critical task, assembling the computer's two circuit boards, so densely packed that each has chips on both sides. Ricoh was involved in the development work from the early stages of the project. Since then, it became a steady partner of IBM's in this product category. The black-and-white liquid crystal display was supplied by Sharp Corporation and other Japanese manufacturers.

The IBM PS/55 Note weighed a little over five pounds and cost from $1680 to $2550, depending on features. That was roughly half the price of the heavier and much larger laptop computer, the PS/2 Laptop, that IBM introduced for worldwide markets just two weeks before the introduction of the PS/55 Note in Japan. The PS/2 Laptop was designed solely by the company's Boca Raton Design Center, Florida, in line with the IBM's old PS/2 guidelines, and emphasis was placed on the similarity to its desktop products, from a functional as well as an aesthetic point of view.

The PS/2 Laptop and the PS/55 Note were quite different from each other, although IBM was selling both in the same market. The former was a typical global product from IBM, sharing many features with its existing products. The latter had unique looks, and was a limited domestic model aimed specifically at the Japanese market. From the viewpoint of IBM's global strategy the former was a mainstream product, while the latter was not. However, the PS/2 Laptop did not sell well, particularly in the European markets, simply because it was bulky, heavy and overpriced. In addition, the product lacked any marked individuality or personality, a factor which was becoming more critical in the personal computer market. To cope with this situation, IBM developed and introduced a European version of the PS/55 Note in autumn 1991, under the name PS/2 Note. The PS/2 Note was welcomed in Europe and sold well.

The PS/2 Laptop was the company's last portable computer developed in America. IBM decided to kill any projects for further developing the PS/2 Laptop series in the US, and to adopt a new corporate strategy of developing small products in Japan for IBM around the world. Since then, much more emphasis has been placed on the design aspects of the products in this category through the new differentiation approach to product innovation.

THE THINKPAD 700C

Measuring only 8.5 by 11.7 inches and weighing 7.5 pounds, IBM's ThinkPad 700C notebook computer was released in October 1992 as the latest model in the ThinkPad product series. The product was developed through global collaboration across three continents and sold in worldwide markets. It was the first IBM notebook computer to incorporate a colour display. The ThinkPad 700C looked very much like the PS/55 Note, but featured many noteworthy technological accomplishments, most significantly:[4]

1. It had a very large screen for a notebook computer, 10.4 inches diagonally, which was the product of IBM's joint venture with Toshiba, begun in 1989. This screen was the largest thin-film transistor (TFT) colour screen available on any portable in the industry, and IBM was the only company that could offer it in 1992.
2. It had a powerful microprocessor that consumed far less electrical power than conventional chips. The microprocessor was based on the Intel's 486 design, but the energy-saving features were engineered by IBM's technology products division in Burlington, Vermont, and the chip itself was made by IBM. The low energy consumption was crucial, allowing the power saved to be used to light the big screen without requiring the extra weight of a larger battery.
3. It incorporated a new pointing device, the TrackPoint, built into the keyboard. The TrackPoint is an original IBM device which acts like a computer mouse or trackball but is faster, allowing the user to manipulate the cursor quickly without removing his or her hands from the keyboard.

The ThinkPad 700C was named *Inforworld*'s "Product of the Year" and "Editor's Choice" by *PC Magazine*. "Overtaking Powerbook" was the headline of a *New York Times* article which read:

> "This year, the ThinkPad appears to be on its way to achieving the unthinkable –
> rivalling the meteoric rise of Apple Computer's Powerbook, the notebook that
> took the industry by storm last year.... The research firm estimates that
> ThinkPad revenues will more than double to $1.4 billion this year, while the

world-wide Powerbook sales will increase 40 percent, to $992 million. If anything, the ThinkPad appears to be gaining momentum recently. *Computer Reseller News*, an industry newspaper, said this week that demand for ThinkPad is outpacing demand for the Powerbooks."[5]

THE DESIGN CONCEPT

The ThinkPad 700C was conceived as an adult's electronic business tool which is powerful and easy to use. Its size allowed it to be easily carried in a briefcase, stored in a locked drawer, stacked horizontally or vertically on a bookshelf and used on a lap, desk or aeroplane. Ease of use in the space-constrained environments of a mobile product was facilitated by the TrackPoint device, since neither extra workspace for a mouse nor extra product size for a trackball was needed. "Ease-of-use in set up, operation and mobility were key design goals," said Tom Hardy, the former manager of IBM's Design Program. "Packaging the large colour display into a small size notebook housing, incorporating an innovative pointing device into the keyboard, and providing front access for diskette, removable hard file and battery pack – all were based on making the user the highest priority."[6]

Conceptually, the ThinkPad 700C design reflects the concept of the traditional Japanese lunch box, or *Shoukadoe Bentou*, the essence of which is a simple exterior with a rich interior. Once opened, the simple exterior reveals a powerful computer with colour display and exquisite attention to detailing. "We wanted a clean, simple design", said Richard Sapper, IBM's consultant on industrial design since 1980, who played an important role in designing the 700C. "When the system's lid is closed, it is as close to a simple rectangular box as we could get. If you took the IBM logo off, you might not recognise it as a computer. It is a simple idea, but it was very difficult to design."[7]

Another key designer in developing the 700C was Kazuhiko Yamazaki, who led the design team at IBMs's Yamato Design Centre outside Tokyo. As with many Japanese industrial designers, he had a strong engineering background. His interest in developing a compact product with many technological features combined with Sapper's strong attachment to a simple form to produce the 700C.

From Tom Hardy's point of view, the ThinkPad product series was the first successful example of IBM's differentiation approach to product design. By this he meant a conscious effort by the company's industrial design teams to add value to IBM products at: (1) point of purchase stage – perceived quality when making the buying decision, such as a product appearance that pleases and informs, an image of user friendliness and innovative characteristics; and

(2) product life stage – usefulness, including ease of use, ease of repair, status conveyed, durability and expandability.

One striking aspect of the ThinkPad products series is its common colour. Black – straightforward, basic – was a perfect match for the system's simple design. Its rubberised paint finish is also distinctive, designed to provide a tactile, more personal feel. "We wanted to begin creating a new image for IBM with these systems", Yamazaki said, "to create new products that stand apart on the basis of clean simple lines."[8] It was the industrial design group which argued strongly for a black computer as a differentiating factor.

For notebook computers, design is critical. "In a way, the notebook is a departure for IBM", said Yamazaki. "It's closer to a consumer electronic product than anything else IBM produces."[9] "Any product with the IBM logo is an ambassador of the corporation", said Sapper, "and each product's design is an integral element of its company's reputation and prestige."[10]

GLOBAL COLLABORATION

The design of the ThinkPad 700C was the result of a global collaboration. The participants included industrial designers led by Kazuhiko Yamazaki at IBM Yamato Design Center, Japan; IBM industrial design consultant Richard Sapper in Milan, Italy; researcher Ted Selker at IBM's Almaden Research Center in San Jose, California; and the engineering team at IBM Yamato, Japan. Design strategy and co-ordination were provided by Tom Hardy and his staff at IBM Corporate Design Program, Stamford, Connecticut. The industrial designers played an especially critical role in the whole process. The three major contributors were Sapper, Hardy and Yamazaki.

Sapper was given the title of industrial design consultant in 1980. His role in the development of the 700C was:

1. to work directly with Corporate Design to establish product "differentiation/personality" strategy for the IBM product line;
2. to work directly with Corporate Design and Yamato Design to establish the common part of the design strategy for a portable product line;
3. to develop the initial "lunch box" concept for the ThinkPad;
4. to collaborate with Yamato Design on developing product details, including incorporating the IBM Research's TrackPoint device and large colour display.

Sapper worked directly with the Corporate Design staff led by Hardy. Based in Connecticut, Hardy and his staff co-ordinated 15 design centres around the world. The centres were maintained by the company's product lines of business: Personal Systems, for example, had design centres at Boca Raton, Florida, Austin, Texas and Yamato, Japan. The role of Corporate Design, in developing the 700C, was:

1. To work directly with Sapper to establish an initial strategic direction for IBM industrial design to emphasise product differentiation through developing "personality" aspects of each product line segment, and then communicate this strategy across the company.
2. To set the initial strategic direction for the design solution of notebook, laptop and other portable IBM products to use common parts, while still providing unique end products for the various applications.
3. To interact with IBM Research to push new ideas into products, such as the TrackPoint pointing device.
4. To guide and approve the initial ThinkPad design concept direction and the implementation of the final solution, including the resolution of design issues.
5. To set the initial strategic direction for consistent product packaging design, operator manual and software tutorial. Emphasis was placed on compatibility with retail packaging directions and software interface established for the IBM product line.

The design team led by Yamazaki at Yamato consisted of about ten designers. "One of the key strengths of our design team is its familiarity with engineering", says Yamazaki.[11] The role of the design team in developing the 700C was as follows:

1. To work directly with Sapper on the major development of the ThinkPad products and its peripherals.
2. To develop the ThinkPad "concept video" in the early stages of product development to show both Yamato managment and line of business management the "personality" aspects of the portable products, including size constraints, mobility needs, status, etc.
3. To interface with the engineering effort in Japan throughout development of the product and with manufacturing throughout pre-production and final production.
4. To work directly with the Corporate Design staff to implement the industrial design guideline document for portable IBM products.
5. To work directly with the Corporate Design staff to review the software tutorial with regard to the IBM software interface guidelines.
6. To work directly with the Corporate Design staff to implement the packaging design and operator manual to follow the corporate retail guidelines.

7. To develop the software tutorial concept for the Japanese market.
8. To interface with the packaging engineers, software programmers and operator manual writers in Japan.

Communication among these three major contributors occurred almost every day in the development process. Besides face-to-face meetings involving prototypes and models, the Sony image system, fax machines, telephones and electronic mail tools were used to facilitate collaboration. The Sony image system transmits high definition images over telephone lines and proved especially useful.

THE CHALLENGES

Yamazaki worked closely with Sapper to fully develop the product and finalise all details. Yamazaki was the primary design interface with IBM Japan's engineering and manufacturing functions, as well as acting as the design team leader to ensure co-ordination at the site level for product peripheral design (i.e. battery charger, expansion unit), packaging design, operator manuals, and software tutorial design. Ricoh Co. Ltd., Japan's leading manufacturer of copiers and fax machines and a company known for its low-cost manufacturing skills, did some engineering work and became the final assembler of the product.

Yamazaki recalls, "The challenge for us was how to combine a prominent design capability exemplified by the PS/55 Note and the early technologies which were emerging in the company's laboratories. We could tap innovative research from IBM laboratories worldwide and put it quickly into the 700C. Things went well in this case."[12]

Two examples of the early technologies available in the company are worthy of note. First the frame of a flat panel colour display was being engineered by IBM without the size constraint of having to fit into an A4-size cover. The initial engineering effort was directed towards replacing the desktop and stand-alone colour CRT display with a desktop and stand-alone flat panel colour display. Originally, the frame (housing) around the flat panel glass that holds all the display components together was being developed to be cheap and simple to produce, rather than as small as technically possible. This large-size frame would therefore not fit into an A4 size notebook product without reducing the overall glass size of the display itself, making for a less than 10.4 inch display. It was industrial design which initiated the effort to redesign the frame, resulting in a compact A4-size product offering a large 10.4 inch display. The engineering was not as simple as the desktop approach, but the final solution gave IBM an important differentiation with the largest colour display in the notebook industry.

The TrackPoint pointing device was another example of the early technologies which were emerging in the company's laboratories. The device was developed by Ted Selker, a computer scientist at IBM's Almaden Research Centre in San Jose, California, with the help of Joseph Rutledge of the company's Thomas Watson Research Centre in Yorktown Heights, New York. Their pointing-stick project started in late 1987. The inclusion of the TrackPoint into a product was due to Corporate Design at Connecticut incorporating the idea into a notebook design model. The model was presented to product management, executives and marketing as an important element of product differentiation. This Corporate Design effort resulted in a technical idea from research being transferred quickly into a marketable product. Prior to Corporate Design's involvement, research had failed to get the attention of product developers.

Each component of the IBM Design Program contributed to the product, with attention being paid to everything the user would see and touch. Industrial designers were responsible for the ThinkPad hardware and peripherals (A/C adapter, quick charger, keypad, expansion unit and carrying case) and for design co-ordination. Graphic designers developed the user's manual, nameplate and shipping carton graphics, while the software look and feel was developed by graphic interface designers. The IBM graphic design consultant Paul Rand, of Weston, Connecticut, worked directly with Corporate Design to establish the product nameplate, packaging and operator manual graphic guidelines, and reviewed the ThinkPad graphic design solutions from Yamato Design Center.

In the early planning stages of the notebook development, the IBM Yamato design team provided a design concept video, a promotional booklet and product design mock-up to communicate the high priority of such customer values as size, materials, colour, ease of use and image. These values constituted the product's "personality". Using the video technique to demonstrate was especially persuasive.

USING OUTSIDE CONSULTANTS

At IBM, almost all product design is created in-house. The company has 15 design centres scattered from Boca Raton, Florida to Yamato, Japan. In Yamato alone about 70 industrial designers work with engineers to develop new product lines. "The key to IBM's design successes lies in hiring the best talent available, and then allowing them to create to the best of their ability. It takes commitment by top management. It takes hard work by skilled professionals and it takes a design attitude being woven into the corporate structure", says Hardy, who had retained overall responsibility for worldwide product and graphic design.

However, IBM does not depend only upon the in-house design capability. To ensure design quality, the company uses outside consultants. In fact, it has a long history of doing this. A good combination of strong internal design teams and consulting experts has been pursued as a principle of operation.

In 1956, Thomas Watson Jr., then the company's chairman, hired the talented industrial designer and architect Eliot Noyes who, until his death in 1977, remained the consultant director of design. Paul Rand, an accomplished graphic designer, was retained as a consultant for graphic design and corporate identity, while Charles Eames became a consultant for film and special exhibitions. These consultants, who were responsible to the chairman, provided technical and design leadership, and their proposals had an impact on the IBM profile that is still felt today. More specifically, Rand redesigned the logo and established a corporate identity system. Eames designed major exhibits including the 1964 World's Fair, and Noyes supervised all product design and also personally designed products with a potential for high visibility, such as the Selectric typewriter. Currently, Richard Sapper is the company's consultant on industrial design, and Edward Tufte advises on information design.

Based in Milan, Sapper is consulted by numerous companies and has had over a dozen of his designs collected by the Museum of Modern Art in New York. Before he was hired as a consultant to IBM, he had had almost no experience of designing computers. A popular industrial design journal, *ID*, described Sapper, thus:

> "Here is a designer at the top of his profession, a self-made practitioner who at the age of 26 left his native Germany and a secure job at Mercedes to seek opportunity (and autonomy) in Milan, now serving as key advisor to one of the most entrenched bureaucracies in the world. Surely Big Blue's maze of organisational hierarchy is no place for a strong-willed design sensibility born of German engineering training and Italian design finesse. But then again, perhaps this is precisely the place for such a designer."[13]

As an outside consultant to IBM, Sapper is responsible for giving general perspectives in the corporate design policy and supervising activities in the company's 15 design centres. He is called in to the company's quarterly design reviews, where representatives from each design centre meet for three days. He is also responsible for designing his own products for IBM. He says "IBM's products should be more recognisable as IBM products. The company must have a completely revolutionary product like the Selectric typewriter designed by Noyes. So I tried to develop such products as prototypes."[14] One of them was the PC Convertible designed in 1986, which led to the portable design concept in 1990. This concept eventually became the prototype for developing the PS/55 Note. Therefore, in Sapper's mind at least, efforts for developing the PS/55 Note were a part of his continuous efforts and the product was not a limited domestic model aimed only at the Japanese market. He expected it to be a global product and enhance the general recognition of IBM products.

From Tom Hardy's point of view, meanwhile, it was crucial to enable the individual designers to be more directly involved with Sapper on a more frequent basis. In 1989, after taking over the Design Program, Hardy began developing a new "differentiation" strategy and determined that in order to make the strategy work, there had to be an improvement in communications and teamwork, particularly between the in-house designers and Sapper.

> "The key objectives were to: (1) streamline and speed up the development process, (2) stimulate innovation, and (3) make Sapper a more integral team member on a day-to-day basis with locations. That is where technology played a significant role. By installing the Sony image system in 1989, 'instant' high resolution, colour interaction was made possible between the designers and Sapper. This tool not only saved time and money, but helped to bring decentralised design organisations together as a stronger and more integrated team. The use of the technology in this manner acted as a tool of empowerment."[15]

Now Sapper is available for consultation with individual designers in any of the design centres. He also acts as a troubleshooter whose judgement is sought when engineers or managers are in conflict with industrial design Yamazaki says:

> "For young designers like me, the existence of Sapper is of great help, because we can take a short-cut within the company's bureaucracy by getting Sapper's authorisation. Sapper is almost an insider because he has a long relationship with IBM. He has faith in his idea of what is good design. He is strong. But, simultaneously, he is not wedded to the old ways. He is also a nice person. He is not interested in monetary affairs."[16]

Good design can be an effective business tool. But for Sapper there's even more to it than that. "Good design makes a difference in your life. You can't help but be influenced by the items with which you surround yourself; their design is part of true quality."[17]

LATER STEPS

To make its personal computer business more competitive, IBM set up a new unit, the IBM Personal Computer Company (IPCC), in September 1992. This is a small but self-contained organisation separated from its corporate hierarchy, which takes responsibility for developing, manufacturing, distributing and marketing the company's personal computers.[18]

Under this new organisation, the company launched several new products in the ThinkPad series. In January 1993 the ThinkPad 550BJ, an A4-size notebook with a built-in printer, was launched in Japan. This was jointly developed with Canon. In March 1993, enhanced versions of the ThinkPad colour and monochrome notebooks, the 720C and 720, were announced. In September 1993, further enhanced versions of the ThinkPad colour and monochrome notebooks, the 750C and 750 were announced, together with a multimedia docking station. At the same time the ThinkPad 750P, an A4-size notebook with pen capability, was also announced worldwide. The 750P converts from keyboard-based to pen-based computing by swivelling the display cover.

These products are examples of the strategy of using common parts and the same basic industrial design concept to develop unique end products. The design concept of the ThinkPad has fostered a series of products, but the original design concept still remains and provides the company with a stable base for developing new products quickly. According to the *Business Week* article, "The company now gets new models (of PCs) off the drawing board every 6 months – instead of 12 to 18 months 2 years ago."[19]

EVALUATION

The IBM ThinkPad series has sold well: sales in 1993 were estimated at US$1.4 billion worldwide, making the ThinkPad market leader in the notebooks sector.[20] In fact, demands were so strong that the company was not able to fulfil all of them during 1993 and 1994.[21] There is no doubt that its distinctive design contributed to its success. "According to a survey in the US, over one-third of purchasers of the ThinkPad in 1993 bought it because of its design. One-third is surprisingly high", said Sapper.[22]

Thinkpad was developed through triad international collaboration across the United States, Japan and Europe. The use of design expertise was nothing new in itself for IBM. The way it happened, however, was genuine as this particular product development focused more on product differentiation and unique features of individual products. Industrial designers played an especially critical role in the whole development process in order to give a competitive edge.

The ThinkPad is a sort of "tradition-breaking" product that came into existence when IBM realised that its "traditional" approach to new product development was less effective for the PC business. With the ThinkPad, IBM managed to utilise both internal and external resources globally to develop a tradition-breaking product. Its innovative state-of-the-art capability in both technology and design was made possible by the huge effort of different locations around the world. The case also suggests that having a strong product can provide a base for quick development of subsequent new products. A similar example in this respect might be the Hewlett Packard printer. The HP DeskWriter was a base for a series of models with resolution improvements, portability and colour as features which were added on, or brought out, as time went by. The key is to have a strong base product.

CONCLUSIONS AND IMPLICATIONS

This case suggests that ideas and expertise may be sourced and combined on a global scale with good results on a commercial and product line level. Long distances may be overcome by modern technology if combined with investments in close relationships with the best competence, in this case represented by industrial design, engineering and management. Moreover, the ThinkPad design process also suggests that firms should be more aware of the creative, interactive and interdependent design development going on in industrial design teams. As this case reveals, innovating product designing is often fostered and led by more than one creative contributor: in this case the industrial design consultant, Sapper; Yamazaki (a crucial link to the Yamato design and engineering resource); and Hardy, head of IBM's corporate design co-ordinating and taking new design managerial initiatives on a world-wide basis.

Needless to say, global new product development is expensive, with many staff working globally, and therefore it may be worth pursuing only for a product which is potentially highly profitable and has wide appeal. It may not be easy for IBM to extend this success to its other businesses. But nonetheless, this case proves that the design element can add an extra dimension to new product development through global collaboration.

Table 4.1   Chronology of IBM's portable computers (1986–1993)

1986	IBM released the PC Convertible the company's first laptop computer. The product was designed predominantly by Richard Sapper.
1987	IBM Research began development of the "Track Point" idea.
1989	Tom Hardy and Sapper began developing a new "differentiated" strategy.
	Sony image system installed.
Spring 1990	Corporate Design and Sapper worked with Yamato Design on implementing a new strategic direction for portable products.
	Sapper developed initial portable design concept, using basic idea originally thought of in 1986.
Spring 1991	PS/2 Laptop announced in the US. This was developed in the US to the old design guidelines.
	PS/55 Note released in Japan. This was the first portable product with the new differentiated strategy.
	Corporate Design connected with IBM Research and the industrial design model of the "Track Point" research idea was developed.
Autumn 1991	A4-size monochrome notebooks announced world-wide. This was the world-wide version of PS/55 Note.
Spring 1992	A4-size notebooks with colour flat panel display announced (with Trackball).
Autumn 1992	ThinkPad 700C, an A4-size notebook with colour flat panel display and new Track Point device announced world-wide.
January 1993	ThinkPad 550BJ, an A4-size notebook with a built-in printer launched in Japan. This was a jointly-developed product with Canon.
March 1993	ThinkPad 720 and 720C notebook enhancements announced.
September 1993	Updated versions of ThinkPad colour and monochrome notebook products (750C and 750), together with a multimedia docking station, announced.
	ThinkPad 750P, an A4-size notebook with pen capability announced world-wide.

NOTES

1. For a detailed account of the case, see Sakakibara (1994).
2. For general discussion on global R&D, see Perrino and Tipping (1989), Hakanson and Zander (1986), De Meyer and Mizushima (1989), and Sakakibara and Westney (1992).

3. For a detailed account of the case see *Business Week*, 11 January 1993.
4. A summary description based on the *New York Times* article, 23 June 1993.
5. *New York Times*, 23 June 1993.
6. From my interview with Tom Hardy, 19 January 1993.
7. *Think*, No. 4, 1992, p. 47.
8. *Think*, No. 4, 1992, p. 47
9. *Think*, No. 4, 1992, pp. 46–47.
10. *Think*, No. 4, 1992, p. 44.
11. From my interview with K. Yamazaki, 2 September 1993.
12. From my interview with K. Yamazaki, 28 June 1994.
13. *ID*, May/June 1991, p. 32.
14. From my interview with R. Sapper, 16 May 1994.
15. From my interview with T. Hardy, 27 October 1993.
16. From my interview with K. Yamazaki, 28 June 1994.
17. *Think*, No. 4, 1992, p. 47.
18. See, for example, *Financial Times*, 4 September 1992.
19. *Business Week*, 17 January 1994, p. 47.
20. *Financial Post*, 8 January 1994.
21. *The Wall Street Journal Europe*, 22 February 1995.
22. From my interview with R. Sapper, 16 May 1994.

REFERENCES

Perrino, Albert C. and James, W. Tipping (1989). Global Management of Technology, *Research-Technology Management*, May/June, 12–19.
Hakanson, Lars and Zander, Udo (1986). *Managing International Research and Development*, Sveriges Mekanforbund, Stockholm.
De Meyer, Arnoud and Mizushima, Atsuo (1989). Global R&D Management, *R&D Management*, **19**(2).
Sakakibara, Kiyonori and Westney, D. Eleanor (1992). Japan's Management of Global Innovation: Technology Management Crossing Borders, in N. Rosenberg et al (eds), *Technology and the Wealth of Nations*, Stanford University Press, 327–343.
Sakakibara, Kiyonori (1994). IBM ThinkPad 700C Notebook Computer, Case at the Centre for Design Management, London Business School.

CHAPTER FIVE

ABSORBING OR CREATING DESIGN ABILITY: HAG, HAMAX AND TOMRA

Birgit H. Jevnaker

INTRODUCTION

How may firms consider using highly skilled specialist competencies, such as design experts, strategically? This challenge concerns access to, and use of, productive specialists with heads to think with and feet to literally walk in-and-out of the corporate doors taking with them the most critical knowledge (Löwendahl 1994). Apparently, old systems of control and management will not do in governing valuable and rare human expertise. Moreover, potentially valuable design allies may not be easily acquired through classic market contracts, since merely where to find a dedicated "partner" is a challenge for the novice user not familiar with the design milieux. Yet such diverse specialist competencies seem to be needed increasingly by old as well as new business firms intending to differentiate and build products and services with a competitive edge. Concurrently, many sorts of competence-seeking manufacturing firms are facing this complex design and human resource challenge.

As in other difficult fields of learning, exploration through collaborative relationships may be worthwhile. No doubt, closer collaboration with most types of visual expertise has been neglected in the past. The collaborative

Management of Design Alliances. Edited by M. Bruce and B. H. Jevnaker.

use of independent design experts, linked to the firm over time to become partly "an insider" as well as crossing borders from the inside-out, represents a socially complex but potentially creative route, as indicated by the practice of Bang and Olufsen, Olivetti and other design-successful firms (Palshöy 1990, Kicherer 1990). Though each firm and design alliance may follow unique paths of building design capabilities, there might be certain practices that may be repeated suggesting the existence of underlying design management abilities. Thus, to capture how firms actually "absorb" (or not) a design capability, i.e. how design resources are "put to use" creating and sustaining value for the firm, how firms work with designers in real settings, may be.

In this chapter, the basic findings from a study of five Scandinavian export-oriented firms and their successful collaboration with industrial design experts will be presented. Through input of, and interaction with, design expertise, and follow-up in product development and marketing, these firms managed to create new benefits for their customers. All cases illuminate that working consciously with "the design dimension" is demanding but not impossible even for novice users of professional industrial design.

Based on this empirical material, the chapter first gives some background on the methodological challenges of identifying and describing the secrets of trial, error and success behind collaborative industrial design approaches. The key result indicators for the five companies are noted, that is visible and commercial results such as unique products, increased sales/profits and other impacts. Then mostly invisible abilities to explore and manage design resources are identified and discussed. The "invisible" abilities are necessary in order to continue to create and communicate competitive product designs. As an example of how to "resource"[1] value-creating, but complex specialist competence from outside the firm, these design cases may have wider interest beyond the particularities of the settings studied.

BACKGROUND: WHY ARE DESIGN COLLABORATIONS VALUABLE?

The firm's relationship with design experts may highlight our thinking, in general, on autonomous experts with *diverse knowledge* grafted to the firm, since the firm needs to mix its own local knowledge with external profitable ideas and early perceptions of more global opportunities. Interestingly, design relates to a current issue in research as to learn more on the linkages between local manufacturing industries and experts belonging to the knowledge-intensive service sector. However, this perspective is not based on a preference, in general, of valuable (and fashionable) "outsourcing" as a substitute for training internal staff or recruiting new people (internalization). Rather, what has emerged from this case study on industrial design, is the *combination* of external design experts with internal competencies in product and business development. Such mixing of knowledge may allow creative connections that may improve both design processes and products.

CREATIVITY AS A CORE ASPECT OF DESIGN

The independent design expert often works *across* sectoral or company boundaries and may contribute fresh views and multi-disciplinary knowledge of critical importance for the creation of new product features and their configurations (see, for example, Lorenz 1986/1990). In particular, industrial design concerns itself with the best knowledge available on the actual *use* of the product (Ainamo 1996), suggesting that designers may be a valuable source for innovations. Although not much studied nor easily measured, previous empirical evidence exists on the commercial benefits of professional design input investments (Potter et al 1991). Nevertheless, innovative designs and developments of new products do imply risks and uncertainties which are necessary to understand constructively. In order to learn from productive (and unproductive) dynamics in business firms, one has to *capture the actors' particular contributions and experiences* in relation to perspectives; in time and space. For product-based firms, the product design and development may be especially critical and tricky to uncover as these vital processes include sensitive information related to both codified and more tacit thinking and acting "back stage" in several localities. Since product development (and design) concerns future opportunities as well as past and current efforts in value creation, it is often seen as a powerful but uncertain area typically kept in secrecy.

FAMILIARITY AS ANOTHER CORE ASPECT OF DESIGN

In order to make new profitable product designs tailor-made for the industrial firm, industrial designers and co-developers typically need to explore both the firm's strengths and its weaknesses in relation to opportunities in a particular target area (so as to make effective trade-offs); that means considering what the firm may be able to produce and market, what they may be particularly good at and so on (strategic resource considerations). Not surprisingly, designers seem to find it difficult to grasp what the client really wants as well as capture its more invisible core competencies and complementary resources relative to its customers and competitors, e.g. the firm's received marketing signals. Tapping into this type of often tacit knowledge may be difficult for any outside consultant since it is often referred to in implicit language or is taken for granted. Moreover, management or whoever is the gatekeeper for design consultants, may not capture what the designers actually need or want to know as both parties may not know the other's field of competence (asymmetric knowledge). Even when the parties want to share their knowledge, they may "know more than they can tell" when they first begin to work together. In particular, the firm-specific knowledge embedded in the corporate cultures may take time to understand as this is often unarticulated or taken for granted, unlike particular production facilities which may be inspected. Yet the firm may want fresh views from the outside to be combined with its firm-specific development capabilities in order to create distinctive new products. Thus, this represents a fundamental dilemma in more complex product design.

Moreover, designers and their clients may work together in design situations characterized by different combinations of creative and familiarity knowledge present. Though these knowledge aspects may change during the design developments (that is, a dynamic situation), the different combinations may, for pedagogical reasons, highlight this fundamental dilemma in design linked to situations ranging from a "random walk" to a combination of high potential for creativity combined with a high score on domain-specific knowledge (see Table 5.1).

Table 5.1   Designer's knowledge combination of creativity and familiarity in relation to the client firm and tendency of performance

Designer's familiarity with the client firm

		High	Low
Designer's Creativity	Low	Lock-In	Inexperience (and less talent)
	High	Innovation Strategic fit	Random walk experiment

Source: Jevnaker, B., SNF (Foundation for Research in Economics and Business Administration)
Note: This table illustrates the suggested favourable combination of high (autonomous) creativity and high familiarity with the client's needs and problems; i.e. favourable so as to constitute a design intelligence that can be transformed into products and services with a competitive edge and strategic fit. The familiarity concept as used here includes firm-specific and industry-specific market knowledge as well as tacit technological development competence. This rich familiarity knowledge is accumulated through designers' work with clients on specific industrial projects over time, building a reservoir for new projects.
The table also suggests that talented designers may be creative without deep knowledge of a client, e.g. new products and/or new user groups/niches may be discovered through small-scale experiments. This situation is more characterised by an experimental or probe-and-learn process which may lead to serendipitous innovative results (but also typically build up familiarity knowledge over time making the next probes less random). The dynamics of these two aspects of design intelligence may thus be highly constructive for business.

UNFINISHED BUSINESS?

Up till now, we do not know how professional design competence actually is combined – or not – with the firms' own competencies and technologies, nor do we know why and how the design-professional approach is sustained or disrupted. The *ad hoc* nature of design purchases has been experienced by many designers (Olins 1987). This is alarming, since a survey of British and Scandinavian design consultancies indicates that about three or four are actually *repeat clients* (Bruce et al 1995). Recent research suggests that firms may not learn sufficiently from their *ad hoc* transactions with designers, e.g. Svengren (1995 and in Chapter 7) points to the problems of the conceptual integration of design in otherwise successful high-tech firms such as LM Ericsson.

Even in large firms with internal design resources, the integration of a qualified design approach is mostly an "unfinished business", as described by the former design manager of Philips, Robert Blaich (1995). Moreover, *non-users of professional design* seem to be most common in the industry of most regions; perhaps with a few notable exceptions such as Japan and Northern Italy (*Design Management Journal* 1993).

Why then is adoption and integration of (qualified) design so rare or so difficult? Whilst the complementary and heterogeneous nature of design competencies among the parties may be beneficial for creative outcomes, the initial *perceived uncertainties* and weak integration may also be barriers for a sustained design-based approach, especially as new product development (NPD) often already has its devoted interests and path-dependent ways of "doing things" (see Henderson 1991). NPD is typically experienced as a risky but exciting business even before the introduction of a "new expert". And, how to organize and *manage* the designer's inputs when it is often difficult a priori to specify the design problems and the direction of what is to be done, as well as capture what is expected as desired outcomes? For instance, the business firm may not know the designer nor industrial design as a field of competence with all its particularities, and vice versa, which may lead to misfits and even marketing blunders (see examples in Dumas 1993).

EXPLORING COLLABORATIVE RELATIONSHIPS

As in other difficult fields of interaction (see Macneil 1980, Bae 1992), this paper suggests that a *relational perspective* may help the designer and the firm to contribute productively together in new product development. Relationships may foster mutual help and repeated efforts to become more familiar and competent, thus facilitating adaptive responses and stimulating creative solutions for the firm's design. However, knowing the unique setting of design and its business environment, is but one fundamental aspect; another is strategic behaviour associated with economic contracting with an external source. As yet, we do not know how to make design genuinely strategic in the multiskilled competencies and specialized interests in product and business development. One major challenge is the interface problem as design is regarded as an "in-between" activity. In order to make strategic interfaces *combining* the most relevant and promising internal and external design-related competencies in a favourable way, we need to explore how a collaborative approach may represent a valuable opportunity in practice. Since the designer and the client may have different perspectives, knowledge and competencies (i.e. an asymmetric and heterogene relationship), their interaction is probably no "quick fix". In particular, in new product development we would expect the parties to need each others' competencies to reduce the uncertainties and barriers in innovative efforts.

What, then, may be achieved through closer collaboration in industrial design? A classical reference could be the collaborative relationship between the industrial design pioneer Henry Dreyfuss and the tractor company John Deere. This led to a product line of tractors that were fundamentally more suitable for the users in terms of the human factor solutions. However, when some of Dreyfuss's main "gatekeepers" and supporters left the company, design seemed to fall back to a less strategic, more operational role (Lorenz 1986/1990). "It's all in the relationship", said Bruce and Docherty (1993), but exactly what is embedded in the firm's relationship with designers? Re-reading the Dreyfuss/John Deere-case,[2] the *relational* social glue, the *spatial* influence (access through geographic mobility and manifold kinds of communication) and the *time* dimensions (evolving relationship, frequent contact) emerge as promising ingredients in an empirical exploration.

In order to uncover the dynamic practices behind the particularities of contemporary industrial design-based approaches in product development, this chapter therefore explores and discusses the firm's relationships with mobile professional design expertise over a certain time period (3–25 years) and with various spatial arrangements.

ON METHODS IN THE STUDY

During the preliminary study[3] of the research reported here, the significance of the *design relationship* emerged as one possible factor contributing to or modifying the results which could be obtained through industrial design (Table

Table 5.2   Significance of the design relationship (strategic selection)

- Was a medium-sized firm (ca. 60–300 employees; and presumed short communication channels between industrial design and the company's management)
- Was working in international markets (with differentiated products)
- Had implemented complex product development
- Had concurrent or otherwise close collaborative industrial design

Source: Jevnaker, B., SNF (Foundation for Research in Economics and Business Administration)

5.2). To identify and describe essential features of collaborative industrial design, data was collected from genuine relationships, i.e. a company and a designer that were actually working together in product design and development. The research design was consciously chosen in order to capture both parties' potential contribution to industrial design as well as exploring the management and integration of industrial design within the firm.

This was a *strategic sample*, in opposite to a random one, and five export-oriented manufacturers were included in the research, as follows:

- HAMAX (consumer-oriented plastics for leisure)
- TOMRA (automated machines for handling beverage containers returned by the consumer)
- GRORUD (window and door metal-based fittings)
- HAG (ergonomically designed office chairs)
- Stokke (ergonomically designed furniture).

Variations in the collaborative approach among the designers and the firms were desirable; whether the designer was located entirely outside the firm as an autonomous designer or design consultancy, or rather partly an "insider" (Kicherer 1990). Using this selection criteria with an eye also on the designer's educational and regional background (in addition to the sampling criteria for the firms), the following sample of *designers* emerge, as shown in Table 5.3.

Table 5.3   Designers selected for the study of industrial design collaboration

- **Roy Tandberg**, part-time employed designer at TOMRA, with education from Art Center, LA, in product design and work experience from the US.
- **Steinar Flo**, independent industrial designer, educated in Norway and Sweden (metal design/industrial design)
- **Ninaber/Peters/Krouwel**, the largest industrial design consultancy firm in the Netherlands (**Wolfram Peters**, educated in TU Delft)
- **Peter Opsvik**, from the industrial design firm Peter Opsvik Ltd., educated in furniture design in Norway and London, and with further studies in ergonomics from Germany

Source: Jevnaker, B., SNF (Foundation for Research in Economics and Business Administration)

The study of the companies and their most important current designer, was implemented by lengthy interviews with top management as well as key developers, designers and marketing people.[4] The aim was to get as close as possible to the management and practice of industrial design, as experienced by the parties involved. The case material illustrates that there is more than one perspective on industrial design, even within the same firm. This is not surprising, but important to highlight. Such a description will give a more valid picture of what goes on and is experienced in practice, rather than the more idealized pictures of product development (Hollins and Pugh 1990, Hart 1995). By coming sufficiently close to practice and "experience with knowledge" – as stressed by Aristotle (Öijord 1992), one may also gain insight into the arena of embedded particular or domain-specific knowledge, coined knowledge by familiarity (Johannessen 1988); for example knowing specific production facilities, knowing the various customers' values and interests, experience of particular forms of use etc., which is not necessarily shared by the designer and all in the firm. This unique familiarity knowledge may still flow into the design development process, as demonstrated in some of the cases.

One may not walk in the same river more than once ("new water emerges all the time"). On the other hand, a certain *continuity* typically exists in established organizations ("the river has not shifted its bed"). Another trained researcher – with the same perspective and approach – would probably have found similar results, given the same access to the companies. This continuity, in the complex practice of product designing, seems to be created partly by telling stories. In all cases, storytelling emerged to initiate the researcher in difficult fields of learning; for instance when tension or surprise were features of the design relationship. This is discussed in greater detail below.

WHAT HAVE THE FIRMS ACHIEVED BY USING INDUSTRIAL DESIGN?

All the firms implemented *path-breaking projects* by the use of industrial design experts. The results can be summarized in terms of five result indicators, as shown in Table 5.4.

Unique Products

Distinctive and genuine *products* have been created for all the five companies. These products are ultimately useful to the end-user; for instance children's

Table 5.4   The results of industrial design*

Result indicators	Achieved (no. of firms)
1. Unique products	All 5
2. Increased sales	4–5
3. Renewed companies	(4; to some degree all 5, but most radically HAG and Stokke)
4. New markets and new customer relationships internationally	All 5
5. Increased knowledge and competencies	All 5

Source: Jevnaker, B., SNF (Foundation for Research in Economics and Business Administration)
*The results were not attributed to the designer alone, although designers made a significant contribution in all cases; see the text below.

bicycle seats, office chairs and conference chairs, reverse vending machines for return drinking bottles, and window fittings. In short, products that are useful in everyday life. Improvements in these types of products are essential to many people, even though the user may not notice – when the products function well.

The collaboration with the industrial designer was the most influential factor behind the product creation at HAG and Stokke. At TOMRA, GRORUD and HAMAX, the interplay among technical experts, industrial designer and marketing/business administrators created the products.

Market Assets and Commercial Results

Four of the five companies have obtained increased *sales revenues,* in particular in export markets in Europe or the US. According to the CEOs in four of the firms, the profit development had been mainly positive since 1990, and this financial development was mainly attributed to the consciously designed products and their commercializations.[5] TOMRA obtained about half of its profit in 1994 from its new product model. During 1994, HAG's profit increased nearly seven times, from 3.9 to 27 millions NOK. HAMAX made a successful entry into the German "Fachhandel." Without distinctive products "in the luggage", this entry would not have been possible, according to the marketing manager. Looking back as far as to the 1970s, one firm (HAG) recognized that they had actually survived by design.

New Image and Relationships

All of the companies achieved *new customer relationships* based on offering the new product designs. Some of the companies have also improved their *image* and reputation due to the distinctive products and how these have been profiled and presented to international audiences. The above results are more fully reported elsewhere (Jevnaker 1995).

Revitalizing the Firm through Design Competence

What has been learnt? In all five firms, the designer's collaborating partners tell stories of learning more about design and industrial design, through the design associates and the new experiences in design development. For instance, one product development manager admits to have known "very little beforehand". Now he appreciates the fresh injection of new knowledge from the independent designer, "an individual without blinkers", and he further elaborates that industrial design is not limited to the appearance or surface of the product: "industrial design, that concerns everything" of the product's configuration, he said.

In some of the firms, important changes in organizational behaviour have been introduced or rediscovered; for instance in the product development process – such as integrating the designer at an earlier stage at TOMRA. At HAG and Stokke, the product designer is also included in the generation of the communication messages and (sometimes) the communication material, and in direct communicative efforts with dealers, early adopters, physiotherapists and other user-oriented groups.

It is worth noticing that not only the CEOs have learned more about design. For instance at HAG, the whole company is "refurnishing" itself, by a systematic and enthusiastic internal training programme, encompassing the top level down to the grass roots. Although only a few of the firms had separate, company-embedded learning processes focusing on design as a core resource, particular *knowledge-based efforts related to design* were visible in all five firms.

Similarities as well as differences were present in the companies' design management experience. At TOMRA, HAMAX and HAG, the companies have developed their own competencies and capabilities in managing design and collaborating with design experts. At Stokke and HAG, a strategic learning of significant importance has emerged, as dynamic ergonomic design thinking through design relationships has renewed and even transformed the companies' business philosophy, changing their *raison d'être* as furniture-makers (Jevnaker 1991). At one of the firms, the design integration was still mainly anchored at the product development level, although top management did stimulate more effective design developments and outcomes were visible.

How and why did the five firms manage to obtain the above results? In particular, we should sensitize our exploration to the conceptual integration of design, a major finding also in Svengren (1995) and grounded in previous research (see Jevnaker 1993).

HOW AND WHY WERE THE FIRMS SUCCESSFUL IN INDUSTRIAL DESIGN?

In general, industrial design-based benefits are attributed to the abilities (or disabilities) of *industrial design experts* to improve the quality, usability, aesthetic expressions and communicative product identity as well as functional and economic aspects of products and systems for industrial reproduction (Dumas 1993, Farstad 1994). From a cultural perspective, it is noteworthy that most definitions of industrial design do not focus on the role of the design-client relationships or include the client's competencies or the designer's social skills in industrial design, although these elements may be mentioned in passing.

From this study, we may appreciate *mutually creative partnerships* as those visible in these five SME (small and medium-sized) firms. Based on the empirical descriptions as elaborated elsewhere (Jevnaker 1995a), a consistent pattern emerged with certain qualitative aspects in the collaboration between the design expert and the firm: it included both a creative *dialogue* and intense *interplay* – even with mutually *interfering conversations* about products, philosophy and visions. Moreover, both parties committed themselves in an entrepreneurial way to achieve material results repeatedly; hence, persistent effort was also present. This suggests how specific, attractive and more sustainable design-based advantages may be obtained.

In the following, it will be discussed how this creative dynamics occurred in practice in the five firms, thus focusing more on the driving forces than the barriers which we know exist in industrial design as applied in a business setting (e.g. cost concerns, "design illiterate" players, organizational politics and tradition-based behaviour, cf. Kotler and Rath 1984). In all five cases, the product design evolution over time was essential for creating a *win-win* situation for both parties. Even though being unique challenges for both parties each time, could these product design developments still hide "rules" or intelligent practices that are favourable from a design-based competitive viewpoint? We did notice certain cyclical procedures or ways of doing things in the industrial design development as well as its implementation. Moreover, these practice rules seemed to be combined with particular competencies or underlying capabilities. In order to understand how the new designs may become strategic in business firms, it may be fruitful to explore both.

UNDERSTANDING PRODUCT DESIGN DEVELOPMENT

The "how's" and "why's" of the firms' successes, encompass abilities and activities by several people, among which the designer clearly was one crucial contributor. All five companies had benefited significantly through their design associates; thus, the concept "design alliance" is appropriate. Indeed, some of the firms had survived and built up a new profitable product line or redesigned existing products into core and distinct products through their designer ally.

- The particular *creative synthetic and catalyst effects* through design relationships are illustrated, as in the case of GRORUD, when a small team with industrial design expertise managed to develop a new and winning product design prospect in very short time (see below).
- This was also evident in the Dutch design consultancy's work for HAMAX. Within 18 months a new generation of bicycle seats for children was finished, drawing on a network of toolmakers in Portugal with the Dutch design firm as catalyst and close follow-up from the Norwegian manufacturer.[6]

Why were these particular design relationships successful in the long run, when compared with other designer relations? Although an important ingredient in some of these cases, it is clear that, for instance, *early product success* is not a sufficient explanation in itself. Success is only part of the companies' stories in product design and development. Most of these collaborative designers had met both successes and challenges in balancing the experimentation and design research for the future with short-term problem-solving and cost- and time-effective design. And yet, the commissioning producers did adopt and integrate the new product designs, and management repeatedly stressed the value of design-intensive product developments. How could this absorptive capacity and conceptual integration be explained? The following four abilities are of particular significance:

1. The ability to *transform* basic product concepts.
2. The ability to develop *entrepreneurial* design relationships.
3. The ability to develop *acknowledged* competence-based relationships.
4. The ability to extend knowledge to (repeatedly) *re-anchor* the design direction in business and marketing strategies.

On the competence side, the ability to expand the existing design knowledge and transform this into new concepts and configurations of ultimate use for the customer, was crucial. Moreover, the extension of this into marketing, strategy and core competencies helped implement the new and innovative product designs. Why did these complementary competencies and assets emerge, assets that should not be taken for granted in design collaborations? This comparative research strongly indicate that *relational competencies* were critical in all five cases, in addition to the personal talents, skills and knowledge of the core contributors. Inspired by theory-informed lenses (see review in Jevnaker 1994a), these relational assets have been summarized into two meta-abilities: *acknowledgement* (Lövlie-Schibbye 1996) and *entrepreneurial mobilization* (see, for example, Itami 1987). These categories capture the dual overall abilities to create a suitable supportive *and* challenging infrastructure (the details of which may vary in each case) and sufficiently diverse knowledge-intensive processes even when venturing into the unknown; that is, when working on product designs in response to future opportunities.

The above four abilities are interrelated and interwoven, but understanding each may reveal some of the hidden and open rules and practices in design-intensive product development. Table 5.5 summarizes the four repeated abilities as observed in the five firms.

Conceptual Transformation

The industrial designers bring *innovative yet practical skills* to the often complex technological and uncertain market competence of manufacturing firms. And in some cases (Stokke and HAG), the designers may contribute significantly to more creative conceptual thinking which may expand existing knowledge and even transform the core knowledge of the firm, as suggested by Hedlund and Nonaka (1993). One of the hidden keys behind this creative

Table 5.5   Four abilities embedded in a study of five industrial design relations

Relationship between industrial designer and client characterized by*	Competence to:	
	transform/expand	*extend*
Acknowledgement	Ability to create unique, core product concepts	Ability to anchor design in core competencies and on strategic levels
Entrepreneurial mobilization	Ability to dialectical, knowledge-intensive and interdisciplinary leverage	Ability to market and explain design through continuous recreation

Source: Jevnaker, B., SNF (Foundation for Research in Economics and Business Administration)
*Both acknowledgement and entrepreneurial mobilization are most effective when mutually developed by both parties in the relationship, i.e. a relational asset.

ability is *empathic design*, that is to explore actual user behaviour and expose oneself to user situations and interact with user groups, although drawing upon existing technological capabilities that are somewhat redirected to give a new service or product for the customer (Leonard-Barton 1995). Examples:

■ The Dutch designers Ninaber/Peters/Krouwel explored the users' need for a seat in front of the bike-rider, a preference associated with Latin countries.
■ Peter Opsvik immersed himself in user requirements as seen from his child's perspective, and later, went on to experiment with a design group to conceive "alternative sitting" for many types of users who needed movement while they were seated, as in offices, in trams, or in the musician's studio.

Entrepreneurial Mobilization through Design Relationships

Furthermore, the research findings clearly illuminate the driving forces at company and product design development level. Sometimes it was hard to tell who initiated an idea, or who managed to explain and transmit it to the associate designer or one of the companies' management and staff.[7] It is fascinating that the case descriptions often point to *more than one party*, or rather the *design relationship*, as crucial for the knowledge generation and exploitation in the designing of products.

In all five cases, the innovative work has been possible because the CEOs (or other key top leaders) have been actively involved and committed as driving forces and as supporters in the design and development process of products. The commitment included key leaders that often are referred to as "promoters", "product champions" and "intrapreneurial middle managers" in the innovation literature, such as managers of product development (see, for example, Burgelman and Sayles 1986, Nonaka 1995). These functioned as gatekeepers as well as ambassadors for the external designer/design consultant.

However, this study also disclose that the independent designers may take on an *entrepreneurial role*. The designer consultant as entrepreneur may be a source of innovation as well as conflicts, due to the strategic influences on the firm's use of its resources and the potential financial risks. Moreover, the traditional developers and internal entrepreneurs of the firm may feel threatened by an external or more "autonomous" contributor creating new meanings and core products of vital importance for the firm's customers.

As in most open relationships, *dialectic tensions* actually were present among a smaller group of company staff and the collaborating designer. The designers, the managers and many of the development colleagues did interfere and discuss critically the evolving product ideas, as well as design and development and even marketing and promotional activities. But overall, tensions or propositions seemed to be expressed in a constructive mode, and did stretch the company's performance, such as at Stokke. This firm developed a new visual communication programme – fine-tuned with the ergonomically sound products – by using expertise in its own international network, including the industrial and graphic designers (instead of an outside advertising agency which was first planned).

The mutually creative mobilization of resources – expressed with tension, but in a relational context with entrepreneurial management support – is an important ability behind these design developments. In this context, the designer may also take on a more entrepreneurial and even business strategy-conceiving role, that overlaps with the firm's own core competencies in defining its core businesses and meanings.

Acknowledged Competence-based Relationship

Interestingly, mutual respect and *acknowledgement* of competence was also a common practice among the collaborating parties. Very little "fights for the honour" of good ideas, design and development work did emerge. The parties attributed honour to the other party, which is often not common in complex and diffuse (undifferentiated) relationships (Bae 1992). Although tensions and frustrations did emerge on both sides, these sentiments did not seem to have reduced the flow of knowledge-creation of vital importance to both parties.

The overall acknowledgement between the design consultant and design promoters inside the firm emerged as a vital component *framing* the exchange and design management processes (cf Lövlie-Schibbye 1996). This finding was actually more mixed, suggesting that acknowledgement is *not* an either/or ability. This was also found in other settings[8]:

■ As told by an industrial designer working internally in one of the firms investigated, the colleagues sometimes gave their personal opinions while evaluating product designs, *forgetting* to notice this designer's competence-based judgements. However, in this firm a system of open rules, management practices as well as fundamental corporate values did emphasize design as the firm's core source of competitive advantage.

■ In another firm, the turnover of engineers in product development projects actually made it difficult to grasp and appreciate the industrial design perspective for co-developers from the engineer ranks, but fortunately, a continuity of commitment existed on higher levels, in particular on the founder level.

■ In a third firm, the (former) top manager and major design promoter even left the company, and still, the particular client-design relationship survived certain tensions at the time.

This more nuanced picture illuminates the authentic *human dimension* of design relationships as it is indeed difficult to be fully acknowledging in *all* communicative situations. And yet, the overall acknowledgement is essential as it may leave a room for diverse and unexpected creativity, as well as wider commitments and maximum stretch of the parties' resources beyond the initial contracts, as observed in several of these design relations. As illuminated at HAG, acknowledgement is actually fundamental also in the daily product design and development work facilitating the inclusion of diverse knowledge and more honest and "silent" opinions which is important for authentic quality judgements.[9]

Knowledge Extensions

The storytelling emerged in these and other complex situations to initiate the researcher into the issues at hand. Stories can be valuable carriers of knowledge, often referred to as a way of transmitting knowledge *within* educational groups. The research reported here illustrates that it may be particularly helpful in *interdisciplinary discourse*, as proposed by Nyrness (1990): this may be a partly hidden practice, as in Grorud's development teams, or highly "visible" as in the re-education of the user, as in Hag's and Stokke's promotional activities.

At GRORUD several stories were told, one of which concerned the design of a window handle, originally not a part of the subcontract. This design task was, however, transformed on the designer's subtle initiative, when making remarks to the industrial customer's proposition that "it was not logic...etc". The story is far more tricky, and was often told in bits and pieces to convey various themes. One part of the story goes as follows:

> The designer had made two new alternative designs of the window handle in question, according to his own ideas – two themes, a conventional one, and one more different. The conventional one was given priority and presented first. "This

is trivial literature", the top manager said, "and this is a poem!", he added, holding the innovative handle in his hands.

Afterwards, an evaluation race was instigated among those who happened to be at work still. All but one (with some reservations) preferred the conventional handle, and yet the senior manager decided to go for the most innovative one. This story illustrates the managerial "gut feeling" to invest in innovative, rather than conventional, design, even though most of the staff did not choose it. It is also a "war story" of how the subcontract was developed and eventually won, despite poor odds at the first decision point, when two other subcontractors were also in the running for the client's custom (the Norwegian firm was, in fact, side-lined). Moreover, the story includes the significant contribution of the allied designer. Initially, he had only ten days to create a new design prospect for the client's potential customer, which he did successfully.

In this case, the windows were often purchased by industrial buyers with architects as associates or staff. The innovative handle turned out to be a good choice in terms of these targeted customers, according to the preliminary feedback. Indeed, the window company was so satisfied with the designer, that he is now also working directly for them, in addition to its subcontractor. This new design alliance is looked upon as an advantage also for the subcontractor as it may generate further commissioned work. So far, the new customer relationship has generated two new projects for the subcontractor. "We would not have got these, if we had not succeeded with the first project", the project manager recognized. He acknowledged the crucial contribution by the associate designer who, interestingly enough, more than once emphasized the skills of this manager.

Hidden and Open Rules

So far, this chapter has focused more on capabilities than rules and procedures. Interestingly, the component capabilities as identified and summarized above, often were in fact accompanied by open or more hidden *rules of practice*, such as:

- the regular inclusion of top management in managerial design decisions in the product design and development work;
- the regular intensive interface interactions among specialist and the managerial level, including briefing, participation and follow-up of external designers by both marketing people and engineers representing production and technology;

- the inclusion of the designers in the firm's contacts with dealers and customers, often including social and entertaining events to increase the social glue as well as competence in the firms' international marketing networks;
- the intense interest and conversations among specialists in noticing and investigating users and other target groups that were or would be exposed to and treat the companies' products.

In four of the five companies investigated, the top management *teams* were involved directly in the major design and development decisions during the process as certain milestones for shared evaluation and decision-making were set up as a rule. This similar way of involving key managers should be noticed by other firms striving to improve their product design development. However, certain differences were also visible among the five firms:

- Two of the firms (TOMRA and HAG) had the rule of making inquiries through networks in order to discover "who is best?" This applied also to the sourcing of design expertise.
- Three firms (TOMRA, HAG and HAMAX) had a close follow-up procedure of the product cost specifications to ensure cost-effective design solutions and more profitable products.
- It is noteworthy that one firm (HAG) had a formal rule of *debriefing* at the end of a product design and development project, to disclose all kinds of experiences during the design and development work. This debriefing was arranged in the factory – not at the headquarters – and included the external designer and the whole project development group. Interestingly, it was arranged by a procedure of group discussions to tease out the successful and the less successful aspects, followed by a plenary session to draw conclusions for further developments. This debriefing was incorporated in the development people as well as inscribed in written archives for future use.
- It is intriguing that only a few firms, such as HAG, had a rule of giving the designer "the last word" in design decisions. The same principle, although maybe less incorporated in the corporate culture, was referred to by the founder of one of the other companies.
- Moreover, HAG and Stokke did launch and implement separate formal training opportunities for employees and the external network of dealers/ distributors with the inclusion of these firms' most important product designer.

Interestingly, some of these "rules" and repeated procedures were more or less silent or taken for granted; for example the researcher had to probe repeatedly to uncover the debriefing procedure at HAG, suggesting that this is part of the "small values" (Leonard-Barton 1995) which may be significant for actually sustaining the innovative and strategic design directions.

KNOWLEDGE AND LEARNING

In some of the firms investigated particular learning-focused activities bridging creativity and familiarity of the parties involved, were valued openly. These firms allocated resources and provided space for a "design inauguration" of staff, dealers etc. – not just once, but *regularly* (cf. inaugurative learning, Jevnaker 1993). Furthermore, four of the five firms did stimulate learning efforts as aspects of other tasks, e.g. arranged through business collective events for mixed groups of distributors and developers from the headquarters, the factories and the international networks. Interestingly, humour was a typical ingredient in the social part of these international seminars and meetings. These interactive learning arenas were important, as the study illustrates that interpretation of the product concepts and the users' situations through first-hand observations and dialogues often triggered the creative concepts and the creative marketing. Moreover, user understanding is a continual challenge for the companies and the designers who do not rest on their laurels. This accords to the new emphasis on *empathic* and user-interactive design, as described by Leonard-Barton (1995) and also by Nonaka (1995), emphasizing the need for explorative search as part of product development processes.

To some degree, the parties had sorted out what both parties could contribute (best). And yet, designers sometimes felt they could contribute even more to the value-creation of these (and other) companies, suggesting a *latent* knowledge creation potential that is still unexploited.

Alternatively, this may be interpreted as the dilemma of the associate designer; who would like to contribute as much as possible, but is not always welcome to all development work at the business operational or strategic level. It is worth noticing the very differentiated strategy of the Dutch industrial design consultancy, Ninaber/Peters/Krouwell. As expressed by Wolfram Peters, one of the partners, it was okay to take on more narrowly defined commissioned work, for instance for small and medium-sized clients, but within certain limits: ". . . for us is important the concept and the models always have to be in the project. When that's not in the job, when it's only engineering or only mould-making, we don't do the job."

LEARNING ALLIANCES

With reference to three design relationships present in this SME material, we may analyse the critical knowledge-related capability of being able to absorb know-how and strategic competence from design sources outside the firm. These emerged as different "prototypes" of learning alliances, but all shared the intention to augment internal knowledge and design ability as described by Leonard-Barton (1995). The three include HAMAX, HAG and TOMRA.

An Outside Partner

The Dutch design firm Ninaber/Peters/Krouwel is a core outside partner for Norwegian plastic manufacturer HAMAX contributing to this client's product design and development activities. This is a fundamental functional area with high strategic importance for HAMAX, differentiating itself by focusing on young families' leisure products, with an in-house resource of only two core development engineers. This indicates that they have a capability gap in design, which is solved by importing and absorbing ideas and know-how from outside designers, a tradition that is not new for HAMAX. However, what is seen as new is the management system of product design projects organizing this value-creation according to selected targets, timing and future needs for profitable new products. This organizing capability is built on continuous and dedicated internal management discussions, as well as idea generation, design, development and testing through networks and partnerships. Interestingly, about 40% of discussions at HAMAX's board meetings is devoted to product development. The small company is learning both from the market (specialized dealers, chains of distribution, market investigations), and from its technology base through suppliers, construction and production engineers etc., and industrial design seems to be in the middle of all this continuous learning effort which mostly is an integrated aspect of the busy daily activity. Thus, it is noteworthy that industrial design within the company has increased its strategic importance as production facilities no longer are seen as the main point of departure – although remaining an essential enabler. Since 1991, a new top manager has incorporated and articulated design increasingly as a strategic factor in keeping up a leading edge in its niche market in plastic sledges as well as building new product lines of children's bicycle seats and accessories.

In this turnaround situation, the Dutch design consultancy has positioned itself as a major contributor in the Norwegian firm's development system, although ideas and competencies are regularly sought in a larger network; for instance by inviting three different design groups to compete at the start of new design projects. Hence, HAMAX is combining their close design partnership with certain competitive "market" mechanisms. Being geographically distanced from each other, face-to-face interactions are highly emphasized as being necessary for deeper insights into the complexities of technology-intensive design and developments, as outlined above. This model seems to be used quite frequently in industrial design, combining professional design partnerships with a testing out of more than one outside source from time to time.

An Outside "Insider"

Peter Opsvik Ltd. is the most long-term and profitable design partnership of HAG, the largest supplier of office chairs in Scandinavia, with an organization also in Greensboro, North Carolina, US. HAG was almost bankrupt in 1973/74 at the time when industrial and furniture designer Peter Opsvik first started to work for HAG. The current owner and CEO, Torgeir Mjör Grimsrud – at the time responsible for sales, took the initiative to this particular design relationship after inquiring in his network "who is best?" He also sustained it even when the former owner and top manager wanted to "send the designer home when finished" with the particular product. Since then, this entrepreneurial manager has been a committed and driving force for fostering both innovatively designed products and a vital corporate design culture vividly expressed through, for example, Swiss designer Bruno Oldani's body-conscious posters and well-designed rhetoric pamphlets communicating the idea that man is not created to sit. HAG is, so to say, living on this paradox but collect the best knowledge out of it as they are continuously exploring user problems as related to dynamic sitting in work environments.

Although HAG is working with about 12 different design groups, and may have ventured into similar directions without Peter Opsvik, this particular designer has no doubt been its most close learning alliance. This is indicated by their often shared and constant knowledge-accumulation in ergonomic chair design since the mid-1970s. Moreover, Opsvik is not only a sensitive explorer of user needs but is a dedicated conceptual experimenter, combining new and old design ideas in new product architecture, not for the sake of newness but for improved functionality. In fact, Opsvik also periodically distances himself from his clients, working independently and long term in an experimental as well as incremental mode. Indeed, his clients, such as HAG, do not need this design source every-day either, but he is willing to work very closely, being flexible and intense during project periods. From the data, this emerged as an interesting relationship as the designer contributes creatively as an outside "insider" in that both are familiar with the company's current and future needs, and at the same time preserves a more autonomous design experimentation sustained over long time periods. This designer is also a "teacher" as he has often inaugurated teaching the corporate staff and networks the ergonomic design thinking behind HAG's and his "own" products.

A Partly Internal Resource

Industrial designer Roy Tandberg's relationship with TOMRA is as a sort of internal consultant design resource, regulated in a part-time work contract. This means that this designer is located in TOMRA's headquarters and may use all the infrastructure as regulated in an agreement with the company. TOMRA's entrepreneurial managers first became aware of improvements in product designs and design as a competitive factor when screening the development of vending machines, and their initial contact with Tandberg started through another design consultancy (Nils Tvengsberg) in 1983. Through this working experience TOMRA's top managers, the brothers Planke, discovered his excellence as a designer and they discussed how to get hold of him. They realized that having a broad area of interest, he would probably not be satisfied with working solely for them with the TOMRA advanced machines for return drinking beverage. "Then I came up with this model", Tore Planke informed, "of combining work for TOMRA a fixed part of his time, supplying him with offices and accounting facilities etc., and then he could use about half of his time as a freelance consultant and he could then take on commissions that he found exciting" (interview 1994). When they heard of his plans to establish his own consultancy, they quickly suggested that he moved to them.

Since then, the designer has, over a decade, committed his work to both TOMRA and other clients in a wider network. His contributions to TOMRA's product designs depend on what kind of development projects are configured and "in the pipeline." The decision to configure the particular participants in development teams is decentralized, but Tandberg has contributed to all but one. When design is a complementary factor to technology, yet still a fairly strategic one, design thinking may still be difficult to grasp for the dominant groups: something which also has been experienced in the engineering ranks at TOMRA as well as at another high-tech company Ericsson (see Chapter 7). Not surprisingly, then, the early integration of design thinking was a current issue at TOMRA during interviews in 1994, and the management had already taken steps to improve in its organizing of new development projects. On the other hand, as seen from the company and from other more distant design partners, this model did get much tailor-made design effort out of its inside design partner: "He is thinking of TOMRA's needs also when working on other projects", an external design colleague commented. The designer also emphasized the accumulation of design experiences and learning since there is a continued need for improvements, adaptations and modifications, thus, he incorporated such ideas also for future improvements. The technology director was a great ambassador for this designer, acknowledging his superior competence as related to industrial design, but also noticing what he had learnt in technology areas over time: "You do not get such rubbish ideas which may not be producable."

KNOWLEDGE CONVERSIONS THROUGH RELATIONSHIPS

All five cases demonstrate the importance of experiential and interactive *knowledge-conversions* as part of product design development; that is, a social interaction between both explicit and more silent or "tacit" knowledge as mutually complementary aspects, according to Nonaka and Takeuchi (1995, p. 61). Based on extensive in-depth interviews, the practice of converting knowledge among a core group as well as a larger network came forward at HAG, HAMAX and TOMRA: Whether design experts were a partly internal resource, an outside "insider" or a more distant partner, selected design choices were delineated, vividly discussed and explained by more than one party. Critical information as well as lively rhetoric was exchanged, while people in the firm's networks were exposed to drawings, models or finished products and communication material designed.

This finding is in sharp contrast to the myth of the individualistic designer working typically withdrawn in his/her design studio and communicating only through his/her designs. In all firms (but to a varying degree), several managers made valuable experiences and learned more how to work with design and designers, and vice versa. In some of the firms, design-related learning was found to be an aspect of problem-solving and value creation as well as part of more imaginative thinking around products and their commercialization. This indicates a corporate design ability that is both receptive and creative to external design expertise.

This is intriguing as other firms have been found to have great difficulties in integrating new design thinking (Svengren 1995), or designers' efforts have been seen as closely related to "blind variation" or experimentation in the business context which may lead to cyclical performance variations and even decline (cf. Ainamo 1996, p. 26 and Chapter 8). It is therefore worth noticing that in four of the five firms, the more or less initial random or emergent strategy in design was changed into a deliberate one. This transformation of new design thinking into business and corporate strategies could take several years to be effective – suggesting a so-called *time-compressed diseconomy* (Dierickx and Cool 1989).

IMPLICATIONS AND FINAL REMARKS

One important implication is that firms should be more aware of the value of design efforts and the related potential knowledge development over time and space. New product designs and their commercialization may be of strategic importance, as demonstrated in all five firms, but to a different degree. Thus, to find and start working with the particular design experts was only the first step, although an important one. Moreover, the research highlights the continued ability to *transform* the combined talents, knowledge and expertise into new core concepts and profitable product designs. A mere on-the-spot access or short-term use of designer's know-how, or his/her models, were not sufficient at least in these five cases to create and sustain any design-based advantage. Most product models do not "sell on their own" without complementary service and follow-up of the quality, making more cost-effective production and distribution and making a range of family products or modules avoiding such products as "lonely wolves", as one designer explained. In particular, in the commercialization of innovative product designs with uncertain consumer acceptance, the design-marketing interface is crucial. In order to facilitate the tricky marketing adaptations and other commitments of resources, the ability to *extend* the design directions beyond the product development teams is critical, making design strategic on several corporate levels. Based particularly on the insights from HAG, it is striking that product and communication design thinking is made alive in each individual staff, manager or distributor through both verbal and visual expressions exploiting stories, examples and dialogues (cultural and communicative categories).

As found in this in-depth study, these transformative and extendable abilities were embedded in genuine *relationships* between the designer and core competent people of the firm. Indeed, the interconnectedness of competences and relationships makes it difficult to see all aspects. For instance, in all five cases, the contact with the industrial designer/design consultancy started as a recommended or network-based relation, leading to the (further) discovery of the designers' creative competencies as well as the need for interactive dialogues and entrepreneurial follow-up efforts over time. Most hidden, though, is acknowledgement, a somewhat fragile relational "asset" that should not be taken for granted in industrial design contexts, but beneficial when present to the extent of actually framing the relationships (Lövlie Schibbye 1996).

The implication for business firms and designers is to explore and develop this *dual design-dynamic capability approach*. This relational capability should not be seen as an either/or present category; metaphorically speaking, it is more like a musician's trained ability to active listening while playing or pausing, to stimulate other musicians and even the conductor. In practice, this means that attending to the *entrepreneurial role* is as creative and disturbing as it may be socially and economically fruitful for the envisioned outcomes, bearing in mind – and in particular in the acting – the mutual opportunity to attend to the *acknowledgement pole*; that is to strengthen both parties by listening, understanding, accepting and affirming the other party (Lövlie Schibbye 1996). Overall, the acknowledgement is fundamental in order to facilitate both *change* and *continuity* in constructive ways, as the party's competences are linked to values and how the designer and the firm perceive and profile themselves ("identity construction") which may have its rigidities as well as capabilities (Leonard-Barton 1995).

In summary, the evidence does not support any "either/or" argument between, on the one hand, the mobilizing and even confrontational behaviour associated with tough entrepreneurs, and on the other hand, the acknowledging behaviour as is often associated with a "soft practice" such as caring or otherwise nurturing relationships (Bae 1992). On the contrary, the case material indicates that both poles need to be addressed in order to recreate, sustain and extend the firms' design directions and be able to make the knowledge-rich *connections* such as those intricate ones between product design and corporate strategy.

For other designers, the *mutually creative* – indeed entrepreneurial – mobilization of knowledge and resources by both designers and their clients should be understood in-depth beyond the personal competence level (avoiding the heroic attribution to either party). For other business firms and managers of design, it is particularly worthy to notice the underlying management ability to recognize and appreciate advanced design expertise as well as their own responsibility in managing and nurturing more profitable and creative design developments.

These creative dynamics influence both parties to stretch constructively beyond existing capabilities, as recommended by Itami (1987). The parties *expand their knowledge* and perform better together than each may do alone. This creates a surplus for future "projects", or a positive external economy (externality), as economists would formulate it. This "hidden treasure" may not be easily copied as relationships are always unique. The understanding of these creative dynamics, and the interplay and "rules" between the designers and the firms, are important to further enhance these mostly *invisible assets*.

"The visible treasure" is demonstrated by the unique products viable on competitive international markets.

ACKNOWLEDGEMENTS

The author would like to acknowledge the *Norwegian Design Council* who commissioned and financed the empirical research material which this chapter is based on, with additional financial support from the *Norwegian Research Foundation*, the *Ministry of Industry*, the *SNF* and the *Confederation of Norwegian Business and Industry (NHO)*. The analytical work in this chapter has also been supported through the project "Scandinavian Design – relationships between designers and Nordic firms", financed by *NOS-S, Joint Committee of the Nordic Social Science Research Councils*, and the chapter was completed as part of the project "Design as a value-creating consultancy in an information-strategic business practice", a collaborative project with Geelmuyden.KieseDesign financed by the Norwegian Research Foundation's programme on service and information. Earlier versions of the analysis in this chapter have been presented in TUDelft, to NordREFO, and to the Barcelona DMI Academic Conference.

NOTES

1. Hedberg et al (1994) introduces this concept to highlight the network approach rather than out-sourcing to market supply.
2. As described by Lorenz (1986/1990) and also Freeze's recent review (1991) of Dreyfuss's close relationships with clients, this case gives insights into the almost silent practice of industrial design.
3. In the initial research phase, information was collected through a focus group, through key informants, through a comparative pilot case study (of two firms) and through an international literature review. The knowledge-based and relational perspectives were chosen as complementary to the industrial design perspective, to frame the otherwise open-ended qualitative study (see Jevnaker 1996).
4. Interviews were carried out with the company leaders (CEOs), the product development managers and the associated key designers. Furthermore, other managers (who vary somewhat in each firm) were interviewed, that is, those involved in the products' designing, development and internationalization; such as marketing managers, project managers, training managers, other functional staff. In two companies (HAMAX and HAG), the whole management group was interviewed in-depth. Most interviews were tape-recorded, generating a material of nearly 1500 pages in total.
5. Although it is difficult to sort out the effects of various input factors, in particular in integrated product development, all the managers pointed to a significant impact over time from the particular designers selected. Nevertheless, we found a nuanced view among the five firms regarding the most dominant factors (ranging from design as the firm's most valuable asset to combinations with technology, marketing and service).

6. During most of this development, HAMAX had an industrial designer/engineer employed as product development manager.
7. This emerged in the focus group conversations and is in contrast to the belief of a "sole creator" in design.
8. I refer here to personal communication with Berit Bae, January 1996.
9. This information is based on follow-up interviews in HAG's product development function, April 1996.

REFERENCES

Ainamo, A. (1996). Industrial Design and Business Performance. A Case Study of a Finnish Fashion Firm. Thesis. Helsinki School of Economics and Business Administration.

Arbeidsgruppen om industridesign (1995). Industridesign som konkurransefaktor for norsk næringsliv (Industrial Design as Competitive Factor for Norwegian Industry), Ministry of Industry and Energy (Secretary: Norwegian Design Council), Oslo.

Bae, B. (1992). Acknowledging Children's Experiences – Focus on the Quality of the Teacher–Child Relationship. Paper presented at the ETEN-Conference, Viborg College, Denmark, 3–5 May 1992, College of Early Childhood Education, Oslo/Norway.

Barney, J. (1991). Firm Resources and Sustained Competitive Advantage, *Strategic Management Journal*, **17**(1), 99–120.

Blaich, R. (1995). Design Management: Unfinished Business for this Millennium. Speech and Abstract presented at the Challenge of Complexity, 3rd International Conference on Design Management, 21–22 August, University of Art and Design Helsinki (UIAH), Helsinki.

Bruce, M. and Biemans, W.G. (eds) (1995). *Product Development. Meeting the Challenge of the Design-Marketing Interface*, John Wiley and Sons Ltd, Chichester–N.Y.–Brisbane–Toronto–Singapore.

Bruce, M. and Docherty, C. (1993). It's all in a relationship: a comparative study of client-design consultant relationships, *Design Studies*, **14**(4), 402–422.

Bruce, M. and Morris, B. with Svengren, L. and Kristensen, T. (1995). Strategic Management of Design Consultancy: Comparisons from Sweden, Denmark and Britain, School of Management, UMIST, Manchester.

Burgelman, R. and Sayles, L.R. (1986). *Inside Corporate Innovation*. The Free Press, N.Y. & London.

Burns, T. and Stalker, G.M. (1961). *The Management of Innovation*. Tavistock, London.

Design Management Journal (1993). Design and National Policy, **4**(3) The Design Management Institute, Boston.

Dierickx, I. and Cool, C. (1989). Asset Stock Accumulation and Sustainability of Competitive Advantage. *Management Science*, **35**(12), December, 1504–1513.

Dumas, A. (1993). The Effect of Management Structure and Organisational Process on Decisions in Industrial Design. Ph.D, London Business School, London.

Farstad, P. (1994b). Styring av markedsrettet produktdesign i produktutvikling (Governance of market-focused product design within product development). Paper of 28.9.94. Institute for Industrial Design, SHKS, Oslo. (IFID was later reorg. under Oslo School of Architecture).

Freeze, K. with Powell, E. (1991). Design management lessons from the past: Henry Dreyfuss and American Business. Article, Design Management Institute (DMI), Boston.

Hart, S. (1995). Where we've been and where we're going in new product development research, in Bruce, M. & Biemans, W. G. (eds) (1995). *Product Development. Meeting the Challenge of the Design-Marketing Interface*, John Wiley & Sons Ltd, Chichester–N.Y.–Brisbane–Toronto–Singapore, 15–42.

Hedberg, B. et al (1994). *Imaginära Organisationer*, Liber-Hermods, Malmö (Virtual Organisations), Sweden.

Hedlund, G. and Nonaka, I. (1993). Models of Knowledge Management in the West and Japan, in Lorange, P. et al (eds), *Implementing Strategic Processes: Change, Learning and Co-operation*, Blackwell, Oxford and Cambridge, MA.

Henderson, R. (1991). Architectural innovation as a source of competitive advantage. *Design Management Journal*. **2**(3), 43–47.

Hollins, B. and Pugh, S. (1990). *Successful Product Design*, Butterworth, London.

Itami, H. with Roehl, T.W. (1987). *Mobilizing Invisible Assets*, Harvard University Press, Cambridge MA and London.

Jeppesen, B. et al (1994). *Dansk design – fra kirke til kafé* the Design Management Institute, Boston. Systime, Herning (Danish Design–from Church to Café), Denmark.

Jevnaker, B.H. (1991). Make the World a Better Place to SIT IN!, *Design Management Journal*, **2**(4), Fall, 48–54.

Jevnaker, B.H. (1993). Inaugurative learning: adapting a new design approach, *Design Studies*, **14**(4), October, Butterworth-Heineman Ltd., Oxford; 379–401. SNF-reprint No. 39/1993.

Jevnaker B.H. (1994). From the Outside. In Building Organizational Capabilities in Product Design, SNF Working paper No. 17/94. SNF, Bergen.

Jevnaker, B.H. (1995a). Developing capabilities for innovative product designs: A case study of the Scandinavian furniture industry, Bruce, M. & Biemans, W.G. (eds), *Product Development: meeting the challenge of the design–marketing interface*, John Wiley & Sons Ltd., Chichester.

Jevnaker, B.H. (1995b). Den skjulte formuen. Industridesign som kreativ konkurranse-faktor (The Hidden Treasure: Industrial Design as Creative Competitive Factor). SNF-rapport 36/95. SNF, Bergen, Norway.

Jevnaker, B.H. (1995c). Designing an Olympic Games in the Face of Chaos: The Case of Lillehammer, *Design Management Journal*, **6**(3), the Design Management Institute, Boston, 41–49.

Jevnaker, B.H. (1996). Industridesign som kreativ konkurransefaktor: En forstudie (Industrial Design as Creative Competitive Factor), SNF-rapport 54/96, Bergen.

Johannessen, K.E. (1988). Tankar om tyst kunskap (Thoughts on Tacit Knowledge), *Dialoger*, (6), 13–28.

Kicherer, S. (1990). *Olivetti. A Study of the Corporate Management of Design*, Trefoil Publishers, London.

Kotler, P. and Rath, G.A. (1984). Design: a powerful but neglected strategic tool, *Journal of Business Strategy*, **5**(2), 16–21.

Kristensen, T. (1995). The Contribution of Design to Business: A Competence-Based Perspective. *Process of Change Laboratory*, Stanford University and Copenhagen Business School. Proceedings from the 1st European Academy of Design, Design Interfaces, 11–13 April 1995, Vol. 4 Design Management, University College of Salford.

Lauvaas, P. and Handal, G. (1990). *Veiledning og praktisk yrkesteori* (Supervision and Practical Vocation Theory), Cappelen, Oslo.

Leonard-Barton, D. (1995). *Wellsprings of Knowledge. Building and Sustaining the Sources of Innovation*, HBS, Boston.

Lorenz, C. (1986/1990). *The Design Dimension*, (new revised ed. 1990), Basil Blackwell, UK.

Lövlie Schibbye, A.L. (1996). Anerkjennelse: En terapeutisk intervensjon? (Recognition: A Therapeutic Intervention?), *Tidsskrift for Norsk Psykologforening*. **33**, 530–537.

Löwendahl, B.R. (1994). Når strategiske ressurser har både egne meninger og ben å gå på (When strategic resources have both own opinions and feet to walk with). *Praktisk økonomi og ledelse*, 3/94, 83–92.

Macneil, I.R. (1980). *The New Social Contract: An Inquiry Into Modern Contractual Relations*, Yale University Press, New Haven, Conn.

Nonaka, I. and Takeuchi, H. (1995). *The Knowledge-Creating Company. How Japanese Companies Create the Dynamics of Innovation*, Oxford University Press, New York/ Oxford.

Nordhaug, O. (1993). *Human Capital in Organizations*, Scandinavian University Press & Oxford University Press, Oslo/Oxford.

Norsk Designråd (1993). Design i norske bedrifter 1993 (Design in Norwegian Firms 1993). Internal report Scanfact, based on survey by telephone from February/March 1993 (N = 347 bedrifter), Oslo.

Nyrnes, A. (1990). Omvegen om språket. Eit essay i og om kunnskapsdebatten, *Norsk Pedagogisk Tidsskrift*, 6, 328–336.

Öijord, A. (1992). Analytisk estetikk – eller jakten på skjönnheten. Tell, Asker.

Olins, W. (1987). Mysteries of design management revealed, in Bernsen, J. (ed.), *Design management in practice*, European/EEC Design Editions, Danish Design Council & Foundación BCD, Copenhagen/Barcelona.

Palshöy, J. (1990). Design Management at Bang and Olufsen, in Oakley, M. (ed.), *Design Management: a Handbook of Issues and Methods*, Blackwell, Oxford, 37–42.

Polanyi, M. (1958). *Personal Knowledge*, Routledge & Kegan Paul, London.

Porter, M.E. (1985). *Competitive Advantage*, Free Press, New York.

Potter, S. et al (1991). The Benefits and Costs of Investments in Design: Using professional design expertise in product, engineering and graphics projects. Report DIG-03. Milton Keynes/Manchester: Design Innovation Group, Open University and UMIST.

Prahalad, C.K. and Hamel, G. (1990). The Core Competences of the Corporation, *Harvard Business Review*, May–June, 79–91.

Schön, D.A. (1988). Designing: Rules, types and worlds, *Design Studies*, **9**(3), 181–190, Butterworth: Oxford.

Snow, C.P. (1963). De to kulturer (The Two Cultures). Norwegian version, Cappelen, Oslo.

Svengren, L. (1995). *Industriell design som strategisk ressurs* (Industrial Design as Strategic Resource), Ph.D., Lund University Press, Lund, Sweden.

Teece, D., Pisano G. and Shuen A. (1990). Firm Capabilities, Resources, and the Concept of Strategy. Economic Analysis and Policy Working Paper. EAP-38, University of California, Berkeley.

Walsh, V., et al. (1992). *Winning by Design. Technology, Product Design and International Competitiveness*, Blackwell Business, Oxford.

Wickman, K. (1996). Drømmen om Scandinavian Design lever endnu, *Louisiana Revy*, 2/96. 18–23.

Wildhagen, F. (1988). *Norge i Form. Kunsthåndverk og Design under industrikulturen* (Norway in Shape. Decorative Arts and Design under the Industrial Culture), Stenersen, Oslo.

Williamson, O.E. (1985). *The Economic Institutions of Capitalism*, The Free Press, New York.

CHAPTER SIX

NOVO NORDISK A/S: INNOVATIVE DESIGN FOR DIABETICS[1]

Karen Freeze

Novo Nordisk A/S was formed in 1989 by a merger of Novo Industri, founded in 1925, and Nordisk Gentofte, founded in 1923. Both had strong traditions in hospital and laboratory research, and each brought different strengths to the new company along with prominence in the development of insulin. Between them, they accounted for all the major innovations in insulin products worldwide and provided nearly half the world's supply of insulin. Nevertheless, by the late 1980s it was clear that insulin was becoming a commodity product: Novo Nordisk's competitors, most notably the American pharmaceutical company Eli Lilly and the German company Hoechst, could provide insulin of equal quality to that of their Scandinavian counterpart.[2] Thus the future in this industry would belong to the company that not only could manufacture insulin of superior quality, but could also provide a range of products and services to meet the manifold needs of diabetics around the world.

DIABETES: THE TARGET VILLAIN

Diabetes is a serious metabolic disease that affects about 100 million people worldwide, including over 14 million in the US. It is characterised by a lack or insufficiency of insulin, a protein hormone manufactured in the pancreas gland. Without insulin, the body cannot process sugar properly. Untreated, diabetes

Management of Design Alliances. Edited by M. Bruce and B. H. Jevnaker.
© 1998 John Wiley & Sons Ltd.

results in death – in fact, it is the third biggest killer in the US behind cancer and heart disease.

Treatment for diabetes involves various means of enabling the individual diabetic to control his or her blood sugar level as tightly as possible on a daily basis, so that the long-term, debilitating effects of diabetes (such as loss of extremities (fingers, toes), blindness, loss of sense of touch) can be mitigated or even prevented altogether. Diet and exercise play important roles, but insulin, in carefully controlled, multiple doses daily is for many diabetics essential to life. With pure, genetically-engineered human insulin readily available, the principal challenge of research (outside of finding a cure for the disease!) is to simplify the task of self-administering this life-giving hormone. In terms of product strategy, this means providing not only user-centred insulin-delivery devices, but all the auxiliary equipment, e.g. blood testers.

To the partnership born in this new competitive arena, Nordisk brought considerable experience with the manufacturing of medical devices, while Novo brought just one insulin delivery device, the NovoPen. But Novo also brought a design and service-oriented culture that would come to dominate the new company and equip it for the challenges of the 1990s.

DESIGN AT NOVO NORDISK: A PROBLEM-SOLVING TOOL

As a company Novo had always paid close attention to its logo and as early as the 1930s began consistently to hire top architects for its buildings. Its founders, the brothers Pedersen, had come from a modest country teacher's family and, when they succeeded in the insulin business, they did as most cultured Danes did: they invested in and generously supported the arts. Until the early 1980s, however, Novo's "design strategy" could be said to be an intuitive matter-of-fact, rather than an explicit, effort. Only when Mads Øvlisen became CEO in 1981 did design become an integral part of corporate policy.[3]

Øvlisen's interest in design apparently came naturally. A son of artisans, he "likes materials" and "enjoys things that are good and shine with genuineness". For Øvlisen design is no "frosting on the cake", but rather a problem-solving tool: "We should not work with design just for the sake of design, but rather to make better products and increase the value of the firm." Good design solves problems: "You can have beautiful graphics, but if they don't solve a problem, then it is not good design." The design prizes won by the company's insulin pens are only partial confirmation of this philosophy:

testimonies of diabetic users, for whom the pens solved a problem, were what counted, for their purchasing decisions would determine the fate of the company's insulin business.

Øvlisen also believed that the relationship between a company and its employees, and between a company and its customers, could be greatly enhanced by a strong corporate identity. This identity had to be expressed by a consistent design that integrated all aspects of the company into a coherent whole. He viewed such a visual identity as a "valuable resource" that told the world what Novo Nordisk stood for, what it demands of itself, and where it wants to go. "One should be able to tell that a building is a Novo Nordisk building, and one should have no doubt that a brochure is providing information about a Novo Nordisk product."

CORPORATE VISUAL IDENTITY TAKES THE LEAD

Øvlisen's greatest ally in this aspect of the company's design strategy is graphic designer Jytte Ulrich, manager of Corporate Visual Identity and guardian of the company's image. Hired in 1977 as manager and graphic designer for the Pharmaceuticals Division's promotion department, Ulrich had single-handedly built the CVI function and headed it since 1986. In preparation for the merger in 1989, her department was given the responsibility of creating a visual identity for the new company. After evaluating the strong visual equity of Novo's traditional logo, management decided to retain its dominant element, the Apis Bull[4] (Figure 6.1).

Working with an outside design consultant, "11 Danes", they developed an updated logo around which to unify the new company. "Everyone was involved", recalled Ulrich. "Mads Øvlisen would drop in and play with it too. He is genuinely interested in hands-on involvement in design, even though it isn't his speciality."

To provide effective guidelines for the CVI program, Ulrich produced a series of brochures detailing the application of the logo and company colours in various contexts, such as stationery, packaging and so forth. "I don't like traditional, thick CI manuals", she said, "People can hardly read them. This way, people take only what they need and can quickly grasp how to apply the CVI standards in their situations."

Ulrich is also guardian of environmental-interior design at Novo Nordisk. In accordance with Øvlisen's desire that CVI be expressed in Novo Nordisk's architecture, she monitors decisions on furniture, colour and art that adorns the hallways and common spaces in Novo Nordisk's workplaces in Denmark.

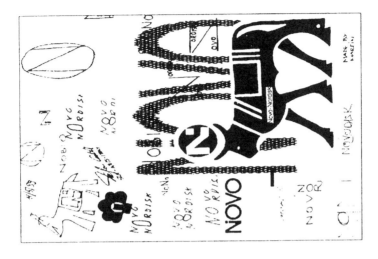

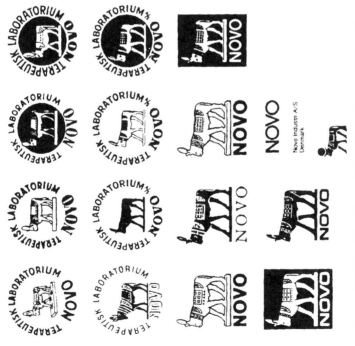

Source: H.Richter-Friis, *Livet på Novo* (Copenhagen, 1991), p.43

Figure 6.1   Novo Nordisk design: Evolution of Novo's logo, left, and right, the new company logo

When a daughter company in the US restored its building lavishly without incorporating any evidence that it belonged to Novo Nordisk, Ulrich was piqued: "Here they've used Novo Nordisk funds and they don't even have the Novo Nordisk name anywhere in sight!"

Ulrich uses external designers whenever she needs help, because her department consists of only two people: herself and an assistant who is not a designer. Although she would like a communications designer on board, she is convinced that she shouldn't have a bigger department. The problem with in-house designers, Ulrich believes, is that "it is so difficult to criticise them. It is good to get fresh views from outside." She has tried to work with a "design panel" of various outside designers, but found that "it is hard to get them to stop competing with each other and work for the same goal."

As a design manager with 18 years at Novo, Ulrich stresses the importance of cultivating relationships: "You can't come in from the street and make good designs. You have to get to know the company." From her point of view, working with designers who really understand the company saves time: "You don't have to give so much information to them, and the job proceeds so much more effectively." Informality is also a key in Novo Nordisk's relationship with design consultants, "They like the fact that we can be very open and direct with each other."

One of Ulrich's frequent consultants is Kim Paulsen, an independent graphic designer and president of MIDD, the Association of Danish Designers. Paulsen expressed his relationship to Novo Nordisk this way. "[Novo] is one of only ten or twelve Danish companies with a massive design tradition. Because the basics are there, you don't waste time. And you know in advance that you *have* to work at a high level for Novo."

DESIGNING FOR DIABETICS: INSULIN DELIVERY SYSTEMS AT NOVO NORDISK

Novo Nordisk's intensely user-centred and highly precise insulin-delivery devices have their origin in the early 1980s, when Novo engineers with design sensitivity, rather than professional designers, followed a hunch. Inspired by an English doctor, they believed that simpler, more discreet insulin injections would be a bonus to diabetics – especially for those who needed to inject themselves several times a day. Their device, introduced in 1985 as NovoPen, looked like an expensive fountain pen and used cartridges to deliver up to 150 units of insulin in one-unit increments. Despite some disadvantages (the user had to click and count dosage units while injecting), NovoPen was a commercial and design success, winning prizes and transforming the everyday lives of diabetics whose regimens included regular (short-acting) doses of insulin. When a company specialising in cases for small devices could not accommodate Novo's needs, they recommended industrial designer Steven McGugan to design a case for NovoPen. With that began the company's first long-term relationship with an industrial design consultant.[5]

Responding to the demand for a similar device that embodied a more practical dosage system and could deliver other types of insulin, Novo developed, with an outside supplier, NovoPen II (called Novolin Pen in the US), a plastic version with a "dial-a-dose" system. This product suffered from a lack of design expertise, however, and was soon improved by Jens Møller-Jensen, a designer whose background was actually architecture. He became Novo's second long-term external design consultant. After a false start, NovoPen II was manufactured by B&O Technology A/S, a Bang & Olufsen subsidiary.

IMPLEMENTING DESIGN AT NOVO NORDISK: THE NOVOLET PROJECT[6]

Enjoying design acclaim and brisk sales for the NovoPen, which had only by chance, rather than any explicit design strategy, achieved such renown, Novo now intended to utilise design resources in every future product. It was, however, a business rather than a design decision that pushed Novo to investigate a new concept for the next generation insulin delivery device: the disposable pen. Competitors were attempting to manufacture cartridges of insulin for use with NovoPen and NovoPen II. Although they had not yet succeeded, Novo assumed it would be only a matter of time before they did. A preemptive move would be to develop a product that could not be copied and in which competitors' insulin could not be used: a closed-system, prefilled, disposable device.

In late 1986, serendipity brought Novo together with Pharma Plast, a company that made disposable syringes and other high-volume plastic medical devices. While Novo had been contemplating a disposable insulin pen, Pharma Plast had already attempted to make one. However, to realise the closed system they envisioned, Pharma Plast needed an insulin manufacturer as a partner. Novo, for its part, needed Pharma Plast's experience with plastics and volume manufacturing.

In 1988 the two companies formed a joint venture, Diabetes Care Products (DCP) and hired Steve McGugan, who had designed NovoPen's carrying case and had worked on various projects for both companies, to work on the design of a disposable pen. McGugan received a two-page brief (Figure 6.2) describing the requirements for a disposable pen. It specified, for example, the incorporation of Novo's PenFill, the cylindrical insulin cartridge developed for NovoPen and NovoPen II, into the new device. It also specified NovoPen needles.

On the surface, the main design challenge was to minimise the number of parts and make the device economical to produce. But an insulin syringe is not a toy, so the real challenge lay in making a device that could achieve zero defects in the manufacturing process. "The difficulty with medical devices is the stringent safety requirements", industrial designer McGugan explained. "When I design something upon which people's lives will depend, something where accuracy is a matter of life and death, then I don't have a lot of choices." McGugan also pointed out that briefs for medical equipment aren't always so short: "Sometimes briefs are very thick and you end up with a very detailed map that you have to follow."

Novo had in McGugan both a knowledgeable and flexible partner. Although he knew a lot about technology and brought his own philosophy to the project, he believed that a designer had to listen to the company and be flexible, not dogmatic about his designs. Klaus Thogersen, a manufacturing engineer from Dansk Technologi (an engineering and machine-building firm) who designed the tools, said of him that, "Steve had a great understanding of manufacturing, and in fact I hesitated to press him too much because he might be too accommodating."

As McGugan began to prepare initial sketches, people from various disciplines were drawn into the project. Four groups were involved:

1. **Core Group**, or steering group, consisting of Novo people from marketing, medical (patient) research, R&D, production, and regulation, who met once a month;
2. **Working Group**, which included people from production, technology, marketing, medical systems and registration;
3. **Technical Group**, with people from Novo, the design consultant, Diabetes Care Products, and Dansk Technologi who met once a week; and
4. **Registration/Labelling Group**, which joined product development people with graphic artists (Figure 6.3a and b).

Working with engineers and production people from the Technology Group, McGugan quickly moved to three-dimensional (3D) models, which the group considered essential for communicating with doctors and pharmacists: "We

---

"NovoPen III" Product Brief

User Features:

Requirements:

- NovoPen III should be an insulin injection system in the shape of a single use pen, delivered with a mounted cartridge. The product should not be re-loadable.
- Novo's cartridges 1.5 or 3 ml should be used.
  Needle for NovoPen should be used.
  The pen should be able to be stored both with and without needle.
- Dose selection should be obtained by turning in 2 unit increments, with 10 units per rotation for 1.5 ml and 10 or 20 units per rotation for 3 ml.
- Dose selection shall be visual/audible and possibly also tactile for each increment.
- Dose selection should be reversible. Reversal should not be possible below zero.
- Dose should be given by one hand and by a simple push.
- It shall be visually/audibly/tactually clear when dose has been delivered.
- It should not be possible to disassemble the pen without destructing the product.
- The construction should ensure that any handling and material errors will not lead to an overdosing and any error that may give an under-dosing should be easy to recognize.
- Selection of a dose bigger than what is left in the pen should not be possible.
- The rubber membrane should allow for disinfection when needle is changed.
- It should be possible to see 2/3 of the cartridge, so movement of the piston and the homogeneity of the suspension can be checked.
- NovoPen III shall have a clip for storage in a pocket.
- It should not be possible unintentionally to expel insulin when the pen is not in use.
- A possibility should exist to make visual and tactile coding of the pens with different insulin.
- Weight should not exceed 35 gram.
- Length should be more than 100 mm at any time during use.
- NovoPen III shall be easy and self-explanatory in use.

Wishes:

- Maximum dose 50 units.
- Scale to show residual amount in cartridge.
- Automatic zero-setting of dose selector.

Conditions:

- NovoPen III should be stored, used and work at temperatures between 0 and 40°C.
- Dust and humidity should not interfere with the use of the product.
- The push button should withstand the specified force.
- Negative dose setting should withstand the specified force.
- The insulin should be protected from light under use and storage.
- Storage of pen without dimensional and other changes: 3 years.
- NovoPen III and the other imprints on the product should resist common disinfectants.

Design:

- NovoPen III shall have a pleasant, discrete and non-medical look.
- The surface shall be resistant towards dirt and pleasant to touch without any sharp edges or other design problems.
- Length less than 156 mm.
- The pen shall carry a label which is visual in the whole lifetime of the product and which carries batchnumber and expiration date.
- Scale number shall be at least 3 mm.
- The product shall carry the name NovoPen III on the clip or another agreed place.

Source: Design Management Institute Case Study, K. Freeze, 1993

Figure 6.2   NovoPen III product brief

never present something on the basis of a drawing", declared Kim Steengaard Petersen, manager of disposable devices.

ATTENTION TO DETAIL: DIABETIC-CENTRED DESIGN

The Technology Group quickly determined that the new pen would consist of seven parts (down from 23 in NovoPen II). The operating principle was a new, simple dial-a-dose system that permitted the patient to administer multiples of two units up to 58 units at once, for a total of 150 units (1.5ml) or several days' worth.[7] (Figure 6.4)

Other features that occupied the designers were colour (they decided on a cool grey); shape (they made the larger version tapered, rather than cylindrical, to minimise apparent size); colour and tactile coding of the device's cap to indicate type of insulin, and many other details.

The tactile coding exemplified user-centred design-thinking. Having determined that each type of insulin would be represented by a different colour cap and label, the team realised that this would not be sufficient for elderly people with poor eyesight. With the help of people at the Institute for the Blind in Gentofte, McGugan developed a tactile code.[8] "With the clock as inspiration", they developed a combination of lines and bumps that could be expanded as new mixes were added.

As was their custom, Novo worked with patients at Hvidøre Hospital (after the merger, at Steno Diabetes Center) during the entire development of NovoLet. They assembled thousands of units by hand and worked with hundreds of patients of all ages to determine whether the prefilled syringe idea was as practical as it seemed. In the end they had more than ten patient-years of experience with the product from clinical trials before launch.

IT'S MUTUAL: DESIGN FOR MANUFACTURING AND DESIGN FOR PATIENT-USER ENHANCE EACH OTHER

One key to NovoLet's success was the incorporation of manufacturing engineering in the development team from the very beginning. Interestingly, several of NovoLet's design details had not only a user-related function, but also served to assist the automation of the production line. For example, the flat part of the lid that surrounded the needle gave the impression that the pen was smaller, surrounded the needle with minimal air while still providing

(a)

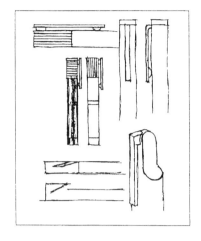

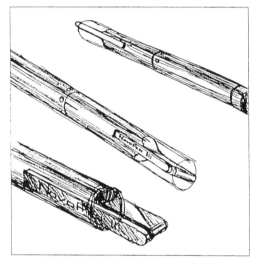

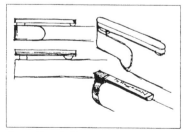

Source: Steve McGugan

Figure 6.3   (a) NovoPen III initial sketches

(b)

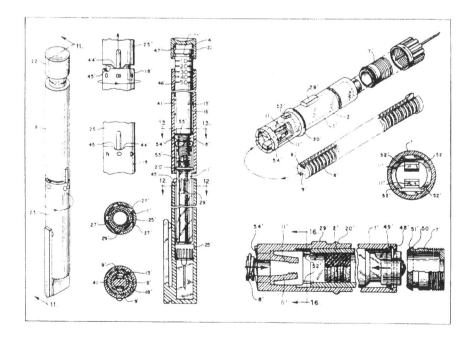

NovoPen III's parts

Figure 6.3 (b) NovoPen III initial sketches

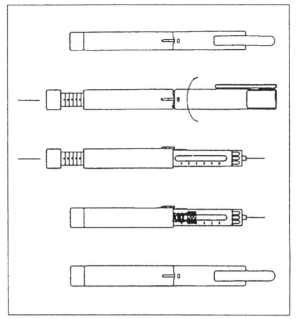

Source: DCP, 1988

Figure 6.4   Engineering drawing of NovoLet's use

protection, and gave patients a convenient place to hold on to the lid as they dialled a dose. It also gave the assembly robot's hand something to grasp as it placed the lid on the pen during production. A small ridge in the base of the pen served as a tactile point to "0", helping the patient to align the pen properly with the scale. The ridge also provided something for the robot to hold onto as the plunger and cartridge were inserted into the base.

Despite these design details, volume manufacturing turned out to be a major challenge. To go from a finished design to a mass-produced, 100% accurate, prefilled insulin syringe was not an easy task – in fact, it would take two years from the initial ramp-up before all the hiccups were worked out of the manufacturing process and NovoLet could begin to meet the volume demands from all its markets. "The problem is", tool designer Klaus Thogersen explained, "that every time you replace people with machines, you discover new variables you have to test for. People automatically see faults wherever they are, whereas machines see only the fault that they are programmed to look for. The result is that you have to develop new types of automatic controls that test for defects after every assembly step." Until reliable testing devices were in place, the DCP assembly plant tested each item individually.

NOVOLET: THE "PREFILLED INSULIN SYRINGE" DEBUTS

A year or so before NovoLet was launched, management decided to position the new device as a "prefilled syringe" rather than as another "pen". For that reason, they did not call it "NovoPen III". "The 'pre-filled syringe' is a familiar concept", explained international product manager Peter Nissen Jørgensen. "To hospital personnel it simply means 'easy to use', and since our largest potential market at the time was hospitals, we decided to position it that way." Moreover, in markets outside Europe, where insulin *pens* had mixed reviews, a pen-like prefilled *syringe* would have a "clean start".

NovoLet was introduced in Holland in 1989 and in Denmark and Sweden in January, 1990. It was so popular that by 1992 it increased the market share Novo Nordisk's pens enjoyed in Denmark to 69% (of total insulin by volume), two-thirds of which were NovoLet. Results in Sweden and Holland were also impressive. (Figure 6.5)

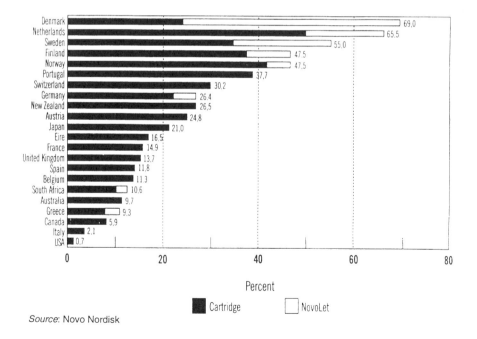

Source: Novo Nordisk

Figure 6.5   NovoLet's market take-up

GOING GLOBAL: NEW DESIGN CHALLENGES FOR
THE AMERICAN MARKET

While NovoLet was enjoying success in European markets, Novo Nordisk's North American organisation was waiting for the new product to be approved by the Federal Drug Administration and to be available in quantities suitable for launch in the US. A key question was whether NovoLet's design – however successful it was in Europe – was suitable for the US market. Diabetes therapy was – or at least had been – quite different in the US, with fewer and larger doses of insulin administered per day than was typical in Europe. Therefore, the 3ml version of NovoLet (which was not ready even in 1994, when the 1.5ml was finally launched in the US) was considered essential. Some of the Novo Nordisk American sales people questioned whether the safety features were clear enough for American users, especially illiterate ones.

In April 1988, Novo conducted initial market research at six sites in the US. The initial reactions were mixed: some people wanted one-unit increments; most wanted some kind of calibrated gauge and coding for type of insulin. Some were afraid the device would be too expensive; after all, it "looked too good to throw away". Novo briefly tested an ugly, transparent version for the US market, "but that was not the answer either".

Although the US input did contribute to an improved gauge on the insulin cartridge and to the coding system, the consensus in Princeton in 1992 was that Novo Nordisk did not pay enough attention to American market research when developing its products. From the Danish side, there was apparently little effort made to communicate the thoroughness of NovoLet's design achievement and the relationship of the extensive, even exhaustive patient research to the final design. Therefore it did not occur to the American marketers to leverage this design depth in when they launched the Novolin Prefilled in April 1994.[9] Within a few months, to their good fortune, modern, multi-injection insulin therapy, for which the Prefilled was ideally suited, was vindicated by a major study published in the US on the long-term effects of close control of blood sugar on the health of diabetics. By the end of 1995, Novolin Prefilled was well established in the US, with $3 million in annual sales. Novo Nordisk's formidable American competitor, Eli Lilly, had just launched its next entry into the insulin pen competition.

STAYING GLOBAL: DESIGN CHALLENGES AROUND THE WORLD

The experience in the US raised several issues about global design that are even more acute in non-Western countries. Although the body of *homo sapiens* functions the same the world over, much of medical procedure is cultural. "In Arab lands", Steve McGugan notes, "colour is very important. If a product is the wrong colour, they won't buy it." Since diabetes is affected by diet, its characteristics in a given population may vary in accordance with a country's cuisine. Japanese diabetics tend to use very little insulin in small doses, so Novo Nordisk is considering developing a smaller pen for them that could also be used as a children's device elsewhere.

The design challenge for global insulin devices is formidable, and needs to be tackled up front. "When we do a product", insists McGugan, "we should aim for a design that helps raise the awareness of design over the whole world." Both functionality and visual appeal should incorporate cross-cultural criteria, he believes. In other product categories, such as toys or domestics, flexible manufacturing systems can be utilised to make adaptations for every market. In medical products, however, such an approach would only multiply dramatically the margin for error. To aim towards *one* design with zero defects is challenging enough; the secret is to incorporate principles of global design from the very beginning.

REFLECTIONS ON DESIGN MANAGEMENT AT NOVO NORDISK: CURRENT AND FUTURE PRACTICES

The preceding discussion of design culture, strategy and practice at Novo Nordisk raises a number of issues, such as how to institutionalise and streamline product design and development, and how to utilise design for competitive advantage worldwide throughout the entire company.

MEETING THE PRODUCT DEVELOPMENT CHALLENGE

Although the NovoLet project was a tremendous success, it was slow and inefficient. Preparation for manufacturing, for example, was a trial and error, learning-as-you-go process, which took almost two years from concept to initial launch, and another two years to achieve mass production with essentially zero defects. In coming years, however, given looming competition from major players, this would not be fast enough. Therefore, in the autumn of 1990, when Stig Jørgensen presented a report to management suggesting that something had to be done about Novo Nordisk's product development process, he was asked to lead a working group to examine the problem. Jørgensen was a medical doctor with a business degree who had spent eight years at Novo and had been involved with NovoLet since the autumn of 1989.

Jørgensen found that Novo Nordisk suffered from the classic problems of industry leaders who have never known competition. Without a sense of urgency, they had had no reason to learn to plan ahead and prioritise, to communicate effectively, to rationalise and speed-up decision-making processes. Project management had not existed as a concept – people became *de facto* project managers haphazardly, not because of any particular ability or training in project management. As a result, in the NovoLet project Jørgensen found that "the left hand didn't know what the right hand was doing". Jørgensen also found that lack of experience in working cross-functionally contributed to a slow development process. "Handing a project over from one function to the next (and sometimes back again) takes time."

Moreover, Novo Nordisk's informal culture, where everyone was on a first-name basis with everyone else, including the CEO, had its downside. Complete decentralisation in order to, as Mads Øvlisen put it, "let people with ideas and drive get on with what they are doing" and "let the creative juices flow", also contributed to the inefficiencies of democratic decision-making. Since everyone is asked about everything in such a culture, it was often unclear who was to make a decision.

By the beginning of the 1990s, however, the competitive scene had changed, and it was clear that Novo Nordisk would have to as well. It had entered truly global markets, and would have to change its product development culture and methodology if it was to compete. The challenge would be to make those changes without losing the company's identity and core values.

NEW DESIGN MANAGEMENT METHODS

By the mid-1990s, Novo Nordisk's product development process had become more formal and more organised, with procedures to follow and milestones to meet. Professional project management is now in place, with project managers devoting full time to their jobs and being compensated accordingly. Communication between Denmark and other markets over new product development issues has been greatly improved, partly due to state-of-the-art electronics and the willingness to use them.

EXPANDING DESIGN RESOURCES

These changes have affected design management as well. Although Novo Nordisk has maintained its relationships with external industrial designers Steve McGugan and Jens Møller-Jensen, whom they consider "house designers", individual project managers may typically hire several designers at the very beginning of a project to develop concepts, and then choose the best of these to be developed.

One illustration of this more competitive design resourcing[10] concerns a recent project within insulin delivery devices. In 1994 Novo Nordisk began work on a new insulin delivery device with technical brainstorming and then hired four designers, including McGugan and Møller-Jensen and a relatively inexperienced designer who, according to Henryk Isbjørg, the Novo Nordisk project manager, said "we thought might have something new to offer". To each they gave a detailed brief, a budget, and access to Novo Nordisk people. On that basis each developed a design model. They were to be paid for their work, and Novo Nordisk was to own the rights to whatever they produced.

After the first stage of the project, one designer's input was dropped. Three designers produced models that were shown to diabetic patients. That initial market research narrowed the choices to two, which were further developed towards prototypes. "This got expensive", product manager Isbjørg noted, "because we had to use teams with each of them and try to keep them separate, so the two designers wouldn't find out about each other's work". With hindsight Isbjørg believes they should have chosen only one design before going further. In fact, in the middle of this stage they dropped one design so they could go forward with the final prototype as a single team.

Although this approach appears similar to a traditional architectural design competition, Henryk Isbjørg states emphatically that it is not: "The designers get paid for their work, and they like this approach."

Designer Steve McGugan, who did not win that final contract, has mixed feelings about this system. On the one hand, he appreciates Novo Nordisk's desire to gather as many ideas as possible, and its right to have its own "visions". He believes, however, in the importance of the corporate image or "family look" of products within a given line. "Then a satisfied customer will recognise a new product as a Novo product and trust it." McGugan believes that this family look is hard to achieve if you switch designers in the middle of a product line.

Novo Nordisk has grown so big now, McGugan points out, that "each area has its pet designer", and that of course influences their choices. The people who made the decision on this particular device did not know McGugan personally, even though he had worked on many projects for the company. "But of course, that means I am favoured in other areas."

Even though he was disappointed at losing continuity with the insulin delivery device line, McGugan agrees that the "competition" was not a waste of time. "I got the idea of making a 'Users' Guide' to go along with the model I submitted. As a designer, you know how something works, but if you can't explain it in simple language, then there's something wrong. Such a users' guide helps you see the weak points in your design. And it also helps marketing people in the early stages. The idea has caught on like wildfire at Novo!" It is typical of Novo Nordisk's still informal style that unexpected innovation can be quickly welcomed and adopted.

DESIGN COMPETITIONS IN COMMUNICATIONS DESIGN

Novo Nordisk has also used closed design competitions for other activities as well. Not long ago the Bioindustrial Group (BIG) faced the challenge of completely redesigning their magazine. They knew that it did not fit at all with Novo's corporate identity guidelines, and they knew they didn't like it, but they didn't know what they *did* want. They hired three outside consultants, including the one that had done the magazine before, and gave them a very detailed, half-day briefing. As one of the people in charge of BIG promotion explained, "We told them who the target group was, what the company's values were, what we didn't like about the old version. We also discussed technical parameters – that it comes out four times a year, that the content and quality of illustrations are extremely variable, and that in fact one challenge is to find better ways to illustrate something as nondescript as an enzyme!"

Two of the three designers (including the one that had produced the magazine before) came up with feasible options, and one was completely off the mark. Finally they chose a new designer, who has completely transformed the magazine, making the graphic design and production process more flexible and lowering its costs.

STRATEGIC MANAGEMENT OF DESIGN RESOURCES FOR THE 21st CENTURY

Although still under development and refinement, Novo Nordisk's design management has evolved a long way towards effectively contributing to the realisation of the company's business strategies. As the only official in-house design manager, CVI director Jytte Ulrich wants to ensure that effective design management becomes institutionalised at Novo Nordisk before she retires. She has therefore gone far beyond her formal responsibilities in Corporate Visual Identity and looked at the management of design throughout the company – in products, communications, environments. In analysing design management at Novo Nordisk, she has come up with frameworks for thinking about product development and has made recommendations as to how time and money can be saved if the company would invest more in design up front. Because of her position, her location at corporate HQ, her track record, she has the ear of senior management and does not hesitate to communicate her views and ideas to them.

One of Ulrich's pet projects is the company's retreat centre at Hvidøre Palace, on the coast north of Copenhagen. Formerly Novo's diabetes hospital, it has been completely reconstructed for employee education, conferences, and the like. Occasionally product development teams have met there to brainstorm. "We should cultivate this method", Ulrich is convinced, "but it is hard to convince people to do it. It is expensive, yes, but it works." Ulrich would like to establish a "creative sand box", where outside creative resources and in-house managers of those resources would come together at Hvidøre once a month, whether around a specific project or not. She has been talking about this with anyone who will listen. "I've convinced Mads Øvlisen that this would save money in the end, but we've got no one to carry it through."

NOVO NORDISK: MEETING THE CHALLENGES OF THE FUTURE

Novo Nordisk's experience with managing design resources over the past ten years suggests a number of considerations regarding design strategy and implementation in large companies.

DESIGN CULTURE AND LEADERSHIP

First, Novo Nordisk demonstrates that the nature of a design culture is important to understanding a company's success and failure in the implementation of its design strategy. At Novo Nordisk, the design culture is dominated by individual management styles and priorities. CEO Mads Øvlisen has vigorously supported design excellence from the top, while corporate visual identity director Jytte Ulrich has provided professional leadership for the design program as a whole. In the product development trenches, design management styles and procedures have evolved from serendipitous beginnings, when Novo first came in contact with Steve McGugan and Jens Møller-Jensen, to a design competition model that is still evolving.

When the company was still small, both Ulrich and Øvlisen promoted unity and consistency in United States. Because of the nature of medical products, which simply have to achieve zero defects, Novo Nordisk cannot afford to make a variety of products on the whims of local markets, but must work to achieve global designs that will be accepted anywhere in the world.

That the company is responsive to innovation and new approaches bodes well, however. The immediate adoption of McGugan's user manuals for design proposals as a requirement for all designers illustrates this attitude, which can only strengthen Novo Nordisk's goal to stay in the forefront of patient-oriented devices.

THE CHALLENGE OF CREATIVITY

Finally, Novo Nordisk, whose major products are "nondescript" enzymes and hormones, may become a laboratory for broader-based creativity, if Jytte Ulrich has her way. For developing user-friendly delivery devices in service of these pharmaceutical and agricultural formulas, the company has achieved renown within the design community and among patients and medical personnel. But company management, exemplified by Mads Øvlisen, believes in going further – in tapping creative resources within the company in creative ways. These resources could be harnessed to solve a wide range of problems, from management of human resources to management of product development to management of global enterprises. If this company, grounded in traditional business and research values, can dare to use non-traditional methods (such as Ulrich's "creative sandbox") to find perhaps entirely new directions and approaches to its place in the world, then it will undoubtedly continue to be one of the premier niche-players among the giants of the pharmaceutical world.

Back in 1986 Mads Øvlisen presented his "Vision for the Year 2000" to Novo's employees and asked them to participate in its unfolding. The vision was further elaborated and presented in the fall of 1989 to the management of the new Novo Nordisk, a company that was poised to become a world player in the health care and bio-industrial fields. Thanks to ongoing, strategic management of design, particularly of product and communications design, Novo Nordisk has established a leading position as the "Diabetes Company" worldwide and won recognition as a formidable niche-player in bio-industrials and medical pharmaceuticals. It cannot rest on its laurels, however, and therein lies its fundamental challenge.

NOTES

1. See Karen J. Freeze (1993), 'Novo Nordisk A/S: Designing for Diabetics', Design Management Institute Case Study, available from the Harvard Business School, Boston, US, for a detailed treatment of the company's history, culture and products for diabetes care. The author would like to thank the Design Management Institute, Boston, US, for their permission to reproduce the figures in this chapter.
2. In the early 1990s Novo Nordisk held a 45% market share worldwide, and 25% in the US, while the American firm Eli Lilly enjoyed nearly 50% worldwide, and dominated the American market with 75%.
3. Øvlisen was a Danish lawyer with a Stanford University MBA degree who married the daughter of one of Novo's founders – and for that reason did not originally want to work for the company. As a favour to his father-in-law he accepted a temporary position in 1972 and liked it so much that he stayed.
4. In the ancient tradition of pharmaceutical companies, Novo had chosen an animal symbol, the Egyptian Apis Bull, to represent the company back in 1926. Since then the logo had evolved through 15 changes; after 1989 it would incorporate its life-long competitor, Nordisk – which, of course, had to get used to "identifying with the symbol they had competed with for over sixty years".
5. Steve McGugan was an American who had been educated at Art Center College of Design in California and had spent several years in Denmark, learning Danish and designing for Bang & Olufsen in-house before establishing his own industrial design consultancy in Copenhagen.
6. Although the project that resulted in NovoLet (called Novolin Prefilled in the US) proceeded under the codename "NovoPen III", I will use the final names, NovoLet and Novolin Prefilled, in this chapter.
7. It worked like this: Holding onto the body of the pen, the patient would turn the cap clockwise in multiples of ten ($5 \times 10 = 50$) plus multiples of two ($4 \times 2 = 8$), up to 58 units at once, for a total of 150 units (1.5ml), or several days' worth. As the cap was turned, it pushed the plunger mechanism up, via a screwlike mechanism reminiscent of deodorant sticks or lipsticks. When the plunger was pressed down, it would dispense the precise number of units through the needle. Then, after the plunger was all the way down and the insulin had been dispensed, the patient could reset the pen to "0" by replacing the cap, and be ready for a subsequent dosage.
8. They couldn't use Braille because most diabetics don't know Braille.
9. This was evident from my conversations with Lori Day, NovoLet's (Novolin Prefilled) US product manager, in November 1993.
10. See Jevnaker, Chapter 2.

CHAPTER SEVEN

INTEGRATING DESIGN AS A STRATEGIC RESOURCE: THE CASE OF ERICSSON MOBILE COMMUNICATIONS

Lisbeth Svengren

Companies with a strong engineering culture have difficulties when trying to change priorities in product development, for instance, trying to integrate industrial design as a privileged element. However, many of these engineering and electronic manufacturers are now in a situation where their products face both technical and marketing challenges. The products are no longer designated for other technical experts – quite the reverse.

Computers and communications tools are used by people who are not interested in the product's technical sophistication, but in how easy it is to use. Other criteria than technical performance decide whether the product will be a commercial success and many of these criteria are industrial design elements, for example user-interface and product identity. Some electronic companies, for instance Sony and Philips, have learnt to integrate industrial design as a means to make their products more consumer-oriented, easy to use and attractive. This chapter will describe how the Swedish telecommunication company Ericsson ventured into mobile communications and how it eventually started to integrate industrial design as a strategic resource for cellular "phones".

Management of Design Alliances. Edited by M. Bruce and B. H. Jevnaker.

LM ERICSSON – A TELECOMMUNICATION COMPANY

Ericsson is a successful company with a global leading position in mobile communication systems. In the 1980s Ericsson entered the market for mobile communication terminals, also called cellular 'phones. This market required, however, different strategies and skills compared to its core business, i.e. telecommunication systems. One of the new resources that management recognised was required was that of industrial design. Being a very technically-orientated company, where product success is attributed to technical factors, it was rather a difficult struggle for Ericsson to integrate industrial design, in a strategic sense, in the conceptual development of the product. Ericsson is at the forefront of the technology, but to develop a design management strategy was a different task. Few, if any, telecommunication companies have a tradition of working with industrial design in any strategic sense. This case study describes how Ericsson managed industrial design and finally created a position for industrial design as a strategic resource. It is a case of how to get from *talking* about design, to *implementing* it as such a resource.

Occasionally Ericsson have collaborated with industrial designers when developing telephone apparatus, but it was not until Ericsson went into the microcomputer industry that a regular collaboration with one industrial design company began. With Ericsson's acquisition of Facit, a company designing and manufacturing PCs, typewriters and office furniture, a collaboration with Roland Lindhé Design AB (RL'D) began. These products were grouped into a new company division known as Ericsson Information Systems (EIS). Substantial investment was made to this venture, which involved, amongst other things, an aggressive entry into the US market. EIS met a grim fate, however, in the price wars and industry turbulence of the 1982–85 period and eventually part of EIS was sold to Nokia in 1988.

AB LM Ericsson is one of the largest companies in Sweden and one of the leading telephone companies in the world. Apart from the venture into the computer industry Ericsson has built its business on the development, manufacture and sales of systems and products used in public and private networks. Ericsson's AXE switching system is in use in over 80 countries, with a 14% share of the world market. In mobile communications, Ericsson has a 40% world market share for cellular networks.

DEVELOPMENT OF A NEW MARKET

Ericsson entered the mobile telephones market in the beginning of the 1970s by developing cellular telephones designed for military and police forces. At that

Table 7.1 Total number of cellular phone units sold worldwide

	1987	1989	1993	1994	1995	1996
Analogue	2	7	14.1	20.3	24.3	27.0
Digital	–	–	1.8	4.8	16.3	38.0
Total	2	7	15.9	25.1	40.6	65.0
Increase (%)		250	127	58	62	60.0

Source: Ericsson Mobile Communications

time there was not a private market for these products. In the beginning of the 1980s one of the senior managers at Ericsson was convinced that the private professional cellular market had the potential for growth. His prediction seemed to be true because, as deregulation and privatisation of telecommunications gathered speed throughout the 1980s, cellular 'phones quickly became a consumer-oriented mass market. From 1987 the total market grew rapidly (see Table 7.1).

The cellular 'phone market is a market with high institutional and technological entry barriers. The entrants are large companies with a base in electronics. The mobile telephone systems chosen in the various countries differ, as do the amount and roles of systems operators. It is fiercely competitive and from about a dozen companies operating in the network in the early 1980s, by the end of the decade, a large number of competitors worldwide emerged. Ericsson, Motorola, Oki, Nokia-Mobira, GE and Mitsubishi were soon joined by NEC, Hitachi, Matsushita/Panasonic, Philips, Siemens, Toshiba, Fujitsu, Uniden and many others in Asia, Europe and North America. The market could be divided into two: one for terminals (i.e. cellular units) and one for system manufacturers. The system manufacturers amount to seven large companies (Ericsson, Motorola, AT&T, NEC, Northern Telecom, Siemens and Nokia).

DEVELOPMENT OF CELLULAR 'PHONES

At the beginning of the 1980s cellular "phones" weighed 7–15 kilos. By the mid-1980s the weight of the 'phones had been reduced to about 5 kilos and they started to be considered as portable "phones". Nonetheless, such cellular 'phones were still in the form of a "car battery". The new characterisation of this product was the integration of different parts in the receiver. In 1986/1987 the first generation of the "pocket phones" emerged. They could fit into a large pocket and soon became the status symbol of young people "on the move", a symbol of "yuppies". In Sweden that led to a nickname for the telephone: "yuppie-puppies" (*yuppie-nalle*).

The size of the 'phone has always been a trade-off between battery efficiency, size and weight. To decrease size and weight was and is therefore the technical challenge. A size-weight-talk-time-efficiency advantage of one supplier was soon challenged and fuelled the proliferation of different products in the market. The recent development of new batteries, e.g. lithium batteries, will further increase efficiency, decrease size and give opportunities to develop new design concepts.

The early development of cellular units was parallel to Ericsson's entry into the information business with the EIS company. This was Ericsson's first step into a consumer market. However, the disappointing experience with EIS meant that the Ericsson senior management was reluctant to embark upon another "consumer product". But the forces to continue with the cellular 'phones were strong, and so within Ericsson Radio System a new division emerged.

ERICSSON MOBILE COMMUNICATIONS TERMINALS

During 1983–90 a number of forces influenced the development of the mobile communications market, including globalisation, a gradual rise in competition (more strong firms entering than exiting the market), and a shift away from cellular 'phones as high-priced industrial products towards inexpensive consumer-oriented work/leisure and functional/status products. In 1987 the price for a cellular 'phone was about 25–27,000 crowns, and in 1996 the consumer prices ranged from 1 Swedish crown to 3000 crowns, depending (in different campaigns and subsidies from operators), i.e. a price reduction of about 92–99%! Ericsson recognised that these trends would place terminal manufacturers under increasing competition to turn out smaller, lighter, and more user-friendly products: "car batteries" would no longer be acceptable. The race was on to raise cellular to the levels of refinement that the likes of Sony and Philips had reached with consumer audio.

Ericsson's first cellular 'phones were designed by RL'D in 1984. The focus of the industrial design work was to emphasise "user-friendliness". The size of the phone was dependent on technical specifications defined by the Swedish PTT and the size of the battery. The ergonomic enhancements focused on display and keyboard design. The outcome was a keyboard with orange buttons that were comfortable and efficient for the eyes, in different lighting conditions. The orange buttons also gave Ericsson's phones a certain character and identity. When the hand-held, portable cellular phones (900c) were developed in 1987, RL'D designed these with a similar look and the orange buttons became a strong distinguishing feature.

FROM RADIO SYSTEMS TO HOTLINE

Cogniscent of the need for a steady supply of radio and logic engineers, Ericsson acquired a space in the new Ideon research park near Lund's university of technology in 1983 and established a cellular telephone R&D centre. This move away from the headquarters in Stockholm also marked a differentiation from Ericsson's engineering dominated corporate culture, where there was still some scepticism at LM Ericsson towards consumer products at that time. Part of the initiative required that the newly established terminals group in Stockholm and Lund dedicated itself to creating an independent, market-oriented business with its own distribution and means of support. It was also necessary to have an organisation that could handle quick decisions. Even more significant, the mobile telephone terminals group was officially spun off from the Mobile Telephone Systems unit to become a business unit of its own – Ericsson Mobile Telephone Terminals (RMOT). This put Mobile Telephones on an organisational par with the four other units which reported to the president of Ericsson Radio System (see Figure 7.1).

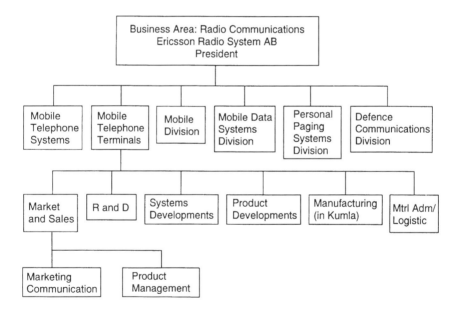

Figure 7.1 Organisational chart of LM Ericsson's business area Radio Communications and its division for cellular telephones Mobile Telephone Terminals (RMOT)
Ericsson's business areas in 1990 were (share of turnover): Public telecommunications (45), Radio Communications (25), Business Communications (11), Cable and Net (14), Defence Systems (4) and Components (1)

DEVELOPMENT OF A RESEARCH DEPARTMENT

In 1985 a researcher at Ericsson's military radio department was given charge of the R&D in Lund. His commission was to organise the research and develop cellular 'phones with the objective of "smaller and better". The R&D manager stated that: "the first products we made were more in order to show Ericsson that we could make them."

The organisation of product development was rather chaotic. The R&D manager recalls: "When I arrived in Lund there was nothing more than a confused laboratory. No one knew how to make cellular 'phones or how to manage development projects. My task was to do something – anything – to create a certain order."

THE CREATION OF A NEW CULTURE AND IMAGE

The management of the terminals group was immediately faced with the challenge to launch the new products. Ericsson had adopted a new corporate identity in 1981 and its use was restricted. LM Ericsson and its several business units produced advertisements with a strong "high tech" profile. The division manager and the sales manager recognised that something different was needed to launch the new cellular product and a Swedish advertising agency was commissioned to brand, promote and advertise the product.

CONSUMER ADVERTISING

The management team and the advertising agency spent many hours discussing the issue. The idea of a brand that would add some excitement to the product, and thus to the company image, was decided upon. The name "HotLine" was proposed. This was not in line with Ericsson's corporate identity and the division manager had to fight for it at the corporate level. He eventually got the campaign and the name accepted by the president of LM Ericsson. At this stage, however, the attempts at giving form and substance to this brand idea were no more than a basis for an advertising campaign, according to the sales manager. He explained:

> "I don't think we realised the long-term effect of this decision. Even if we knew that HotLine was not only to be used for a short-term advertising campaign, we were actually not aware that it would have such a deep and long-term effect on all marketing thereafter."

The brand HotLine conjured up the image of a red telephone line directly connecting the Kremlin and White House – presumably creating an image of mystery, international intrigue and the ability to contact someone instantly. A catchy red logotype was designed. The ads showed shadowy trench-coated figures, and copy reminiscent of 1940s-style vintage detective thrillers (see Plate 6). It was assumed that this image would appeal to the affluent male business user and a frequent traveller. The image of a new product also aimed at showing a new technology and product to the external audience as well as to further build knowledge and a technical innovative spirit internally.

The "HotLine" identity was very different from that of competitors at the time. But most importantly, it was different from the traditional, business-oriented communication for Ericsson products, and some Ericsson people were uncomfortable with that difference. Some "genuine" Ericsson people regarded the RMOT people as "outsiders" and they were perceived as the maverick business unit of the corporation. Paradoxically, however, this gave the unit a certain freedom within the Ericsson corporation.

BUILDING A NEW ORGANISATION

In late 1987, the entire management team, with the exception the plant manager in Kumla, was relocated to Lund in south Sweden. Thus Marketing and Sales, Financial, R&D and general management including customer service support were centralised in one building, at a considerable distance (600km) from Stockholm and Ericsson's main headquarters.

The move to Lund was both a crisis and an opportunity for the new business unit. Many employees who had been with Ericsson for a long time chose not to follow their jobs south, with the resultant upheaval it would cause domestically. This left many positions vacant. In addition, as the unit entered a phase of rapid growth, many new positions were created. The vacant positions were filled quickly, often with young people with no Ericsson background, nor experience in other larger traditional Swedish industrial companies.

A NEW CULTURE EMERGES

It soon became apparent that RMOT was on its way toward developing a distinctive culture that was significantly different from that of Ericsson's tradition. The influx of new people, the provincial culture and physical distance from Stockholm, a pervasive university-influenced jeans-and-T-shirts R&D

atmosphere, and the small size of the group contributed to this evolution of a special identity. More fundamentally, the conditions of short, rapid product development and market cycles, the end-customer orientation, and high-volume production served to separate the unit from most of Ericsson's other operations, where long, stable product cycles, industrial/government customers, and low-volume project focus prevailed. The "HotLine" identity symbolised this development.

In 1988 a new position of marketing communication was established. The incumbent's immediate task was to create a team in Lund to bring focus and depth to the HotLine concept. At this point, various versions of the detective character and the HotLine essence of mystery and romance were being used in a number of countries, but without co-ordination from Lund. However, the advertising character, internally named "Harry", however, ran into problems. Although Scandinavians could cope with the aura of brooding mystery, Harry also conjured up images of the Mafia and devious intelligence agencies in Continental Europe and Asia, and it was decided that Harry must be replaced. It was possible to drop the concept of HotLine and introduce another brand concept, but overall the management team felt that generally positive reactions to HotLine exceeded the negative ones, and given the enormous amount of time, money and energy spent on HotLine, it was decided to keep it. The original rationale for adopting this concept had not changed. The market still consisted of mainly male buyers. In addition, HotLine was, from the very beginning, a great success on Ericsson's Nordic home markets. As the internal and external uses of HotLine became clearer to management, it came to be viewed increasingly as a major strategic investment which was accruing equity.

DEVELOPING STRATEGIC CONCEPTS

In the spring of 1988 the volume of business had reached a level that it was necessary to develop strategic plans and refine business concepts. Research and product development were of course important but so too were manufacturing and distribution. The new digital cellular 'phone system, which would enable the use of cellular 'phones across country borders, would soon be realised. Ericsson was involved in a pan-European project called the Group System Mobile (GSM) to develop a digital standard initially for Europe. The larger teamplan was to have this standard system accepted also outside of Europe.

The cellular 'phones were still in their infancy and emphasis was put on technological efficiency, software programs, etc. The final design of the 'phone, especially customer interface features such as keyboard display, comfort to hold, overall appearance, etc., were not considered until the latter stages of the product development process, once certain technical features had been decided upon.

PRODUCT DESIGN – AN INTERESTING BUT FUTURE TOOL?

The R&D manager at RMOT was very interested in industrial design. He believed that both aesthetics and ergonomical criteria would play a greater role in a few years time. His reasoning was as follows:

> "The first cellular 'phones were built like an old police radio with a lot of mechanical constructions. What else could be expected by mechanical engineers? But in the future cellular 'phones will become personal objects. The 'phones can be linked to other communication media, computers, fax machines, etc. The choice in development is between primary and secondary functions. We have chosen to prioritise verbal communication. Already today we can make 'phones as small as arm wrist watches. The barrier is the net system and a lot of bureaucrats at the Telecoms who fragmentally develop different net systems."

As recognised by the R&D manager, a collaboration between R&D engineering department and industrial design was needed in order to achieve the goal of attaining a distinct and appropriate product aimed for the consumer market. The R&D manager thought it was necessary to have a local industrial designer – "in the neighbourhood" – to facilitate regular contacts. Instead of continuing the collaboration with RL'D based in Stockholm the R&D manager therefore chose to commission Rickard Lindahl Design, a small industrial design company located in the neighbour city Malmo.

The marketing communication manager had a great interest in industrial design as well and discussed the possibility of using certain elements on the 'phone to support the HotLine identity. This would integrate the marketing and product development process which so far had been sequential rather than integrated. The marketing communication manager wanted the graphic design of information, advertising, logotypes etc., to express the same character as the product design. Market research and intelligence had so far been handled as *ad hoc* projects. In 1988 a product manager as a staff function was employed, responsible for research and intelligence. He described his initial job thus:

> "As I was rather lonely in the beginning my task was to go to all those meetings where the projects progressed – there were many projects and many meetings. I gave my input verbally because there was never any time to sit down and write reports, specification or analysis – everything just rolled on. I had to see too that I was present at least to inform about market issues."

SECOND GENERATION CELLULAR POCKET 'PHONES

By 1989/1990 the second generation of cellular pocket 'phones and the first real "pocket" 'phone was to be launched. The model was internally named "Olivia". A few months before launching Olivia the design was discussed between R&D, Product Development and Marketing. Marketing rejected the design. It was perceived as being too different from previous models and so did not reflect the identity of the previous 'phones. To build up brand equity, the marketing communication manager believed that a continuation would be necessary. The final "Olivia", therefore, had some resemblance to the previous cellular 'phone – for instance, it retained the orange buttons and the logotype. At this stage it was the the smallest 'phone on the market with 18 cm length and a weight of only 420 grammes (compared with the 630 grammes of the previous design). It also had the longest connection time.

Olivia was very well received but competitors soon caught up and launched even smaller 'phones although with shorter connection time. Motorola launched a very small 'phone, the MicroTac, with a new design concept. MicroTac featured a flap-top that covered the key pad which, when pulled down, revealed the 'phone and also lengthened it. This flap-top had no impact on communication efficiency but was psychologically appealing. Many users liked this feature because it gave them the feeling that they were talking into a "proper" 'phone. MicroTac was very successful and Motorola increased its global market share from 20 to 30%.

THE FUTURE GENERATION OF CELLULARS

So far, product design was "technology driven" but ergonomic design became increasingly important, i.e. hand-held friendliness, key pad display readability, symbols, etc. However, the Ericsson team expected that a "breakthrough" in design that would be more flexible in size, form, colours, and its *gestalt* of features was a future possibility. The market was also moving towards a mass distribution system wherein cellular, phones would become a commodity akin to cameras, radios, videos and so on. In this context the HotLine 'phone would become only one of many products for consumers to choose from.

Consequently, the managers of RMOT decided to commit a substantial amount of investment into developing the next generation 'phones that would be global, ergonomic and entail neurocomplex brand semiotics. Their confidence was based on their success to date, but why did RMOT management raise the stakes and tackle both greater global integration *and* a more complex brand symbology? The manager of market intelligence pointed out that one major reason was the very satisfactory progress in the Lund laboratory of the development of the next generation cellular 'phone. This was at the leading edge of digital technology, and this knowledge gave a tremendous confidence to the organisation.

In early 1990 a large number of personnel involved in product development and marketing gathered at a seminar organised by RMOT to discuss design integration and industrial design on a strategic and operational level. One of the issues on the agenda was to formulate an industrial design policy, the outcome of which impacted on the design elements of HotLine. Four design characteristics were delineated:

1. compact (robust)
2. elegant
3. balanced
4. credible.

Together, these features were intended to convey an impression of "high product quality", an impression that should be supported and amplified through the market communication and a mix of packaging and display systems. This meant further conceptual developments for the communication strategy.

SECOND GENERATION OF "HARRY"

Before discussing the industrial design policy RMOT decided to change advertising agencies because of a globalisation of the cellular 'phone strategy. The Copenhagen office of a large international agency was chosen. The new version of HotLine, officially launched in 1990, represented a conscious attempt to modify Harry's look, feel and essence. A concept statement, "A Special Brand of Freedom", became the unifying brand essence, to communicate the freedom that a cellular 'phone could add to one's professional and private life. But marketing segmentation was still not an issue.

The first series of advertisements made extensive use of sweeping natural landscapes and mixed work-leisure situations to show this. Most importantly, a new persona, "Harry II" was designated. He was a friendlier, more relaxed individual. His trademark hat was the same as before, but he wore the hat differently so as to show more of his face (see Plate 8).

Parallel to this development a new joint venture was established and this was to have a great impact on RMOT's future in Lund.

ERICSSON AND GENERAL ELECTRIC INC. IN A JOINT VENTURE

In late 1989 LM Ericsson had embarked on a joint venture with General Electric in the US. Ericsson owned 60% and GE 40% of the new Ericsson GE Mobile Communications in the US. The GE cellular telephone was a low-priced cellular 'phone that differed completely from that of HotLine. The marketing and product development strategies of the two products needed to be co-ordinated. As a consequence, HotLine's R&D manager moved to the US in late 1990 to co-ordinate and manage research whereas product development of HotLine still remained in Lund. HotLine was launched in the US as the high quality brand but this failed due to insufficient resources in marketing and sales in the USA. Instead, RMOT and GE decided to focus upon the GE brand as a low-priced brand in the US market and support this with Ericsson's technology. HotLine kept its high quality profile in the rest of the world. Collaboration between Ericsson and GE was therefore focused on product development and research and not marketing.

CHAOTIC TIMES

In Lund the move of the R&D manager was considered a great loss. He was a visionary person who had managed product development from one generation to the next. Additionally, in the end of 1990, the division manager unexpectedly left the company. He was a very charismatic leader; he had been the spokesman of HotLine and protected the "freedom" of the division in Lund. Both the R&D manager and the division manager were strong personalities that matched and were complementary to each other. The Product Council that had been established to facilitate integration of product development, design and marketing suffered from these losses.

It was decided that the new division manager should be placed in the US, while in Lund an administrative manager was placed in charge. The first person in this role was only temporary and was soon followed by another who did not stay long. Hence, RMOT in Lund lacked a clear leadership which could develop, communicate and support visions for product development and marketing.

CO-ORDINATING DIFFERENT CULTURES

A new Product Council was established with members from HotLine and GE to oversee design and product development issues. The Product Council comprised the division manager, the market and sales manager for Sweden, the marketing and sales manager at GE, the R&D manager and the designer Richard Lindahl as members. This council were supposed to meet every sixth week, altering Lund in Sweden and Lynchburg in the US as meeting places. The product manager was made subordinate to marketing and sales. Most of the time ready solutions were presented to the council. The product manager described the situation as follows:

"Our job was to have an overview and control to avoid collisions when building the brand, and everything that is visible to the customers. Everything should have the same spirit. . . . The council was established but was never allowed to work. We tried though. . . . It was quite difficult for certain engineers to accept our role and furthermore everything went very quickly. Suddenly, there were accessories with a certain design concept. We did as much as we could but we were always behind. . . . The engineers were always far ahead. 130 persons supported by managers who are knowledgeable about the technology compared with four people on the marketing side – it doesn't matter how fast we run. We had no chance to catch up."

Coordination of the product design between GE and Ericsson's made in Lund also caused problems. There were different perceptions of good design and good quality. The product development manager in Lund described it in the following way: "It is difficult with the Americans. They have a different notion about what is modern and good design compared to we Europeans. Their design has to be more robust, heavier, forms that reminds me of the 1950s. Like jukeboxes. . . ."

Attempts to overcome conflicts were made, for example the sharing of projects, so that GE used the Swedish design for the back of the product but designed their own frontage.

White key buttons were used in the US because orange buttons were not appropriate for the US market. This jointly designed product was also launched in Sweden as a low-priced product with a red colour to differentiate it from Olivia. The 'phone was not well received by the market and was soon withdrawn. All these problems led to a rift between the US and the European divisions and eventually, the Swedish division in Lund, became responsible for everything but the US market, while Product Development still reported to the R&D manager in the US. Some co-ordination and collaboration of Product Development remained between GE and RMOT.

RMOT ENTERS A NEW STAGE OF GLOBALISATION: THE DIGITAL ERA

The introduction of the digital mobile communication system in 1992 further enhanced the dramatic growth of the market (see Table 7.1). RMOT was ahead of competitors in this new technology and the European digital mobile standard, the GSM standard. New market opportunities existed in Europe. Product life cycles were expected to become even shorter, and prices were likely to fall for both the 'phones and operation charges. So far the barrier to real growth was the relatively high charges for using cellular 'phones, compared with conventional fixed 'phone systems.

The senior managers of RMOT realised that they had a technical advantage and they wished to fully exploit this to capture the newer market opportunities. Germany and France were relatively new markets with a very low penetration of cellular 'phones and these markets were new to RMOT. Also Ericsson, as a company, was not known in these countries. However, "HotLine" did not have global appeal – for example in Germany. "Hotline" was associated with the telephone service line to call for support for computer problems and "Hotline" in France was associated with a brand name for underwear! A new marketing communication strategy had to be discussed by RMOT managers. The marketing communication manager recalled the situation as follows:

> "Ericsson was unknown but the name sounds Scandinavian with positive connections. We had to utilise that when we entered new markets. Germans mixed cellular, phones with wireless 'phones that you use in the garden. We had to explain the product and the system. We had to be closer to the product with close association to what the product was. The Harry-ads required many associations before you got to the product. You used to look at the hero, now we put you in the clothes of the hero and look at the product.... We wanted more of the Ericsson character. We decided to have Ericsson as the only name. We wanted to communicate the large telephone company and what all that meant in image, especially outside the Nordic countries. We also had to compete on the basis of industrial design and external features."

Plate 9 shows a "post-Harry" advertisement where Ericsson is brought forward as a brand name instead of HotLine.

In this period the RMOT management decided to go a step further to implement an industrial design policy. The marketing communication manager together with the product manager had for a long time argued that they needed more resources to integrate industrial design issues. In 1992 it was decided that these two managers would have the overall responsibility for product and graphic design. They also received a budget for developing the industrial design function.

THE SEARCH FOR A NEW DESIGN PARTNER

In the spring of 1993 efforts for reorganisation of design began. The team that consisted of the marketing communication manager and product manager started to look for a new design collaboration that would match the technical department and one that offered a broader international basis. They started to look at different European industrial design companies. Important for the choice of partner was not only design skills but also strategic understanding, conceptual and project management skills and a knowledge of mass production techniques.

Three design companies were considered: one located in London, one in Stuttgart and one in Milan. They were all invited to Lund to present themselves to different management teams. The marketing communication manager described the process:

> "We met all design companies three times with different programmes for each meeting. We went deeper and deeper into the process and tried to expand our knowledge about which competence they could bring to our company. The engineering and production departments were involved throughout the process to judge the professionalism and skills of the designers."

At the end of May in 1993 all managers in RMOT, including the R&D manager, gathered to listened to the presentations and to decide upon their partner. The R&D manager remained, however, negative to the change of design partner. The choice was finally made to engage Eden Design (European Designer Network), a network with different designers, engineers and management consultants located in different parts of Europe. The industrial designers who would work with RMOT both lived in Milan. An Eden project manager was placed at their Copenhagen office so as to be physically closer to RMOT in Lund (travelling time of about one hour).

The intention was that Eden would work more strategically with both concept and design development, in collaboration with the engineers in Lund. It turned out that this was not always easy to achieve because of scepticism and lack of trust from the R&D manager towards the new designer partners. In addition, the collaboration with the existing small Swedish design company continued. In October 1993 the third generation product, a very small 'phone

(12.7 cm, weight 193–200g) designed by the Swedish design company and known internally as "Jane", was launched (see Plate 10).

The brief for Eden's work was changed in the middle of the project and so Eden had to reorientate their design to meet new market criteria. Their new task was to give form to the surface part of the 'phone. This led to disappointments on both sides. The engineers at RMOT had a positive attitude towards industrial design and recognised the importance of it, but could not deal with any strategic role of the industrial designers. A product manager within the marketing department elucidated:

> "The way we have used design so far it doesn't matter if we have Lindahl or Eden. In the long run we would probably have seen the difference. The question is, however, if we are mature for Eden's competence, if we are prepared to integrate the designers that deep in the strategic development process. For the moment I don't think we are. It would mean that we would give away some of the control of the image and it would mean involving them in everything."

For a long time the design collaboration was rather chaotic because the industrial designers did not receive any information nor any clear goals for their work. For the designers at Eden, they were not allowed access to future plans, nor were they encouraged to discuss the concept of the product and its market development. The marketing communication manager proposed a roundtable meeting for all those concerned with product design and marketing and strategic development. The meeting was postponed several times, from the autumn of 1993 to May 1994. Meanwhile, a reorganisation of the business unit took place.

ESTABLISHING DESIGN MANAGEMENT

In the end of 1993 Ericsson created a new business area for their cellular 'phones: Ericsson Mobile Communications, with headquarters in Stockholm. Ericsson Mobile Communications now owned 100% of GE. All management functions, except for product development and product management which remained in Lund, were located to Stockholm. The R&D manager remained in the US. Hence, marketing was moved to Stockholm but the marketing communication manager wanted to stay in Lund. He argued for a new position to be created in Lund; that of an industrial design manager. After several discussions and lobbying with the new managing director in Stockholm he finally achieved his goal and was given a position as "coordinating manager of industrial design and marketing".

In 1995 Ericsson Mobile Communications had grown to the extent that they had to make a further division between their activities in Europe, North America and Asia. One design partner for each region was established. Lindahl Design continued to work for the European team in Lund; in the US Ericsson had an internal industrial design group and in Asia a design company in Singapore was commissioned to work for Ericsson. The Eden designers remained for a while as speaking partners to the design manager in Lund.

Meanwhile Motorola launched their new design called "Flare", in several different colours and Nokia continued to create new cover designs. Nokia's colourful and personally designed phones were a great success. It was obvious that the market began to be segmented and that the number of female buyers had increased to a great extent. Ericsson's move, as a result of the collaboration with a new advertising agency in Sweden, was to launch Jane (GF 337), with a flap-top decorated with famous art pieces, for instance Miro and Keith Haring. Ericsson's sales manager claimed that the result was satisfactory.

INTEGRATION OF DESIGN AS A STRATEGIC RESOURCE

In 1995 a Design Council was established at Ericsson Mobile Communications headquarters in Stockholm. The council members were the managing director, the marketing director, the purchasing director, the regional managers (from the US, Asia and rest of the world), the product development and the R&D director. The designer partners participated and the industrial design manager, whose department was enlarged by an assistant, prepared the meetings. This development was significant because it was a beginning of incorporating industrial design as a strategic resource, i.e. industrial design would become part of the norms and routines of the design activities with the company. After a year in office, however, the industrial design manager moved to other functions within the company and the industrial design department was left with one person, a young woman with a background in marketing. She continued to work with co-ordination issues. The collaboration with the R&D manager in the US was intensified. Senior managers in Stockholm began to realise that they had to speed up the strategic utilisation of industrial design and the young woman was officially made responsible for co-ordination of industrial design. In the beginning of 1996 the Design Council was integrated with the Product Council. The managing director stated that:

> "Industrial design is strategically important for us. We can no longer have a situation where the technicians come to marketing with a ready product. They cannot face us with a *fait accompli*. Marketing has to have time to do research,

develop the market segments and have a say. The market is more segmented now and we have to integrate marketing aspects also in product development. We have to see to the whole product and the development process where industrial design is an important issue. As such industrial design should be equal to other parts of product development."

DISCUSSION

It is obvious that the management process outlined here cannot be regarded as a systematic, carefully planned process. The case study shows the complexity that a multinational company within a fast moving industry has to face and deal with. Quick decisions and fast moves are required. But in Ericsson's case it led to a situation where every project was handled like an emergency and no one had time to wait for information from others. This situation also reduced the possibility for the industrial designers to be able to influence the strategic context for design solutions. Also there was a lack of co-ordinated goals that could guide the industrial designers in their work. Discussions about industrial design were brought up without involvement of any industrial design expertise. At RMOT neither a design management nor an industrial design policy was developed to guide product development from a marketing point of view. Marketing was equal to advertising. Both the division manager and the R&D manager had strong opinions about design issues. It was not, however, clear who had overall responsibility for design matters. Management interfered every now and then on design issues. As stated by the product development manager:

> "Design is troublesome because everybody has opinions about it. Everybody also has different tastes. It is difficult to find the right way but it is necessary to have some who are strong on these issues. The division manager and the R&D manager were both strong. The industrial designer as well, but he had to listen to what the others said. A certain tactic from his side was necessary... and sometimes he succeeded."

As long as all functions were located in Lund it was somewhat easier to co-ordinate different issues. After the division manager left the company in 1990, the R&D manager was the only person who had an overall view of product development and he moved to the US. With modern communication facilities this should not create significant problems, but product development in Lund lacked strong visionary guidance. The R&D manager was regarded as the one who had this continuity and vision for development.

Technological issues never ceased to be first priority and industrial design was not a driving force. It was not until industrial designers had the trust of the R&D manager and the support of the managing director that industrial design issues were integrated in a strategic sense. It is probably true that no telephone company – out of tradition – has paid industrial design any strategic interest. Technical performance is the driving force and the manufacturers have no direct contact with the users. The product's aesthetic is an automatic outcome of the design work and no goal as such. Despite this, everybody in the organisation has opinions about aesthetics and many are those who interfere in decisions on aesthetic issues. This is valid for most organisations. As stated by the industrial designer: "I have to be present in the organisation to be able to lobby for certain decisions regarding design."

Industrial design is a resource to enhance product semantics and brand equity and in this sense aesthetic issues are important. Research and development focuses upon software design, communication facilities and efficiency. Ericsson has rather pursued a wait-and-see game for the product design. Since its introduction in 1993 Ericsson has kept the basic industrial design concept of Jane as their premium product. Olivia is sold as a low-priced product. One advantage of having two basic models is that they become easily recognisable, i.e. they receive a certain identity. But in a fast-moving market with new segments there is a demand for variations. Companies who supply different market segments will also achieve higher volumes. Despite the fact that Ericsson management recognised the emergence of a consumer market as the volume market to target, they did not explore the possibility of utilising their industrial design capabilities to fully exploit the consumer market, nor to develop a strategic vision for design elements, nor to build industrial design as a competence in the longer term. But is it possible to do this within a relatively short period of time – six years – in a situation where speed is the major driving force besides technological development? There was little incentive to change because the market demand was so high, then everything was sold that could be produced and production capacity was doubled several times. The cellular 'phones received good reviews in consumer tests, and the business press described them as the most successful products in modern Swedish industry. But once the market becomes more competitive and as growth steadies, then for how long can a competitive position be maintained by technically proven products that are not well segmented in terms of design? Although industrial design was seen as important its strategic use was postponed for too long. Meanwhile, strong competitors entered the market who were recognised as having good design and marketing skills (for instance Sony) – and gained market shares. The reorganisation within Ericsson that was initiated in 1993 was necessary for improving the conditions for industrial design.

This study demonstrates the necessity of having a top management, which both actively and regularly supports the integration of the design function as a strategic resource. Industrial design decisions seem to be based on an intuition of what is visually right and wrong. Industrial designers have a professional visual training but others who have not got a professional background in design also have opinions of what is right and wrong. As a result of this, and as the case study also shows, strategic integration of design has to be based on trust for design as a repository of professional knowledge.

ACKNOWLEDGEMENTS

The author wishes to thank LM Ericsson and the Design Management Institute for their permission to reproduce some of the figures and tables in this chapter.

Plate 6

Plate 7 One of the first "Harry" ads launched in 1987/88

Plate 8 A picture with the second "Harry" launched in 1990

Plate 9   Advertising after "Harry"

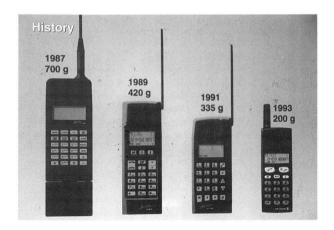

Plate 10   Four models from 1987 to 1993. The 1991 model was internally called "Olivia" and the 1993 model was named "Jane"

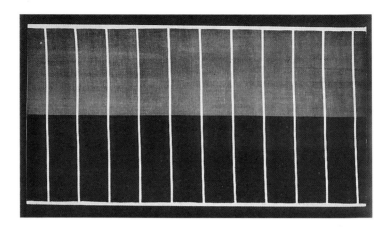

Plate II Vuokko Nurmesniemi's textile pattern from 1954. Copyright Museum of Applied Arts, Helsinki

Plate 12 An example of geometrical abstraction influences in Maija Isola's textile pattern from the 1950s. Copyright Museum of Applied Arts, Helsinki

Plate 13 Vuokko Nurmesniemi's dress from 1957, exploiting her own textile pattern from 1954

Plate 14 Annika Piha's dress from 1965, exploiting Vuokko Nurmesniemi's textile pattern from 1954

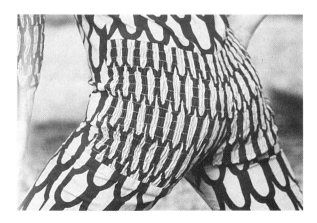

Plate 15 Opt-art and pop-art at Marimekko: Annika Piha's overhauls from 1966

Plate 16 Annika Piha's "Maoist uniform" from 1968. Copyright Museum of Applied Arts, Helsinki

Plate 17 Decembre's bags. Copyright Museum of Applied Arts, Helsinki

Plate 18 Pentti Rinta's men's suit from 1972. Copyright Museum of Applied Arts, Helsinki

Plate 19 Liisa Suvanto's op-art dress from 1974. Copyright Museum of Applied Arts, Helsinki

Plate 20 Katsuji Wakisaka's naivist textile pattern from 1974. Copyright Museum of Applied Arts, Helsinki

DESIGN AND COMPETITIVE ADVANTAGE: THE CASE OF MARIMEKKO Oy, A FINNISH FASHION FIRM

Antti Ainamo

The management of the dynamics that exist between design and competitive advantage in the case of Marimekko Oy, a Finnish fashion firm, is the theme for this chapter. Marimekko is a success story, an award-winning company, and a model for many design-intensive companies both in Finland and worldwide, but the company entered a sustained period of decline in the late 1980s. The article tells the story of how Kirsti Paakkanen, Marimekko's new owner in 1991, began to rejuvenate the firm.

Marimekko Oy's roots were in Finnish art, crafts and design. Its history was marked by being a forerunner of Finnish internationalisation. Armi Ratia, the designer behind the founding of the firm in 1951, was a colourful personality who had helped to create Marimekko as a national institution.

Despite its glorious past, Marimekko's net losses had been about 20% of its net sales since 1986 under the ownership of Amer Group. Kirsti Paakkanen acquired Marimekko Oy for a nominal sum in 1991 from this Finnish Conglomerate. Her challenge was to rejuvenate Marimekko. Besides the personal challenge, she had invested into Marimekko the proceeds from her divestment of Womena, an advertising agency that had specialised in advertising to and by women.

Management of Design Alliances. Edited by M. Bruce and B. H. Jevnaker.
© 1998 John Wiley & Sons Ltd.

After her acquisition of Marimekko Oy, Kirsti Paakkanen told her stakeholders that it was time to manage the firm, instead of letting it drift. She talked about turning on its head the administrative hierarchy where designers, as the group in the firm closest to the users, led the firm. Kirsti Paakkanen explained that Marimekko was a symbol of Finland and its image. She blamed the business administrators of the 1970s and 1980s for the depression that was gripping the country. Kirsti Paakkanen reminded her stakeholders of Marimekko's glorious past under Armi Ratia's design management, especially in the 1950s and 1960s, during which time Marimekko and Finland as a whole were both internationally renowned for their innovative design.

The first step that Kirsti Paakkanen took was to organise a fashion show at Svenska Teatern, a theatre in the centre of Helsinki. Margareta Haverinen, an opera singer, sang at the fashion show to signal the rejoining of art forms in Marimekko's design. The occasion sought to encapsulate some of the flair of the original Marimekko; it was a big success and the event, which attracted a large audience, had favourable media coverage which portrayed the rejuvenation of the firm. Kirsti Paakkanen became a popular lecturer in management, and a role model for new Finnish industrial policy in the media and amongst Finnish managers.

Kirsti Paakkanen concluded that there had not been enough entrepreneurship in Finland, nor enough respect for designers or workers: this attitude, she felt, had contributed to the national economic recession at the turn of the decade. For her, the Helsinki Stock Exchange influenced the short-termism of Marimekko's managers, and of Finnish managers in general. As a symbol that this was now to change, she delisted Marimekko from the Helsinki Stock Exchange, promising that she would re-enlist the firm in three years, or she would "buy a one-way ticket to Timbuktu". The intention to re-enlist with the Stock Exchange was out of respect for Armi Ratia, the founder, who had originally listed Marimekko on the Helsinki Stock Exchange.

By 1992, Marimekko's accounts showed a net profit, thus strengthening Kirsti Paakkanen's assertions that she had indeed rejuvenated the firm.

MARIMEKKO'S HISTORY

Marimekko was established in 1951. At that time, Finland was undergoing substantial post-war reconstruction; many Finnish companies were late entrants to international markets and so were focused on "catching-up" with the international design competition that had begun elsewhere in the late 1940s.

Marimekko is, with hindsight, a particularly important first-mover in its own country because it competed on the basis of its design prowess at a time when other Finnish companies for the most part did not.

Marimekko was established by two designers as majority shareholders, Armi Ratia and Riitta Immonen, with their respective husbands, Viljo Ratia and Viljo Immonen, as minority share owners. The firm was capitalised in 1951 at FIM 300,000 ("old", i.e. pre-1963 nominal value).

A CONFUSING START: THE FIRM'S EARLY FAILURE 1951–1955

The prime driver for the establishment of Marimekko was that, in 1951, the sales of Printex Oy were lagging. Printex was a small crafts-production-based textile firm, of whom Viljo Ratia, Armi Ratia's husband, was the majority share owner. Viljo Ratia asked his wife whether she, as a designer, would be able to think of ways to increase Printex's sales and business success. Armi Ratia became enthusiastic about the idea and she established with her husband "Marimekko", a design project, to look at the problem.

Mission: To Increase Sales

Armi Ratia became so enthusiastic that she institutionalised the design project into an independent legal entity, or Marimekko Oy, as a sister firm to Printex. Marimekko's mission was to develop, design and market textiles that were manufactured by Printex. It was her idea to identify and show, "opinion leaders", the kind of fashionable dresses that could be made from Printex textiles. The idea was that design awareness of Printex's textiles would diffuse from these opinion leaders to the "average woman", who would buy the Printex textiles to make their own clothes for themselves and their families.

Armi Ratia was not just a product designer: she had a strong opinion about what it was that modern women needed, and this acted as a catalyst for other designers. In the development of the basic design concept, Armi Ratia's role can thus be seen as a "heavyweight" design manager in charge of coordinating the development, design and marketing of fashion shows and the one-off clothes during and after the fashion show. Riitta Immonen, in turn, designed the stage set for the fashion shows,[1,2] but never worked full-time for Marimekko.

A Reputation for Innovativeness

The Marimekko fashion show was organised at the Kalastajatoippa Hotel in Helsinki in May 1951. In the final analysis, the products shown may not have represented world class "good design", yet for the Finnish audience, the fashion show represented innovativeness that met contemporary demands. As Finland's first-ever fashion show, it represented the best available knowledge of design artistic quality ("good design") within industrial textiles and textiles in Finland.[3] Fashion-wise, Finland was still in the sombre colours of the post-war era, and there was social demand for the kind of bright colours and fresh artistic activity that Marimekko was introducing. Marimekko's approach to a product was different from that of conventional Finnish mass manufacturers whose concept was based on simply copying textile patterns and clothes from abroad.

The fashion show was a cultural event that received much public attention,[4] raised awareness of Maija Isola's designs (Printex's designer since 1949), and resulted in favourable media coverage, both at home and abroad. The fashion show formed the basis for Printex's and Marimekko's interaction with lead customers, celebrities and the press, as well as presenting its new, forward-looking identity. By the end of the year, Tapio Wirkkala, the internationally-awarded designer of *Iittala* glassworks, was proudly wearing a hand-made man's shirt by Marimekko. Thus the seeds of future prosperity for Marimekko were sown.

Financial Crisis

Financially, however, Marimekko's first year was not successful. The fashion show ended up promoting not a demand for textiles as intended, but a demand for clothes. There were no clothes in stock, nor did there exist any capabilities to manufacture the clothes in anything but one-off show pieces. Marimekko's net sales are not available for the first year, but it is known that fixed costs, salaries and wages were not covered by sales. Instead, there was a net loss of FIM 500,000 – insufficient to cover Marimekko's initial capitalisation of FIM 300,000. Its bankruptcy was avoided by finance from Printex, but this meant, in turn, that Printex was very hard-pressed; even its very survival was threatened.

Many a conventional firm would have lost momentum in this context, but Armi Ratia insisted that Printex and Marimekko should maintain their reputations as trendsetters. A small office and show-window were rented for Marimekko at the Palace Hotel, which was the main hotel for the press, administration, etc., during the 1952 Helsinki Olympic Games. The office and show-window placed Armi Ratia and Maija Isola in a good position to absorb international influences and make contacts. In that year, Marimekko already managed to show a small net profit.

The next year, 1953, Armi Ratia hired Vuokko Nurmesniemi, a third designer to work full-time for Printex (the first being Maija Isola and the second being herself).[5] Nurmesniemi was an avant-garde designer; a trendsetter in art and design. During her first year at Printex, many of her products demonstrated her gift of combining architectural and sculptural forms in both textiles and clothing in complex ways that few individual artists working in Finland could match (see Plate 11).

Stretch

Modern textiles and clothing at Printex and Marimekko were manufactured and marketed both under the Printex and Marimekko brand names, contributing to the reputation of both firms. With the catalytic support of Armi Ratia, Maija Isola and Vuokko Nurmesniemi stretched to the limits, Printex's and Marimekko's meagre material resources moved ever closer to the international artistic avant-garde, finally overtaking it in the mid-1950s.

Maija Isola was influenced by the geometrical abstraction (constructivism) in figurative arts, a trend that was only in 1957 to become internationally famous in the paintings of artists like Jean Dubueffet but already visible in the work of the Finnish artist Ahti Lavonen (see Plate 12). Vuokko Nurmesniemi developed Marimekko's initial design concept into an ideological concept by which people, especially women, would be freed from the Finnish right-wing establishment in which "home, religion and the Fatherland" were above everything else. Freedom from this maxim had special significance in Finland because the nation had begun its independence with a civil war between right-wing and left-wing coalitions, the wounds of which are only now healing.

In 1953, Marimekko showed a small net profit, but lack of Government licences to buy cotton cloth hindered sales. Attempts to export failed that year but the next year the firm sold some of its products to the Liberty department store in London. In Finland, Marimekko and Printex began to sell outside the Helsinki area, although the Stockman department store in Helsinki alone still accounted for 70% of sales. There was still no capital for even the smallest investments in manufacturing, but Marimekko's improving profitability ameliorated the problem of its negative equity capital, and was sufficient to enable Armi Ratia and Viljo to organise another fashion show for promotional purposes.

Armi Ratia enlisted the help of a graphic designer to design a new logo for Marimekko. The logo used a standard *courier* font in lower case letters, not capital ones ("marimekko"), to signal that Marimekko was a collective concept, rather than the contemporary individualism of the 1950s (see Figure

marimekko®

8.1). The visual repetition of the logo in Marimekko's communications enhanced the value of Printex's and Marimekko's products, and their products started to become internationally known among experts of design that year. Marimekko's net sales increased to FIM 5.2 million.

"Take-off"

Net sales the following year, in 1955, more than doubled, amounting to FIM 12 million.[6] Stockmann remained the firm's major customer, while sales outside Helsinki increased. Profitability remained at the same level as before. Marimekko's equity finally rose out of the red into the black. Now investments could be made into production machinery for Marimekko.

THE GOLDEN AGE OF COMPETING WITH DESIGN: RAPID GROWTH 1956–1968

With Marimekko's new machines, there was a move away from pure crafts production to batch production. Higher volumes increased awareness of Printex's and Marimekko's designs. The two firms embarked on a "golden age" of design that was to continue until 1968. Throughout this time both firms were at the cutting edge of best available knowledge of artistic quality in design, virtually leading the avant-garde movement.

Rapid Sales Growth and Initial Internationalisation

In 1956, the media attention in Sweden of Printex's and Marimekko's exhibition in Stockholm was enormous. Accounts showed that good design was associated positively with competitive advantage. Marimekko's net sales increased by three-quarters to FIM 20.9 million (old nominal value) that year. Profitability was maintained. Only taxes hindered the fear of showing a net profit.

A photograph of a girl in a dress designed by Vuokko Nurmesniemi was chosen as the symbol for "Finnish Design" (i.e. the marketing concept for Finland's design-intensive exports) for 1957 (see Plate 13).

In 1958 came an even bigger design breakthrough. Printex textiles and Marimekko clothes were exhibited at the Brussels World Exhibition where Armi and Viljo Ratia met Ben Thompson, architect and owner of Design Research, a Cambridge, Massachusetts based retail shop that was pivotal throughout the 1950s in shaping tastes for the "Scandinavian", or the functional oriental modern design, in the United states. The shop was well positioned for promoting modern design. Thompson had, as an architect, worked with Walter Gropius, the founder of the famous Bauhaus school of design.

In Finland, it soon became a "must" in fashionable homes to have curtains by "Marimekko". (Of course, curtains were textiles and thus, in reality, manufactured under the Printex brand, but consumers had difficulties in telling the difference – it was Marimekko that was equated with "looking Finnish".) Marimekko was considered an exponent of international and Finnish design at the same time, due to its ability to combine elements of international and Finnish art and design.

Viljo and Armi Ratia's tenacity in the face of continuous crisis finally paid off financially for Marimekko. Marimekko pulled out of financial difficulties in 1958, eight years after it was founded. Net sales doubled, amounting to FIM 60.5 million; profitability in relation to net sales doubled. That year, share capital was tripled from FIM 300,000 to FIM 900,000. Even better, this development was not at the expense of Printex because Printex experienced a similar favourable development.

Full-scale Internationalisation

Armi Ratia hired a new designer, Annika Piha, in 1959, who used geometry and architecture as sources of inspiration but favoured large patterns, a very recent emergent international trend in art and design. All the designers communicated with representatives of painting, sculpture, geometry, international cultural tradition, and architecture, as well as those communities that were conventionally considered outside that of design, such as business, journalism, popular culture and politics.

It was probably Armi Ratia's interaction with journalists that led to Jacqueline Kennedy, the wife of the American democratic presidential candidate John F. Kennedy, to buy nine Marimekko dresses in 1960.[7] Marimekko's net sales soared from FIM 81.3 million in 1959 to FIM 114.6 million in 1960. Exports amounted already to 10% of net sales. With this favourable development, investments and share capital at Marimekko were doubled.

Armi Ratia felt that Vuokko Nurmesniemi was not very valuable for the further development of Marimekko and, after recurring disagreements between these two designers, Vuokko Nurmesniemi left the firm. Armi Ratia pushed on and hired another designer in 1960. Liisa Suvanto was to stage the corporate identity or visual look for Marimekko in photographs, exhibitions and fashion shows with such "Finnish Design" techniques as straw and stones to express the harmony that existed between Finnish nature and Finnish art, design and culture, a combination that brought Marimekko's stage design close to the work of, for example, Timo Wirkkala.

In 1961 and 1962, Printex and Marimekko had exhibitions in Boston, New York, Paris, Stuttgart, and Stockholm. A subsidiary was established in Sweden and several shops in Finland. These were under the Marimekko brand because even though Printex and Marimekko both expressed the same ideas in physical artifacts, the Marimekko brand was better known. It was Marimekko that the *New York Herald Tribune* named "uniform for the intellectual". It was Marimekko that was featured on the pages of *Vogue* magazine. Marimekko became the dominant brand over Printex.

Marimekko's net sales for the year ending in 1962 amounted to FIM 217.8 million. Profitability remained constant as a percentage of net sales. Exports continued to develop favourably, and presented over one-third of overall sales. Armi Ratia started entertaining the idea of a "Marikyla", having been inspired by discussions and trends and lifestyles with her architect friends. This Marshall-McLuhanian type of social experiment would be a "global modern village", where "mari-people" would enact their "lifestyle". The village was to serve both as a place to live for employees and as a "research laboratory" for additions to the Marimekko product range. An experimental design project was established to develop this idea with Ratia's friends.

Lifestyle Marketing

Interest and enthusiasm in Marikyla in social circles and the media was enormous. Innovativeness at Printex and Marimekko was now institutionalised at higher levels than simply the product level. Other firms with similar management mindsets to Marimekko's could license Marimekko's brand name and share in the activity of producing the new lifestyle. This arrangement allowed diversification from textiles and clothing to candles, glassware, ceramics, jewellery, etc. Retail shops became increasingly important for Marimekko as means to diffuse this diversity into the marketplace.[8]

Marimekko successfully leveraged the interest of the media into competitive advantage. Net sales in 1963 increased to FIM 2.6 million (current nominal value – the Finnish Markka was converted in 1963 by knocking off two zeros). Profitability was stable. Exports increased two and a half times. Net sales in 1964 grew to FIN 13.5 million, and profitability stayed at the record ratio reached for three financial years in a row. Virtually non-existent long-term debt showed that the firm was very solvent. Increases of share capital raised it in 1964 to FIM 126,000. Net sales in 1965 increased to FIM 4.8 million. Profitability was maintained.

Armi Ratia testified in Danish magazines: "woman is sexy...not a dress." Articles in the Finnish media said: "Marimekko is a charming challenge to all conventional codes. The challenge is thrown to young girls, grandmothers, leisure, work, public offices, home and the school. The challenge is thrown to everyday life. The challenger is Marimekko...a flying banner against all conventionalism and codes." There were persistent rumours that an American millionaire was trying to buy the Marimekko brand from Armi Ratia and Viljo Ratia. Californian newspapers wrote "Happiness is a Marimekko" and a retrospective of Vuokko Nurmesniemi's design was held. There were features in the American *Vogue* and *Life* magazines, and Annika Piha's dress was on the cover of French *Elle*, British *Queen* and Italian *Bellezza* (see Plate 14).

Maija Isola's textiles at Printex remained important. Her geometrical dress and Annika Piha's pop-art lady's overall had worldwide artistic success, and her design excitingly moved close to "pop art" (an art philosophy that regarded contemporary everyday things as worthy of works of art, e.g. Andy Warhol's painting of popular brand soup cans and Leichenstein's paintings that look like they're from enlarged comic books) and "opt art" (a form of geometrical abstraction that emphasised optical paradoxes, e.g. Cunningham's staircase that collapses into itself, for Vasareey's black and white painting of embracing zebras) (see Plate 15).

However, this general interest in Marimekko design was a sign that the ideas on which it was based were fast diffusing into popular culture. The meaning of Marimekko's design was changing. Societies were internationally becoming as collective as Marimekko's design had intended. The materialisation of Armi Ratia's vision was strongest in Finland where Marimekko's style was strongest. The "social revolution" of the 1960s was coming to an end, and Marimekko's style that demonstrated the individualism of the 1950s was becoming outmoded.

Maintaining the Momentum through Continuous Investment

Armi Ratia sought in several ways to break Marimekko's conventional way of implementing its design concept to maintain momentum. Marimekko involved themselves with a Finnish construction firm, and the Marikyla prototype house and sauna were produced in 1966. However, this in the end proved too expensive. Also, Armi Ratia and Viljo Ratia began divorce proceedings. Armi Ratia employed Ristomatti Ratia, her and Viljo Ratia's son, to be the first male designer to work full-time in Marimekko or Printex and eventually to be CEO of Marimekko. Printex's accounts were merged with Marimekko's that year with Viljo Ratia becoming a minority shareholder.[9] The result of the accounts merger was that Marimekko documented record profits at 8% of net sales.

Annika Piha considered that design was still important for Marimekko. In an interview at the time, she said "... there must be freedom of movement. If one feels like running, there must be freedom to run; if sitting, there must be freedom to sit." She began to work on a new product concept.

In 1968, Annika Piha finalised her "Tasaraita" clothing concept, which rejuvenated not only design, but the firm: a sort of continuation of the Marikyla experiment, but creatively combining this experience with 19th century Mediterranean influences and with considerations of Marimekko's design heritage and printing technology. The result was a kind of "Maoist uniform": unisex T-shirts, pyjamas and dresses for women, children and men, with striped tricot (knit cotton) cloth as a "trademark" (see Plate 16). In the international marketplace, the product concept set a new world-wide trend, and was quickly adopted by designers, intellectuals and opinion leaders. Marimekko received the prestigious Neiman-Marcus award for design that year.

Yet Marimekko denounced their initial design concept with this newer design concept. Marimekko now became linked to the depersonalised anonymity discourse in arts. There was no reference at all to the originality of the individual designer, nor to any difference between sexes. The product concept was to capture the process of "standardisation" of intellectual thought in Finnish society in the 1970s and early 1980s that was to lessen appreciation for the kind of "elitist" design that Marimekko had represented throughout its history. Net sales in 1968 increased 30% to FIM 13.7 million. Profitability remained on the new record-high level that had been reached the previous year. Share capital was increased, now to FIM 234,000.

THE SWAN SONG OF DESIGN: GROWTH TO PROFITABLE MATURITY 1969–1974

In the aftermath of his divorce with Armi Ratia, Viljo Ratia left the firm and there was the introduction of professional business administrators from outside the immediate family. Changes in design were needed because the global "social revolution" of student and labour unrest in 1968 had fundamentally changed the nature of Marimekko's environmental context. The social and economic demand for the kind of "elitist" design Marimekko produced was declining. On the other hand, the demand for Marimekko's designs in Western markets meant that its markets were now greatly expanded for any given product. Indeed, sales and profitability reached its highest-ever level, at 10% of net sales.

Armi Ratia had employed Katsuji Wakisaka, from Japan, and Pentti Rinta, straight from the main Finnish design school, in an attempt to give a new "good strong shake" to design thinking in Marimekko. Katsuji Wakisaka and Pentti Rinta were the second and third male designers at Marimekko (after Ristomatti Ratia). Japanese design was a totally new component in Marimekko's design. Promisingly enough, Katsuji Wakisaka and Liisa Suvanto soon began working on new design concepts.

Establishment of a Spin-off Organisation for Design

In 1969 Ristomatti Ratia (designer, and son of Viljo Ratia and Armi Ratia) and Armi Ratia felt that a transfer of products he had designed at Marimekko to a new spin-off firm would have several advantages. The arrangement where products were transferred from Marimekko to the new firm would slow down Marimekko's sales growth and maintain the firm at a manageable size. At the same time, specialisation would provide both Marimekko and the spin-off company with the freedom to explore new opportunities and offer a larger product range.

In 1970, *Decembre Oy* was the design organisation institutionalised as an independent firm, and was wholly owned by Ristomatti Ratia. This new firm specialised in plastics and other new materials. Its main product was a line of plastic shelves for books, coat hangers, bags, etc. Marimekko could further its industrial processes, its penetration of the marketplace, as well as embark on new courses of experimentation. As some of the pressure for creating a new product had shifted to Decembre Oy, this meant that Katsuiji Wakisaka, for example, had the freedom to specialise in textile design greatly appreciated by experts: powerful colours created a kinetic impression and a fluidity of movement and boldness.

Meanwhile: "Everybody into Tasaraita"

Marimekko's 20th anniversary fashion show was held at the same place where the first fashion show had been held in 1951 – at the Kalastajatorppa Hotel in Helsinki. The theme of the fashion show was "Everybody into Tasaraita". A leading Finnish newspaper ran a feature "Everybody into Pallo tricots". "Pallo" was another series of clothes similar to "Tasaraita", designed by Annika Piha. Net sales in 1971 were FIM 17.7 million, or an increase of more than one-third. Profitability hit a new all-time high, both in absolute and relative terms. Share capital was increased seven times over, from FIM 234,000 to FIM 1.6 million.

That year, Decembre's bags line, designed originally at Marimekko in 1968, became a huge success (see Plate 17). The following year, these bags were ranked as a "world's best product" in the United States.

At Marimekko proper, experiments continued to expand the firm's design knowledge. Several dresses designed by Liisa Suvanto used textiles designed by Katsuji Wakisaka as its platform, and vice versa. A men's suit designed by Pentti Rinta became a true "uniform" for the intellectual man. It appealed to male designers, intellectuals and opinion leaders who had risen to social or political prominence on the wave of the 1968 events and who for reasons of image refused to wear a conventional suit. The suit was a big commercial success and manufactured for ten years. It sold particularly well in Finland (see Plate 18).

International Licensing

In 1972, a licensing agreement was signed for manufacturing textiles in the United States. During the next year, licensing agreements were signed with another firm in the United States and in Japan. The "Tasaraita" was now developed by Annika Piha into a version more suitable for fully industrial production. Maija Isola and Pentti Rinta made an attempt to return to a minimalist design aesthetics, at Marimekko, but these products were unfortunately less well received than expected, whereas products produced by Decembre, marketed by Marimekko, sold particularly well around the world that year. Net sales in 1972 were FIM 21.1 million, with an increase of 20%. Profitability remained at a satisfactory level.

In 1973 licensing royalties from Japan and now the United States were half of the book-value's net profit. Otherwise profitability declined from 12% of net sales to 7% of net sales. Although the year was one of investments in both manufacturing and promotional activities, sales still increased by a quarter to FIM 26.2 million.

"Donating Marimekko to the People of Finland"

At this point, Marimekko was, at Armi Ratia's initiative, listed on the Helsinki Stock Exchange. In Liisa Suvanto's words: "We donated Marimekko to the people of Finland." Upon going public, Marimekko's share capital increased from FIM 1.6 million to FIM 5 million.

That same year Katsuji Wakisaka designed a naivist textile pattern, based on cars, that was a continuation of the Marimekko lifestyle concept, and became a huge success both artistically and commercially, selling especially well in the United States (see Plate 19). Liisa Suvanto designed woollen dresses that received favourable criticism, but sold less well (see Plate 20). Armi Ratia employed Fujimo Ishimoto, another male Japanese designer, to expand Marimekko's knowledge of how to design women's clothing.

Global economic turbulence, initiated by oil markets, did not effect Marimekko. The firm was now well positioned in its markets. Exports continued to amount to half of net sales. In Finland, the economy was doing well because of Soviet trade that was relatively decoupled from Western markets that were encountering the oil crisis. There was local demand and appreciation of Marimekko's design at ever higher levels in Finnish society. A new flagship shop was opened on Helsinki's Esplanade, the most exclusive shopping street. Urho Kaleva Kekkonen, the President of Finland, opened Marimekko's new factory. Net sales increased by more than a half in 1974, to FIM 39.9 million. Profitability bounced back up to its "normal" level at 13% of net sales, up from the disappointing 7% of the previous year.

SEARCH FOR NEW IDEAS: REACHING PROFITABLE MATURITY 1975–1980

In the mid-1970s, the utopia that Marimekko represented had become market reality. Especially in Finland it was now true that when an old Marimekko shirt wore out, a new one was bought typically from the nearest Marimekko store. Marimekko was an ideology for a future collective society, and the "rock generation" (those born after the war) had already, by 1973 or 1974, implemented that ideology: sexual liberation, equality, lessening differentiation between art forms, and collective leftist ideals.

However, as an interviewed design expert put it in 1992, "it is in the nature of utopia, that it cannot be chased for a second time." Such was the demand for Marimekko that it could not maintain its distinctiveness and remain socially meaningful. The architectural influences that had affected Marimekko's design since the 1950s became commonly-used elements within industry across the Western world in the mid-1970s. Social demand had permanently changed. The original design concept was in need of total rejuvenation: "Tasaraita" was not enough.

Armi Ratia sought to rejuvenate design and the firm by reviewing and widening the social circles from which Marimekko's design sought its ideas.

She extended Urho Kaleva Kekkonen, the President of the Republic of Finland, an open invitation to more often attend social events at the Bökars country estate. Kekkonen accepted the invitation gracefully. He had adopted a stance close to intellectuals, opinion leaders and politicians who had risen to powerful positions within Finnish society during or after 1968. As a result, Marimekko's social gatherings and parties increasingly included participation of the post-1968 elite. Net sales in 1975 grew by 5% to FIM 42.1 million. Profitability remained at a high level.

Presidential Export Award

The firm's exports developed favourably in 1975. That year exports accounted for nearly a half of net sales. The firm also developed its international operation, opening a franchise shop in Amsterdam. For such accomplishments, President Urho Kaleva Kekkonen gave Marimekko the Presidential Export Award that year. This was a special recognition reserved for an inter-nationalised Finnish firm, which was regarded as an example for other firms.

In 1976, a sales subsidiary was established in Germany, followed by another in the United States the next year. Exports in 1976 grew more than did sales in Finland, measuring 45% of net sales, which totalled FIM 45.5 million.

That year Katsuji Wakisaka and Liisa Suvanto cooperated in a series of blueprints for clothing in which Katsuji Wakisaka designed the textiles, and Liisa Suvanto the dresses. There was also similar cooperation between Katsuji Wakisaka and Pentti Rinta.

In 1977, a design and marketing subsidiary was established in the United States. Net sales amounted to FIM 51.5 million, with profitability to net sales maintained at a relatively high level. That year, a textile designed by Fujimo Ishimoto was well received, both artistically and commercially, especially in the United States.

Net sales for 1978 were only FIM 49.8 million but accounts proved that Marimekko's absolute profit performance had improved permanently to new record levels as a result of internationalisation. The improvements in profitability meant that there could now be investments in a new integrated visual identity for production, offices and retail shops that year. These investments were accordingly made.

Professionals take over Role of Founder

Autumn 1979 witnessed the death, after a brief illness, of Armi Ratia, the design manager and founder of Marimekko. Marimekko's profitability that year dropped temporarily to 5% of net sales, while net sales grew to FIM 51.3 million. Armi Ratia's role as the original design manager and founder, of course, could not be wholly filled by others. Armi Ratia's duties as the person in charge of design were taken over by Hilkka Rahikainen, one of the more recently employed female designers. Before becoming ill, Armi Ratia had hired Marja Suna, another female designer, to rejuvenate the women's clothing line. The firm had opened a flagship retail shop in New York, and under a licence agreement, a Swedish firm had started making Marimekko bed sheets.

In 1980, new Marimekko franchise shops were opened abroad. The strategy was that the main markets were Finland, Northern Europe and the United States. Total net sales grew by over a quarter and amounted to FIM 65.7 million. There were new product lines in men's shirts and ladies' woollens, and the older style tricot clothes continued to sell well. Profitability to net sales set a new record high of 14%. Licensing was growing three times as fast as conventional exports, and licensing income grew by a third, with the increase coming mainly from the United States. Germany grew into a larger export market than the United States, where market position stabilised. Two new retail shops were established in Finland. Marimekko's design thus maintained its momentum.

END OF SEARCH: RECORD-HIGH PROFITABILITY 1981–1985

As a whole, the 1980s were marked by new design surfacing from around the world. Marimekko's designs could not be as unique and progressive as they had been in the 1950s, 1960s and early 1970s. Also, with the founder having passed away, the entrepreneurial verve was lost.

Yet it was precisely within this difficult context that Marimekko proved to be a truly excellent firm. By continuing to adapt its production and improve its industrial efficiency, it enhanced its profitability and reached a new record level in 1981. Net sales grew significantly, amounting to FIM 75.3 million. Return on investment that year was the best of all the firms listed on the stock exchange, and Marimekko was accordingly named the best firm on the Helsinki Stock Exchange. Marimekko had, through its strong brand, simply reached a position where it was not vulnerable to small, temporary changes in its product markets.

Net sales in 1982 grew by one-fifth, amounting to FIM 90.7 million, with profitability maintaining a very good level. Licensing royalties increased by a quarter from the United States and by one-fifth from Japan. The next year, growth of net sales slowed down only slightly, amounting to FIM 103.3 million. Exports to the United States increased by almost half, as did Marimekko's total international licensing royalties. Share capital was increased from FIM 5.0 million to FIM 7.5 million. Marimekko began to license its bed sheets out to a British firm.

Acquisition of the Earlier Spin-off

In 1983, Marimekko acquired Decembre, its spin-off established in 1970, which had successfully manufactured and marketed Ristomatti Ratia's bags and rucksacks. Such internalising of good design was necessary because it provided Marimekko with design solutions on which to expand its business. In the 1980s, apart from a few isolated examples such as Fujimo Ishimoto or Paivi Helenius, Marimekko's best designers failed to produce "good design" products that also sold well.

The growth in Marimekko's exports came from the United States and Germany in 1987. Net sales stayed roughly on the level they were during the previous year, growing to FIM 108.3 million. Profitability to net sales declined somewhat, but not seriously. There were financial resources for investments in the rejuvenation of clothing designs, the overall Marimekko image, and retail shops, and these were all accordingly made.

"Sell out"

As 1985 drew to a close, Ristomatti Ratia, Antti Ratia and Eerika Gummerus, the children of Armi and Viljo Ratia, decided – surprisingly – to sell their firm's shares to Amer Group Ltd, a Finnish conglomerate which was to acquire 95% of Marimekko. Amer Group was, in the eyes of many Finns, identified with the tobacco industry (it licensed, among other brands, Marlboro cigarettes from Philip Morris). Such American-style mass marketing was not perceived to be compatible with Marimekko's design concept.

It soon became apparent to Amer Group that, despite Marimekko's reputation and its commercial activities and profits, the company had been declining starkly throughout 1985. The Group quickly shortened Marimekko's financial year from twelve to six months, supposedly on the basis that this harmonised accounts with those of Amer Group. According to Marimekko's annual report for 1985, demand conditions were temporarily unfavourable, but profitability was expected to rise from its current level to 4% of net sales.

RAPID PERFORMANCE DECLINE 1986–1991

At the beginning of 1986, Amer Group completed the acquisition of the majority holding of Marimekko, promising to respect the independence of Marimekko, and to provide only management and financial resources. In assessing the compatibility of Amer Group and Marimekko, both Amer Group and Marimekko received substantial media attention. Amer Group's managers seemed to enjoy this attention, promising to rejuvenate Marimekko and raise profitability to previous levels with the capabilities it possessed for managing mature brands.

However, the belief that design stalls could be subjected to scientific appraisal failed to rejuvenate the design reputation. Instead, in the process design lost its emotional resonance and individualistic expression.

Unsuccessful Attempts to Enhance the Firm's Reputation

In 1986, the Museum of Applied Arts in Helsinki organised the "Marimekko Phenomenon" exhibition. There was talk of the exhibition symbolising Marimekko's decline because the emphasis of the exhibition was on the firm's "golden age" from the mid-1950s to the late 1960s, and the design direction for the future was weak.

Marimekko's profitability remained negative. Net sales in 1986 were FIM 94.4 million. The design reputation of Marimekko was felt to be lost forever and was reflected in the rapid decline in profitability, which sank to minus 38% of net sales. Marimekko's 1986 annual report claimed that there was still potential for those Finnish firms which were well-positioned, despite the growth of imports. But the drastic deterioration continued. Net sales in 1987 failed to grow and amounted to FIM 96.5 million. The grievousness of the situation began to dawn on the public.

Exports and licensing royalties that year decreased. According to Marimekko's new management, but demand conditions in Finland were unfavourable, they were optimistic that the market would soon improve. Marimekko would in its operations put emphasis on the establishment of a franchise network in Sweden, Germany and the United States.

There was a change in the length of the financial year, partly to cover up for the company's loss-making activities. Net sales in the six-month 1988 financial year were roughly the same as during the previous six-month time span (now 51.0 million). Profitability was negative by over 7.1 million.

Coping with Unfavourable Demand Conditions

In 1989, to offset the ever-deteriorating demand, Marimekko acquired two new business entities: Marja Kurki/Lahjakurki and L & E Peterzens. The strategy was to focus Marimekko's operations on a combination of lower costs and higher sales. That year net sales still declined by one-tenth to FIM 85.6 million because the acquisitions did not yet impact the accounts. Exports and licensing royalties declined to 21% of net sales.

The acquisitions showed on the accounts the next year. Net sales increased by almost one-third to FIM 109.6 million. However, profitability did not improve significantly, nor did it the next year. Thus Marimekko's profitability consistently failed to show any improvement.

Still in 1991, net sales and profitability remained about the same. Amer Group closed Marimekko's flagship store in New York, and that year the celebration of Marimekko's 40th anniversary was low key. Employees had been warned that everyone would be laid off for two weeks in July, a previously unheard-of situation in the company.

REJUVENATION: 1992 ON

Because Marimekko was a national institution, Amer Group could not simply close it down, despite the phenomenal losses Marimekko was making. However, it chose to divest itself of the company and to refuse to make public the terms of a divestment. Marimekko was but a very small and insignificant part of the Amer Group, and not a concern of investor relations of Amer Group. Its accounts could be delivered to public registrars after a time lag and this made it into less of a public concern. It did thus not become publicly known that Marimekko continued to follow the strategic choices made by the administrators of Amer Group, as well as receive intellectual, material and financial support supplied from the Group. Even after Amer Group sold Marimekko to Kirsti Paakkanen Amer Group's financial officer continued to be Marimekko's Chairman of the Board.

When Kirsti Paakkanen took over Marimekko she successfully built up its past reputation to overcome the defamation it had experienced under Amer

Group's ownership. She used Armi Ratia's old speeches from the mid-1970s to make the point that there was a need for more effective and efficient routines to bring about a positive performance. This change in fortunes would sustain financial leverage whereby to create capacity to innovate. She made it clear that "it is useless to manufacture shirts ('Tasaraita' tricots) in an affluent country like Finland and then try to sell them in a high-street shop profitably." Kirsti Paakkanen made sure that there were design projects that were closely related to manufacturing and marketing capabilities. She implemented Amer Group's initiatives to outsource clothing production in the Far East and Estonia. Thus, Kirsti Paakkanen repositioned Marimekko and brought about a small growth in its profitability.

SUMMARY

The life story of Marimekko shows the evolution of a company, from its origins in crafts-based design to main production. Central to the early growth and success of this company was creative design and the ability to constantly innovate and produce exciting avant-garde designs that reflected the social changes of the times. The vision of the founders, especially Armi Ratia, was a major driving force that built up the design competence which was a major source of differentiation, and targeted "opinion leaders" to give a strong public image to Marimekko, both at home and abroad. When Marimekko ran into decline, its new owner Amer Group could not regenerate Marimekko's flair and design reputation. Amer's management activities proved too rigid and focused on financial control to create a climate for designers to express themselves and produce innovative designs. Only when a new owner, Kirsti Paakkanen, took over Marimekko and renewed the spirit of its original owners did design as the fortunes of Marimekko once again flourish.

APPENDIX: Design and Business Performance at Marimekko Oy

According to Ainamo's (1996) original research, between 1951 and 1995 Marimekko underwent swings in its business performance which can be associated with its design performance. Tables 8.1–8.4 and Figure 8.2 illustrate the dynamics that exist between design and competitive advantage. In these exhibits, the quality of design ("good, medium or bad") has been assessed with the help of a panel of experts and competitive advantage as being reflected in the firm's profitability (high, medium or low (EBDIT) profitability to net sales).

Table 8.1   Synopsis of some significant events

Mission: to increase sales	1951
A reputation for innovativeness	1951
Financial crisis	1951
Stretch	1953
"Take-off"	1955
Rapid sales growth and internationalisation	1956
Lifestyle marketing	1962
Maintaining the momentum through continuous investment	1966
Establishment of a spin-off organisation for design	1970
"Everybody into Tasaraita"	1971
International licensing	1972
"Donating Marimekko to the people of Finland"	1974
Presidential Export Award	1975
Professionals take over role of founder	1980
Acquisition of the earlier spin-off	1983
"Sell out"	1985
Unsuccessful attempts to enhance the firm's reputation	1986
Coping with unfavourable demand conditions	1989
Breaking the rapid decline	1991

Table 8.2   Breakdown of the life cycle periods and competitive advantage periods

	Design			Competitive advantage	
1.	Creation of concept 1951–1954	M	Early development 1951–1955		L
2.	Golden Age 1955–1968	G	Rapid growth and internationalisation 1956–1968		M
3.	Swan song 1969–1973	G	Maturity 1969–1985		G
4.	Search for new ideas 1975–1980	M			G
5.	Decline 1981–1991	B			G
			B	Decline 1986–1991	B
6.	Rejuvenation of concept 1992–	M	Breaking of vicious cycle 1992		B

Design: G="good", M="medium", B="bad" (expert panel assessments)
Competitive advantage: L=low performance (EBDIT less than 5% of net sales);
M=medium performance (EBDIT 5% or more than 5% of net sales, but less than 10%);
H=high performance (EBDIT 10% or more of net sales Benchmarks based on interviews.

Table 8.3   Some designers and time span when their design projects were most significant

Designer	Time span	Design projects	Type
Armi Ratia	1949–1979	1	Textile
Maija Isola	1949–1965	5	Textiles
Vuokko Nurmesniemi	1953–1959	6	3 Textiles
			3 Clothing
Annika Piha	1964–1972	9	Clothing
Liisa Suvanto	1975–1976	8	Clothing
Ristomatti Ratia	1970–1971	2	Furniture
			Bag
Katsuji Wakisaka	1971–1976	8	Textile
Pentti Rinta	1969–	2	Clothing
Fujimo Ishimoto	1977–1979	4	Textile

Note: "Time span" refers to time span in which most significant examples of design were made rather than specifications of employment at Printex, Marimekko or Decembre.

Table 8.4   Marimekko net sales, profitability and internationalisation

	Net sales	Profitability (EBDIT)	Internationalisation
1951	N.A.	−5,840	International media attention 1951
1956	209,159	11,408	Exports to Sweden 1954, Swedish subsidiary 1956
1961	2,178,633	141,812	Breakthrough in exports, incl. America, 1959
1966	11,578,242	720,662	Licensing begins 1963, Retail shop in Denmark
1971	17,709,249	2,268,416	International licensing 1972 in America and Japan
1976	45,535,574	2,255,848	German subsidiary 1976, American subsidiary 1977
1981	75,362,400	12,702,000	Licensing royalties from FIM 7.4 million in 1980 to FIM 12 million in 1984
1986	94,427,000	−12,657,000	Franchising begun, Flagship in New York 1986
1991	73,694,000	−15,585,000	New less international strategy 1991
1992	85,934,000	1,496,000	Increasing international subcontracting 1992
1993	96,535,000	3,910,000	Focus on domestic retail shops 1993
1994	90,256,000	14,367,000	Increasing amount of retail shops in Helsinki 1994

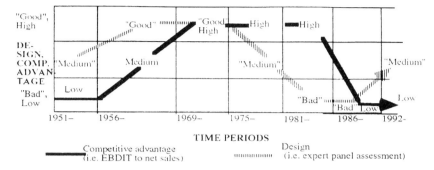

Figure 8.2 Combinations of design and competitive advantage during the empirical case

REFERENCE

Ainamo, A. (1996): Industrial Design and Business Performance: A case study of Design Manangement in a Finnish Fashion Firm. Helsinki School of Economics and Business Administration, Helsinki.

NOTES

1. In designing the dresses, Riitta Immonen was helped by Armi Ratia and two other designers.
2. Riitta Immonen was not responsible for the textiles, only the stage sets and the dresses. The textiles featured in the exhibition were from eight other textile designers, one of whom was Armi Ratia.
3. The fashion show was made memorable to the people present by the overall stage design of co-ordinated sequences of textiles, clothes, models, lights and communications. Marimekko utilised the best visual techniques. The products themselves were not that unique, but "stage design" (exterior and interior architecture and props) was co-ordinated in a way that communicated a design concept of great integrity.
4. Riitta Immonen, the artist, in fact felt embarrassed that her "ready-made" designs attracted such commercial interest.
5. Vuokko Nuniiesniemi had designed for Printex and Marimekko on a freelance basis from 1952 onwards. For example, she had been responsible for developing the shop-window display at the Palace Hotel.
6. Growth of net sales is, in this case, always compared to the previous financial year, except where otherwise noted. The distinction is important where lengths of financial years vary.
7. Jacqueline Kennedy's reasons for buying Marimekko may have been partly political wisdom. By buying "affordable" but well-designed dresses from Europe, she communicated to the American people that she dressed also in other than elitist French *haute couture*. For Marimekko, this brought great media attention around the world; the firm was established as good design that "encompassed the nature of the 20th-century experience" (Bauhaus).
8. Wholly-owned retail shops in Finland and Sweden began in 1962 to account already for 50% of Marimekko's sales.
9. Armi Ratia had come to own a substantial amount of Printex's shares. Viljo Ratio originally very few of Marimekko's shares. Thus, upon merging the accounts, Armi, not Viljo, Ratia became the majority shareholder.

PART THREE

DESIGN EXPERTISE
PERSPECTIVES

INTRODUCTION

Margaret Bruce

Design and business can be regarded as diametrically opposed, design being related to aesthetics, self-expression and individual creativity, business being associated with the profit motives, rationality and objectivity. Design and business have been treated as belonging to two distinct paradigms or "ways of seeing the world". Design has been viewed as being creative so that it cannot be subject to management processes in the way that other business areas, such as marketing and finance, have been. Nonetheless, the mounting evidence that design expertise can affect long-term business performance has led to attempts to investigate and identify design management processes in order to integrate design into business processes. Two of the papers in this section address the issue of the nature of design competence and its relationship to business. Kristensen compares design-based companies (e.g. Braun, Philips) with less renowned design companies and considers the cultural background of the design-based organisations that have resulted in their effective use of design, so much so that design is "taken for granted" as a necessity, not an afterthought. He develops a conceptual framework that relates design competence with different business concerns, namely exploration, development and resource management. With this framework, Kristensen articulates the interlinks between design and business processes.

Borja de Mozota begins by exploring the differences between design and management – "opposing cultures" – and then discovers key areas of overlap – "convergence paradigm". It is the nature of this convergence that she attempts to unravel in her contribution. Finally, she argues for a science of design, "Designence", which has the connotation of design being a core

Management of Design Alliances. Edited by M. Bruce and B. H. Jevnaker.

discipline that embraces other disciplines, such as Quality, Creativity, Marketing, Strategy, etc. In other words, for Borja de Mozota, design is not a marginal activity but is the core competence that differentiates more successful companies from those that are less successful.

The final paper by Bruce and Morris in this section is not conceptual. It presents salient results from a comparative study of design professionals in Britain, Sweden and Denmark. From the study, stark differences in design and business relationship are in evidence, which have theoretical and practical implications. In Scandinavia, close and long-term relationships with design suppliers or partners are cultivated. This relationship is critical to the continual development of products and the design–client relationship is regarded as providing a core competence. Once it was lost, it would be difficult to replace. By contrast, in Britain design has become akin to a commodity that can be purchased "off the shelf" as required by the client. Hence, arms-length and one-off relationships are the norm. Often design is bought on price with little intention of investing in a longer-term relationship.

CHAPTER NINE

DESIGN MANAGEMENT LESSONS FROM THE PAST: HENRY DREYFUSS AND AMERICAN BUSINESS[1]

Karen Freeze with Earl Powell

"We bear in mind that the object being worked on is going to be ridden in, sat upon, looked at, talked into, activated, operated, or in some other way used by people individually or en masse. When the point of contact between the product and people becomes a point of friction, then the designer has failed. On the other hand, if people are made safer, more comfortable, more eager to purchase, more efficient – or just plain happier – by contact with the product, then the designer has succeeded."

Henry Dreyfuss' *Credo*, 1950[2]

"In one way or another, directly or by imitation, the great majority of businesses in this country use industrial designers."

Henry Dreyfuss in a speech to the Harvard Business School, 1950s

Henry Dreyfuss' buoyant enthusiasm as he addressed "hard-headed businessmen who may be considering – or perhaps should be considering – the possibility of employing the services of industrial designers" seems anachronistic forty years later, when the profession would be happy if but half of American businesses understood the value of design. Notwithstanding his

Management of Design Alliances. Edited by M. Bruce and B. H. Jevnaker.
© 1998 John Wiley & Sons Ltd.

miscalculations about the degree to which industrial design had permeated American industry, Dreyfuss' speech exhibited a perceptive understanding of business and industry and an extraordinary ability to communicate his cause to that audience. Five years later, he pulled these ideas together in *Designing for People*, which we have rediscovered on our historical journey into industrial design's past.

In our effort to communicate the importance – nay, the crucial necessity of – professional design in products, communications and environments, we look for "proof" – evidence that will convince those who pay for (or should pay for) design services, whether from internal design departments or from outside consultants. What is obvious to designers is far from obvious to most managers and chief executive officers who make decisions about where their money goes, and design often ends up near the bottom of the heap.

Industrial designers have lamented this situation for years. The Design Management Institute owes its existence, in fact, to the acute need for communication between business and the design community. In the course of the TRIAD Design Project research into companies that do utilise design resources effectively, the institute discovered a number of characteristics common to these companies, despite wide differences in industry, location, and size. Calling these characteristics our preliminary research findings, we put them in a five-point, nutshell summary that went something like this:

In successful companies:

1. design and designers are supported from the top;
2. designers are involved in all stages of product developments;
3. designers facilitate communication through formal and informal means;
4. designers are closely involved with future user of the product;
5. designers are uncompromisingly attentive to detail.

Through illustrations and examples drawn from the TRIAD case studies, we developed an exhibition on design in product development that addresses people from business, industry, and education. Our goal at the outset was to have the thirteen case study companies (among them Braun, Digital, Canon) inspire others to ponder the value of effective design management.

Little did we know (or remember) that our findings were not new. In fact, what we were "discovering" and articulating was both deliberately and ingenuously presented in Henry Dreyfuss' *Designing for People*, back in 1955. Since he opened his office in 1929, Dreyfuss (1904–1972) and his clients had been practising effective design management principles and – unlike many designers – Dreyfuss was able to articulate them. What he did not anticipate was that somehow, somewhere along the line, what he practised and preached would be lost to the next generation of managers – not completely, to be sure, but lost enough so that American products, for the most part, are losing on the design front to European and Asian products as the twentieth century draws to a close.

Most designers undoubtedly read *Designing for People* in 1955 when it was first published, or in 1967 when it came out in paperback. It takes a re-reading in the 1990s, however, to appreciate its often-prophetic voice, and to wonder at its optimism in many cases. In trying to understand the management style of the man behind the book, we talked with several of his colleagues and clients. What emerged is a portrait of a creative and charismatic leader who modelled every one of our five "characteristics of effective design management" well before many of us were born.

SUPPORT FROM THE TOP

It may be Dreyfuss' connections at the top of American industry that made him appeal to Harvard Business School audiences in 1950, 1954, and 1965. Henry Dreyfuss knew what was going on in the upper echelons of the business world and had something to say about the role of his profession in its success. In the first speech, which contained much of what would later appear in *Designing for People*, Dreyfuss covered all the bases, emphasising the bottom line "industrial designers are employed primarily to increase the profits of the client company." He was adamant that the top managers whom he was addressing "must be convinced of the value and necessity of industrial design". "In fact", he continued, "if it is not top management that makes the final decision on the employment of a designer, or if top management is not genuinely convinced of his value, then my urgent advice to industrial designers would be to refuse the assignment, even if it's offered. The designer who enters an organisation without the understanding and blessings of those at the top ties his hands and limits the contribution he can make."

One of Dreyfuss' ideal clients was John Deere, America's largest manufacturer of agricultural machinery. Hired through the efforts of the Waterloo Tractor Works' chief engineer in 1937, Henry Dreyfuss Associates is still working for Deere today. The golden years began in 1955, when Bill Hewitt, an art and architectural aficionado, became CEO. During Hewitt's tenure of 27 years, Dreyfuss and his colleagues became fully part of the Deere corporate family, influencing every aspect of the company's business and helping its bottom line.

Dreyfuss' relationship to chief executives reflects a period of America's business history that evokes nostalgia among those – both clients and consultants – who now have to deal with big legal departments. "Our relationship was based on mutual trust and faith", he wrote, and contracts were there only to clarify a few things. One of his biggest contracts, with New York Central Railroad, was sealed with a handshake only. Another, with *McCall*'s magazine, just never got written in the 12 years Dreyfuss worked for them.

Such relationships must also be seen in the context of Dreyfuss' own ethical standards. "Henry was a man of singular purpose and immense willpower tempered by an extremely well-focused ethical nature", recalled former associate Niels Diffrient, "Everything was above board." Former partner Jim Conner concurs: "He was as honest in his approach to business as he was to design."

The importance of maintaining and nurturing these design–business relationships is a dimension that did not emerge from the TRIAD research. Henry Dreyfuss knew how to do this and enjoyed doing it. He was a charismatic "people-person" who knew how to communicate and sell his ideas. He believed in his mission – to make things better – and was able, according to Jim Conner, "to help management understand that you don't paste ID on top of a completed engineering design". According to his own account in *Designing for People*, Dreyfuss began in 1929 by writing "innumerable" letters to the heads of companies – and then, perhaps somewhat brashly, following up on them in person. It only took a few clients with a wide variety of challenges – railroad cars, tractors, telephones, clocks – for whom Dreyfuss did what he said he would, and his reputation was secured. After that he had to do less marketing – clients tended to come to him – but he never ceased cultivating and keeping in touch with an enormous network of clients, potential clients, friends, colleagues, and other contacts. "As soon as he got on a plane", his partners recall, "he'd get out a black felt-tip pen and start to dash off notes – just a few words and a little drawing. He'd do that throughout the flight. That's how he stayed in touch – and people loved it."

Despite his closeness to the industrial magnates of the time, Dreyfuss was, according to his colleagues, "very accessible". He could talk to people at any level and seemed to enjoy doing so. After all, it was these people for whom he was contributing to better, safer products, and a more amenable environment at home and at work. In doing so, he believed he was raising the standards against which Americans would judge the products they bought.

COMPREHENSIVE INVOLVEMENT IN PRODUCT DEVELOPMENT

Dreyfuss and his colleagues never worked any other way than through total involvement with product development "Henry couldn't have just 'styled' anything if he'd wanted to; it wasn't in him", recalls Jim Connor. By his own account, Dreyfuss didn't accept clients unless he could participate fully in every aspect of the design process, without exception. (One wonders if this requirement contributed to the relatively limited size of his office; perhaps Dreyfuss kept it small not only because he wanted to be able to stay close to every project, but also because he was interested only in clients who really understood what he could do.) Once hired, he and his colleagues gave first priority to establishing "friendly working relations with all departments" – e.g. marketing, engineering, manufacturing, advertising. Without such relationships – "and this cannot be stressed too strongly" – the product cannot fully succeed. "Diplomacy should be the designer watchword", he said in the early Harvard speech. The real test of the designer "lies in proving that he can integrate himself with all departments in the organisation. He must convince them that he is not in the glory business, that he will not accept undue credit, and that he considers a completed design not 'his' design, but 'our' design."

Dreyfuss was happy to tell the attendees of the Harvard Business School in 1950 that engineers are especially appreciative of designers. However, "it was not ever thus. More often than not, in the early days, engineers had to be cajoled by executive and sales personnel into accepting the designers. Now engineers have practically eliminated the necessity for such wheedling. The engineer, in fact, has assumed the role of the designer's best friend and severest critic – and that is as it should be." Note: this is 1950, Henry Dreyfuss speaking.

Dreyfuss himself was able to practise this principle of total involvement most profoundly with clients for whom he worked for decades, such as John Deere, AT&T, Polaroid, and Honeywell, to name just a few. With them he could follow the results of his work in the marketplace over time. However, he also had numerous small, short-lived projects that he took just as seriously. In the early years he was personally involved in all stages of the product, especially consumer products with strong aesthetic dimensions that would be used by thousands or even millions of people. "He was not mechanically inclined", explained Conner, "and would defer to one of us after presenting a design to a client like Polaroid or Deere, whose products had a heavy technical component." Dreyfuss clearly recognised his limitations and surrounded himself with designers who, like his partners Bill Purcell, Don Genaro, Jim Conner, and Niels Diffrient, had technical backgrounds in engineering or other disciplines as well as design.

"Involvement in all stages" was not restricted in any way in Dreyfuss' mind. Nor did it begin and end with a specific project. Especially for his long-term clients, Dreyfuss was never off the job. "We keep you in mind" was the office's motto and was written in letters of agreement and contracts. But for him it was a pleasure to discover something new in some out-of-the-way place and which could translate into a design innovation for a client. One day, as his son John Dreyfuss tells the story, he was driving along a highway and saw a flower on a hill beside the road. "He stopped the car, climbed up the hill, and picked the flower. 'Why did you do that?' his companion asked the non-athletic Dreyfuss as he descended back towards the car. 'I'm going to send it to Don Hall [of Hallmark Cards]. He might like the colour.'"

COMMUNICATION FACILITATOR

If Dreyfuss, who started out as a stage set and costume designer, hadn't discovered industrial design, he would probably have moved to another field that required the singular ability to communicate with many disciplines and to integrate diverse and dispersed information into a coherent whole. He was extraordinarily capable in that role, loved it, and yet he was not arrogant about it. As he put it, in language clearly dating from the 1950s:

"It might seem to some that the designer lays claim to a special omniscience, an infallibility, through which he blithely presumes to offer a solution to any problem. He makes no such claim. He takes pride in a skill based on experience and an alertness sometimes interpreted as vision. He approaches every problem with a willingness to do painstaking study and research and to perform exhaustive experimentation. He is equipped to work intelligently with the engineer, the architect, the physicist, the interior decorator, the colourist, and the doctor. He must know how far to go and when to stop. He must be part engineer, part businessman, part salesman, part public relations man, artist, and almost, it seems at times, Indian chief."

INVOLVEMENT WITH USERS

Industrial designers do not need to be told about the importance of close involvement with the future users of a product. Their profession is often defined as having to do with the user-centred aspects of a product. This essential aspect of their job, described in such a natural and obvious manner in Dreyfuss' book, is not, however, well appreciated by many people in management. Dreyfuss described his own consumer research in this way:

> "I have washed clothes, cooked, driven a tractor, run a Diesel locomotive, spread manure, vacuumed rugs, and ridden in an armoured tank. I have operated a sewing machine, a telephone switchboard, a corn picker, a lift truck, a turret lathe, and a linotype machine. When designing the rooms in a Slater hotel, I stayed in accommodations of all prices. I wore a hearing aid for a day and almost went deaf. I stood beside a big new gun at Aberdeen proving grounds when it was fired, and was catapulted off my feet. Members of our office have spent days and nights in airport control towers and weeks in a destroyer during manoeuvres. We ride in submarines and jet planes. All this in the name of research!"

Alongside this impressionistic, subjective research was an impressively thorough study of ergonomics – called "human engineering" at that time. A pioneer in this science, Dreyfuss recognised that he was "designing for real people" from the beginning, and felt that it was essential to know as much about the human body – its anatomy and physiology – as possible. The office's anthropometric charts, nicknamed "Joe and Josephine", represented archetypal people whose parts and capabilities had been measured and documented in every dimension. They were born in the forties and evolved over the years, helping the designers to fit the design to human forms, and exemplifying Dreyfuss' commitment to designing for people. The most dramatic example of their early service came as a result of World War II when Dreyfuss was hired to redesign the interior of a tank and to carry out other military design assignments as well. In the years following the war, Dreyfuss was a severe critic of the automobile styling craze, as he pleaded for comfort, convenience, and safety.

On the lighter side, Dreyfuss liked to tell stories about his adventures in consumer research – including those times when he turned out to be wrong. He once played store clerk in a drugstore in order to see how customers reacted to a clock he had designed.

> "My first customer was a woman, and I showed her our model and a competitive clock of the same price. I watched her weigh a clock in each hand, I was confident of her choice, for we and our client's engineers had laboured hard and long to

make our clock light, believing the lightness was an expression of its excellence, I had a sinking feeling as she bought the heavier clock. But it brought home the lesson that to some people weight can be a sign of quality, also that the designer must appreciate that some things demand weight and some lightness, and he must determine when each is a virtue."

ATTENTION TO DETAIL

Like every good designer, Dreyfuss was compulsive about detail and insisted on that quality from everyone in his office. (That may account for a remark by the head of design in a large American corporation: "I'd hire someone who had worked for Dreyfuss for a year or more on the spot, without even talking with him. If he had survived that, I knew he was good".) This concern for detail, and for the designer to have a say in all matters great and small, was not limited to the office's design projects, but to the running of the office as well. Whenever he travelled (which was often), he received a daily package of mail containing copies of every piece of paper, every communication, that had gone in and out of the New York office (if he was in California) and vice versa. This desire to be in control was sometimes hard on his associates: "If he had an idea, you had to carry it out", remember his colleagues unanimously. "But he was reasonable. If you had another idea as well, and it was better, he'd accept it."

The business side of the Dreyfuss operation was similarly well run and well controlled. But here it was Doris Dreyfuss (known professionally as Miss Doris Marks) who kept track of those pieces of paper, those communications that went throughout the office, especially in California, and who advised her husband on all business matters. She was, according to Henry's colleagues, "a brilliant manager", whom Henry called after every meeting. Doris Dreyfuss was, as befit the times, a woman who wished to remain in the background. Nevertheless, she was Henry Dreyfuss' *alter ego* in a complete and complex way, and it would be interesting to understand her contribution more clearly.

In the New York Office Doris Mark's counterpart for local matters was Rita Hart, who managed the East Coast Office with a different style but with equal facility for forty years. The management lesson here: someone needs to keep track of the business side of design – and it pays to have someone first rate.

FURTHER OBSERVATIONS

Henry Dreyfuss worked with some of America's industrial giants and created, through his firm, some of the most persisting and pervasive products Americans have ever owned or used. Who doesn't have or at least didn't grow up with a Bell telephone? How many Americans have never seen a Honeywell round thermostat? And how many found a Polaroid camera under their Christmas tree since 1960? Because of these products, in which Dreyfuss could see tangible evidence of industrial design's contribution to the lives of millions, he seemed to believe that the battle of the good design was being won. He saw "American taste" as improving steadily, due to well-designed mass-produced products; he believed that the design process was so logical, so inherently sensible, that no rational person would consider developing a product, however large or small, without the services of an industrial designer.

So what happened in the forty years since Dreyfuss first articulated his vision? Ample evidence from both the popular and the business press of the 1930s through to the 1950s reveals that industrial design was seen during the period as important and worthy even of cover stories. Not until the mid-1980s was it rediscovered by the media, however, and only very recently can it be said that it is beginning to receive feature-article status again. What accounts for the forty-year hiatus? Was Dreyfuss' rosy vision too conditioned by his optimistic view from the top – his relationship with chief executive officers of major companies? Was he blinkered by his love for his work and enthusiasm for the cause? Did early successes lead to complacency among designers, including Dreyfuss and his colleagues? Did the founding fathers of industrial design fail to communicate to the younger generation of designers the need to sell their vision to business and industry? Or was it the design-conscious CEOs who failed to communicate the design dimension of company strategy to their heirs? Why didn't Dreyfuss' message from the 1950s stick? And what can be learned from it that is relevant to the 1990s?

Dreyfuss' main points, repeated again and again in his speeches and interviews (and pleaded for by today's industrial designers), have not lost their relevance. Industrial designers must have support from the top; they must be team players; they must be involved in all phases of product development; they must understand every user interface thoroughly; and they must be able to exercise their passion for detail. Moreover, they need to cultivate the client's trust through uncompromising ethical standards, honesty in design, above-board negotiations, clear communications, and design effectiveness. The designer's purpose is still the same: "to increase the profits of their client company". As Dreyfuss told Harvard Business School students in 1950, "That may sound unduly crass and materialistic but", he added, "it just happens to be true".

However, today's business environment (which reflects society as a whole) is different from what it was in the 1950s. And that difference presents a formidable challenge to designers if they try to live and work by values established a generation or two ago. Society is more complex, and business is encumbered by rules and regulations, interest groups and competitive pressures that did not exist forty years ago. Individuals – or so it seems – have less influence than they did then, whether in government or business. "Back then, when a single man was responsible for a company, the product was more important to him", explains Don Genaro, current senior partner of Henry Dreyfuss Associates. "Today, so many products are like anonymous commodities, and senior management just can't relate to them the same way."

Moreover, the United States is no longer the leading industrial nation in every field. Only recently did it begin to emerge from more than two decades of decline in manufacturing. It has an alarming trade deficit and an eroding industrial base, as many manufacturing segments leave the country for other shores. But those may be the very reasons that design is beginning once again to receive attention in the press. Industrial design in the United States was born in the middle of the Great Depression. It was a severe economic crisis that encouraged business to turn to designers for help. This may very well happen again in the 1990s, in the middle of an economic recession and with intense competitive pressure from abroad.

But even if American industry does turn to design to regain its competitive position today, will good design become a permanent, integral part of American business and industry? Will a design consciousness finally permeate American society? Or will we find, thirty or forty years from now, that educating managers and the public about the design has to start all over again? How can the management style – and strategy – of today's designers and design managers differ from Henry Dreyfuss' and his generation so that their influence will be sustained beyond their own careers, beyond the products they design? How can design be so institutionalised in manufacturing industries, in business, and in the people sphere that it can no longer depend on charismatic individuals, whether designers or top managers? Outstanding leaders come and go, and the fate of their companies often reflects that fact. To counter this inevitability, certain dimensions of company strategy should be so integral to a company's character that they remain unaffected in recessions. To put it another way: these strategic dimensions – including design – must be institutionalised into the very character of the organisation. Fundamental to this process is the maturing of design management as a recognised profession. Moreover, design management must become a part of a management education throughout the country. Give us a few more years, and – this is *our* vision – the Henry Dreyfuss legacy will be at home again.

NOTES

1. For various kinds of archival materials and generous amounts of time we are indebted to Henry Dreyfuss Associates, past and present, including Jim Conner, Don Genaro, Niels Diffrient, Jim Ryan, Brad Agry; to Russell Flinchum, City University of New York; to John Dreyfuss' son, and to William Field, Jon Craine, past and present designers at Polaroid.
2. Printed as "The Industrial Designer and the Businessman," in the *Harvard Business Review*, **28**(6), November 1950.

CHAPTER TEN

THE CONTRIBUTION OF DESIGN TO BUSINESS: A COMPETENCE-BASED PERSPECTIVE

Tore Kristensen[1]

INTRODUCTION

"I decided I could put my stamp on IBM through modern design. Dad had always paid close attention to IBM's appearance. It was a key to his success." IBM's Tom Watson expressed these sentiments in the 1950s (Watson 1990, p. 257). Sometimes this is the case and sometimes the opposite is true. It raises the questions: Why and when are the appropriate conditions met for "good design to be good business"? There are several ways of addressing these questions. In this chapter, design will be viewed in terms of the modern resource-based theory of the firm, or *competence theory* (Barney 1986; Reed and De Phillippi 1990; Leonard-Barton 1992). This is a theory of sustainable economic performance stressing both the product markets and factor markets. The former is common in the discussion on design, the latter concerns design as a competence traded by the firm, e.g. buying design consultancy services and/or integrating design in-house.

Management of Design Alliances. Edited by M. Bruce and B. H. Jevnaker.
© 1998 John Wiley & Sons Ltd.

This chapter is about the design expertise and competence as applied in business and encompasses both product design and corporate identity. The individual expertise of the industrial designer is considered as it connects with other business expertise, notably marketing, production and so on. There are overlaps and differences between design and business and some of these are identified and discussed here. Design competence is also a characteristic attributed to an organisation. In such cases, design is not only localised in particular departments or offices, but is embedded in the knowledge transcending the whole organisation. In conclusion, design's contribution to sustainable competitive advantage is examined.

NATURE OF DESIGN EXPERTISE[2]

Design may be represented by a single person or a team of professional designers. A designer is a person who uses creativity as a main capability. Designers and artists share creativity, but they use it differently. Creating art is a process with its own intrinsic purpose and artists are driven by their need for self-expression (Collingwood 1938). By contrast, design typically serves an extrinsic purpose: there is a need owner who pays for a design service. The designer is a craftsperson in business, working alongside business people who are educated in management, economics or engineering.

Designers are associated with (good) taste (Dormer 1993; Holt 1977). Aesthetics is about expression, but is often confined to a judgement about taste. Clearly, there is a large overlap between artists and designers. Both are able to express emotions and cognitions with the help of representation and visualisation (drawing, making physical objects in various forms, materials, texture, etc.). Both are experts in stimulating the senses. But the difference should be stressed – the *purpose* is different (Wallheim 1980; Collingwood 1938). While important, aesthetics does not account for the practical, analytical and conceptual competencies of design. Creativity, applied to conceptualisation and visualisation, are the superior qualifications of professional designers. To make models with two or three dimensions is part of a designer's skill-training and it makes the designer excel in communicating complex ideas.

The inability to communicate well, particularly across multiple functions – engineering, marketing and design, with their respective jargons – can be a serious problem for organisations, as several critical reports have highlighted (Hein and Myrup Andreasen 1985; Hayes and Wheelwright 1987; Wheelwright and Clark 1992). Lack of efficient communication prolongs lead-times, adds to a number of product iterations and costs and can sometimes result in project failure.

Consider the idea of rapid prototyping in product development. Here, the use of simple visual models is a means of interfunctional communication. "A block of wood speaks" (Leonard-Barton 1991) is a metaphor for effective communication. This communication is neither verbal nor formalised, but visual and tactile. Visualisation may be the fundamental dimension of the professional competence needed. The total competence necessary for the development of new products is found in teams[3] where professions (marketing, production, finance, design, etc.) come together (Wheelwright and Clark 1992). The "seven blind men and the elephant" serves as a good description, because each has his/her own language and jargon. Thus nobody sees the elephant – even in a team.

In the past, design education used to be crafts based, and now design education is becoming increasingly conceptual and computerised (and this reflects the division between the "head" and the "hand" in industry, i.e. designers are planners, rather than makers). Conceptual thinking requires intellectual discipline and the learning of "formal" methods similar to that of engineers (e.g. Alexander 1964; Jones 1970; Hein and Myrup Andreasen 1975). In other cases, design students are attached to a "mentor" and learn by doing project work. Most design education is a combination of these.

For many years, a debate ensued about the nature of design. Alexander (1964) distinguishes between "selfconscious" and "unselfconscious" design. The former is the rational form of working where scientific methods based on cybernetics and systems design are capable of solving design problems better than anything else. Unselfconscious design, on the other hand, is linked with primitive societies where crafts, trial-and-error and learning by imitation of prototypes were predominant. Alexander leaves little room for intuition, adaptation and practical hands-on learning. Computer design and technology-based innovations seem to reflect Alexander's view very well, although criticisms are emerging of Alexander's extreme view (Steadman 1979). This kind of debate has been reflected in management where rational choice models are presented in contrast to intuition and these may be presented as extreme ends of a spectrum. Just as a modern business view reconciles opposing views, the same has happened in design debates. Crafts-based organisations seem to reflect conditions whereby the two aspects of design are recorded. Crafts-based design concerns direct interaction between the craftsperson and the user, for instance a blacksmith making customised tools for the local community or a boatbuilder making vessels for fishermen (Kristensen 1994). While these examples drawn on the past, the phenomenon repeats itself in modern computer systems design, advanced measurement instruments, machine tools etc. as a "lead user" may influence the technical trajectory of an industry (Von Hippel 1988).

An important requirement of the designer's competence has to do with quality. Quality management and lessons from design history focus on standards and norms of quality respectively. To a large degree the latter are internalised and specific to the cultural context (Kristensen 1994). When design is learned as a craft, the novice observes the mentor and subsequently learns by doing, thus becoming part of the designer's "tacit knowledge" (Clark 1997; Polanyi 1958). The requisite quality depends on the ecological context, for example, a boat to be used by a fisherman in the North Sea may have different tolerances than similar products for small lakes in the tropics. Of course, the quality norms may be disturbed by competitive and technological pressures.

DESIGN AND BUSINESS

Some of the differences between design and business expertise may invoke conflicts, e.g. user needs versus market demand. The purpose and goals of design are compared with those for business in Table 10.1.

Designers are engaged in conceptualising, visualising and practically developing new designs. This is what they have been educated to do. Similarly, business executives are educated in analysing, assessing and making decisions about business and typically they are trained in calculus, analysis of markets and assessing strategic, tactic and operational consequences of alternative decisions. In some cases, one individual may possess all the expertise, even both business and design expertise. In other cases, one person may only have some of the appropriate expertise.

Table 10.1   Types of expertise

Design expertise	Business expertise
Design creativity/awareness	Commercial creativity/awareness
Conceptual – Emotional	Analytical – Synthetical
Visual	Quantitative
User-focus	Market focus
Quality	Production
Need	Demand

Business competence can be divided into at least three different elements:

1. *Entrepreneurship:* identification of new opportunities and exploiting them in the form of new products, markets, channels of distribution etc. This is probably the most creative aspect of business.
2. *Management:* Often "management" is used as the umbrella concept – covering the others. I want to restrict management to the handling of resources and structuring the tasks and assigning people to them, and supervising the process – these are the important aspects of management. As for design, this is a matter of project management.
3. *Judgement and investment decisions:* Project selection and taking risky decisions and allocating funds and staff so that people use their time and talent. Designers may meet all three aspects of business expertise and/or co-operate with the people possessing them. Clearly, making judgements about design requires knowledge about design. The business end of design means assessing the chances that a particular project has for success and does not require that the person making the judgement is also capable of designing. Similarly, a designer may be good at his/her work without the ability to judge whether it will succeed in the market.

Overall, design and business goals complement each other, although at times they may contradict. Both commerce and design are creative types of activities. Both may use creativity for problem-finding or problem-solving. But the *use* of creativity is different. Companies are concerned with finding new opportunities for their business; earning a profit by offering a product to a market. Design is concerned with finding needs and designing and improving products. There are overlaps, but profit is not only the prime goal of design, but also the utility, aesthetics and other qualities of artefacts as experienced by individual users. There is much to say about profit as other business goals. Profit is only one such goal and not even the most important. (Collins and Porras 1994, p. 47 ff). Commercial creativity is concerned with economising scarce materials for serving business purpose. It is concerned with private profit goals, but designed artefacts are typically more oriented towards the expressive, functional and aesthetic use of creativity within economic restrictions. Today, it is rarely the case that a designer can perform his/her tasks without having regard for commercial concerns.

Finally, the designer is focused on the individual or typical user and his/her needs, whereas the business person is focused on the market and the business goals. The designer's primary concern must be to deliver good design and that of the business person must be preoccupied with business goals and meeting financial targets. Formulated in "absolute terms", business is oriented towards exploitation, and design towards exploration. In less absolute terms, both design and business interact in an "exploration/exploitation trade-off" (March 1993). Conflict between designers and business people is well known, but not well documented. There are plenty of anecdotal examples, but so far I know of no systematic research on this topic. In a number of cases, constructive conflict resolution has occasionally destroyed the process or drawn on third-party intervention (top management). One example is a Danish designer working for a producer of furniture. The conflict appeared when the producer, in the midst of the process, demanded a chair that could be sold at a price of 30% lower than initially agreed in the design brief. Such a cut affects just about everything conceivable in the project. As a result the project ground to a halt and created mutual acrimony that still exists after years. In some cases, organisational slack and selective attention according to the behavioural theory of the firm (Cyert and March 1963, p. 36) has provided solutions because slack resources reduce tensions, and make possible solutions such as new projects, just as new resources create new options. Thus, Ainamo (1996) has defined design activities as a creation of "slack-resources", which kickstart experimentation, rejuvenation, new visual signs, commitments, culture signs, etc., and can create new spirit and happiness in the workplace.

This has merit in the sense that design is an innovation activity (exploration) that has provided a ground for later exploitation. In a very useful study of Marimekko (see Chapter 8), Ainamo has demonstrated that periods of exploration and exploitation follow each other sequentially.

Good design may not lead to good business by itself and good business without good products and well-designed solutions may result in rather short-term benefits. Therefore, good business and good design can be regarded as two facets of the same thing. The contrast concerns the specific aims of business and the use of visual competence. Design is also used for other purposes than business, e.g. political, ethical, ornamental, etc. One can do business without the use of expressive or visual skills, but it is often instrumental to its purpose. Kristensen (1994) argued for the use of terms like "durability", "simplicity", "user-friendliness", "sustainability" for design in the "knowledge society", which are akin to the virtues of the "crafts-based society". It is a matter of the metaphoric use of terms, because society, in particular with technology and global industrial competition, has changed. These changes, have facilitated a convergence between the market focus held by business and the user focus held by design, because the increase in flexible manufacturing makes "customised" or individual products possible within the economy.

To summarise, both design expertise and business expertise serve an extrinsic purpose; they complement each other, but their goals generally only partly overlap. The designer's conceptual and visual creativity are "typically" aimed at satisfying the individual need of a (single) user. Business expertise is directed towards business aims, entrepreneurship, managing the business and selecting investment opportunities, i.e. the goals are essentially concerned with market demand and production.

THE BUSINESS PROCESS

Business activity can be broken down into three distinct elements: *exploration*, *development*, and *implementation*. In practical projects the elements appear in genuine "concurrent" processes, where sometimes one is dominant and sometimes all three take place simultaneously. Each business element is linked to aspects of competence as shown in Table 10.2. The vertical axis represent tasks to be undertaken in the course of design projects. These tasks are not necessarily undertaken sequentially, but some tasks, e.g. exploration, typically come before development. The process is iterative and each step can be repeated as necessary until the final result is satisfactory. Each phase of the business activity is discussed with regard to design competence throughout the remainder of this chapter.

EXPLORATION

Need-finding connects the firm's core competencies (Prahalad and Hamel 1991) with new opportunities. Typical explorations are extensions of existing inventory of knowledge and these rarely lay the foundation for a whole new industry (Clark 1985, pp. 238–240) but result in regular or incremental

Table 10.2 The competence of design in the process

	Exploration	Development	Implementation
Design activity	Search and record	Studiowork/ Development	Practical problem solving
Business activity	Finding need Problem definition	Multiple drafts/ Modelling	Team dynamics/ Concurrent design
Expertise	Process of change	Concepts/ Visualisation	Diligence/ Communication
Outcome	Contextual hypotheses/Ideas/ Questions	User/Product concepts	Specifications on production/Marketing

innovations, just outside the scope of present business. The design activity concerned is searching and recording knowledge around present and similar technologies and user contacts. The purpose is to find and define a need for which a product concept is developed. The advantage of a designer is concerned with both knowledge of the users, the technology, and the conceptual and production process. The process of need-finding is closely related to understanding meaningful connections between the function and aesthetics of tangible objects and framing the conceptual foundation in view of the user's perspective (Clark 1985, p. 244). The process of innovation itself may be facilitated by changing the "ways of seeing" the world. Such framing effects (Tversky and Kahneman 1981, pp. 128–137) may influence the effective identification of options. This can happen, for example, by an overly risk-averse attitude, based on a conservative evaluation of present activities compared to alternatives. Focusing on the "bottom line" and already established successes may prevent new developments. An example is the Danish toy manufacturer LEGO. For LEGO the plastic building bricks meant a tremendous success. Despite this, the new direction in children's play and preferences for electronic games and "edutainment" took them by surprise. The way out of the dilemma has meant a complete change of management, new corporate identity and engagement in research in children's play and education. While LEGO has used design persistently during many years, the present situation has strengthened its use to yield new products.[4] Subsequent action has increased its potential and market position for the 21st century.

The foundation of a business is usually created by the conjunction of (technological) possibility and need. The purpose of exploration is to be aware of new opportunities and changing user needs and market demands to develop hypotheses of the nature of the context in which the business take place. The process may take a linear form, e.g. market research, in which hypotheses of consumer buying behaviour are developed and tested in order to assess market demand. The knowledge necessary in the early explorative phase concerns both present business and the way society changes and how this alters business. The advantage of design and business knowledge together is a synergy between sensitive awareness, as in the artist, combined with more analytical approaches by business educated/trained people.

The process may also be a non-linear one; a *hermeneutic* learning process (Winograd and Flores 1986, pp. 70–78); Piore et al 1994, pp. 6–8). Such a process is associated with pre-understanding of the current situation and adding knowledge by recognising patterns that yield new insights. Such knowledge is fallible and "breakdown" in relation to the design is an essential aspect of the learning process (Winograd and Flores 1986, pp. 69–71). Thus exploration is not restricted nor is it a delimited part of the process, but is integral to the whole design/business process. Breakdowns serve as new incentives for reiterating the need-finding and problem definition. With product function, we do not have to think about it – it is an extension of the body, but as soon as there is a problem in function, meaning (i.e. understanding the function) or the product's image as a social marker, we are aware of it and must reconsider how well it works. This is an opportunity for further design and development – to bring the product back in such a form that we can "forget" it again. It means that negative feedback and breakdowns are opportunities that we may not get otherwise. Norman (1992, p. 80) adds to the discussion by pointing out the necessity of balancing negative and positive feedback.

Having established a body of knowledge of need and solutions, the next step is to find linkages between the two. In some cases, need (or technology) is given but situations require exploration. More commonly, the process is iterative until an idea or preconception is reached. Such exploration can take various forms and desk research, computer research of databases and process of change research are typical, as well as studiowork. Experiments in laboratories, shops, market trials, consumer panel tests, are other examples of explorations.

Design may be of particular importance in the "fuzzy front-end" of the product-development process. An essential element of design is need finding. This is identification of the end-user problems and the linkage of these to business concerns. This operation is creative and based on intuitive non-linear thinking. It is a creative activity that itself cannot be represented by analytical models, although such models may be useful for collecting and selecting data and helping to structure a problem. The design process consists of non-linear thought processes and starts as an explorative process, not based on specific (or formal) models but rather as a recognition of patterns in the mind of an alert and sensitive person. The activities entail seeing images based on a mix of perceptions, memory and projections. Projections are both desirable and non-desirable states where both cognition and emotions support each other (Damasio 1994, pp. 98–100). Once variables and parameters have been identified, linear thinking can have a part to play, for example via marketing models and quantitative aspects of business decisions. Although sophisticated, such models only deal with making the best decisions given that they are already defined; not with how they are framed, how goals are set and how alternatives are developed.[5] Thus, the designer and the business person complement each other very well. The outcome is in the form of speculation, hypotheses and ideas that need further exploration and testing.

Linear models are useful in the later phases of simulation of configurations and verification of already identified attributes (Urban and Hauser 1993). However, in order to analyse a need, this must be identified in the first place and there is no account in the literature of technologies from marketing or engineering that helps in this early phase. The differences in linear and non-linear approaches form strengths where the two reinforce each other, typically, in a learning cycle. Non-linear operations introduce innovative thinking and linear approaches stress the rigid thinking and attention to constraints.

There are overlaps between design and other business functions, e.g. marketing for exploratory activities. Search activities can be undertaken by designers using the visual/intuitive methods (Agger 1993) referred to as design research, such as when a designer investigates present needs, environmental descriptions, competitors' products, new materials etc. systematically but without the use of formal models. Marketing people involved with marketing research or engineering research may be compiling very similar knowledge, but typically are aided by some kind of formal models (quantitative marketing research) or checklists. These types of knowledge can complement each other, but may also be part of an ongoing conflict between Marketing and Design. There are examples of barriers to or duplication of effort, e.g. where Marketing has compiled a great deal of knowledge about customers, but has not made that knowledge available to Design (Jevnaker 1996). There are various reasons for this. Sometimes the designers do not ask the right questions. Sometimes Marketing hides information, such as an aspect of the organisation's political contact – this may occur in particular where designers constitute a marginalised group (Leonard-Barton 1992).

The next operation is that of need verification, where preferences are mapped and trade-offs between different ideas and specifications are made and documented. This is typically an operations and marketing task. Ideally, the identification and verification of needs and their context should be explored by experts in various fields working together. However, little is known about how differences between various experts are perceived, and how the whole concept or image is created. There are, in the literature, rather few attempts to bring multiple forms of knowledge together in one framework, the exception being Barabba and Zaltman (1990).

DEVELOPMENT OF PRODUCT AND USER-CONCEPTS

The boundaries between analytical and synthetic activities are transparent. Need finding is not based solely on novelty: it is dependent on existing knowledge in the field, whereas development is essentially a synthetic activity, consisting of the conceptualisation of multiple solutions and further development to produce a physical entity. It is often required to develop multiple drafts or alternatives from which the one perceived as the "best" may be selected (see Kristensen, 1990). As design is involved, visualisation and perhaps physical models (Leonard-Barton 1991) serve as the object for selection. The outcome of development is a product/brand for the market, or a new corporate identify and/or image, and so on.

Concept formulation may concern a single product, or a whole business concept. The product which one has in mind must be represented by drawings, rough models, mock-ups and verbal descriptions. This is where designers have much to offer by virtue of their training. Designers spend a great deal of their time dealing with concept formulation. This may not be the task of a designer working alone; other members of a product development team may contribute ideas, insights, thought and expertise to this process. The sequence of multiple drafts is important in the development process for two reasons: it narrows down the number of solutions by elimination, and it expands the general knowledge about the product and the user.

Market positioning of the product is an important strategic operation. A product or communication concept is positioned against the target group's perception of cognitive space, whether this is concerned with the product's attributes or the broader range of the communication frame. It means placing the impression of the firm (image) and/or product (brand) in a favourable position in the mind of potential customers. The cognitive aspect of the operation is to make the potential customer aware that a solution to a problem exists, even when the customer may be unaware of the problem and may be receptive (or not) to the design. Here, graphic design serves as an important factor as it is concerned with communication of concepts and position. It means that market positioning is about persuasion and seduction. This is where the designer's expressive abilities are significant. Understanding cultural codes and people's emotions is often required and communicating visually is critical to the symbolic representation of the concept (Eco 1977, p. 59 ff).

The purpose of positioning is to influence the customers' preferences to lead them to purchase. Positioning in the customer's mind may be followed by a search for more information, trial of the product and subsequently a buying decision. The communication provided by the designer (and other communication specialists, notably advertisers) concerns all forms of advertising, displays, exhibitions, packaging and product design. Making the product appealing is one of the most persuasive acts, to ensure that financial commitment follows market positioning (Ghemawat 1991) and that customers are not attracted by alternatives whilst making their decision to purchase, or not. Design can contribute constructively to finding which values and norms can be used for an analytical and creative basis for customer choice.

The dimensions can be defined on the basis of the product concept; the idea or image of the product. It can be formulated physically, verbally, formally, symbolically, analogously or metaphorically. With innovations, conscious use of metaphors can bring about interesting results. Metaphors are about using language creatively by cross domain mapping (Lakoff and Johnson, 1980) thus reframing the semantic content and deliberately exploiting the ambiguity. Using a metaphor means relying not only on semantic ambiguities, but also the emotional tensions that are created. An advertising campaign may evoke nostalgia, with scenes from the past as a background for positioning of new products. A product concept may revolve around "polite self service". For example, Wittenborg Vending Machines tries to evoke the safe, polite, nicely dressed image of the good servant, while in reality they are selling a machine that dispenses tea, coffee and similar beverages. The advantages are that it creates a strong, creative, emotional, easily communicable image that is not easy to forget.

IMPLEMENTATION

Implementation is about getting things done in practice. It is usually concerned with specialisation and co-ordination (Piore et al 1991). The "linear approach" assumes that the division of tasks can be completely and non-problematically co-ordinated and reintegrated in the process. Much evidence (Piore et al 1991; Hein and Myrup Andreason 1985) contradicts this. Following Piore et al we rather assume that the linear approach only partially accommodates the need for division and coordination and reiteration and feedback cannot be avoided. It means that a combination of the linear and the non-linear approach is necessary. Human resources emphasises how people and teams of people co-ordinate their work. From the perspective of "slack resources" (Cyert and March 1963) the concern is how resources can be transformed into productive work and not wasted effort.

Various methods facilitate the organisation of human resources in accordance with the firm's goals. The simplest way of controlling resources is by direct observation. This can be achieved in small firms where the owner/ manager participates in daily operations. In larger firms where there are hierarchies, managers can observe a few people under their remit. Although "three wave" companies have looser and less hierarchical forms, the principles of control are similar. There are obvious shortcomings to direct supervision. One is that this is not feasible at all times and that it is not always possible to identify the contribution of each individual. Conceptually, the control of resources and management of projects is achieved by models like concurrent design, integrated product development, project management methods, etc. The concept of such models is the sequential and simultaneous performance of a task, according to their interrelations. Some tasks must be performed sequentially, but others may be carried out simultaneously, in order to reduce lead time. Such project management tools integrate teamwork at a conceptual level. But in addition, other incentives may be required to integrate and manage the process. One way is the use of organisational culture; its values, norms, myths, metaphors, etc. Indeed, the term "corporate identity" embraces the deliberate and purposeful activity of uniting the firm's identity in an overall programme. Such an identity programme may consist of mission statements, uniforms, graphic design, with all the visual forms generating a coherent, symbolic structure. Corporate identity thus serves the function of integration of the organisation internally and conveys the essence of its corporate personality externally. It reflects and reinforces the organisation's norms and values and has a role to play in the control of norms, so that such values are internalised and become a part of the individual's personality and morale. One begins to "police" oneself. In this situation, a means has been found for the (partial) loosening of control of the individual employee's work, when neither direct observation nor measurement is possible. Philip Selznick (Selznick 1957, cpt 3) refers to this process as "infusion", that is the process whereby the organisation's values and norms are institutionalised by, for example, ideologies, elites and interest groups within the organisation.

Corporate identity programmes can be regarded as deliberate manipulations of organisational culture. In this, design provides the expressive aspects of the corporation, underlining the corporate strategy by providing symbols and visual cues. Design is intended to create coherence and credibility, integration and unification (Olins 1986).

Design's contribution to the appropriability of resources is basically through visible symbols, enhancement of the credibility and attractiveness of the firm's products and/or brands. Brands with a simple but strong visual appeal (product and graphic), are likely to attain higher awareness and customer loyalty than others. If one ensures the loyalty of the customers through a preferred product, brand or design, this indirectly gives a strategic advantage over the competitors.

PUTTING THE BUSINESS PROCESS TOGETHER

In sum, the business of design consists of exploration, development and implementation. It is the process by which the firm's core competencies

(Prahalad and Hamel 1991) connect with new opportunities. The purpose of exploration is to search and record in order to develop hypotheses of the nature of the context in which the business take place. The process may take a linear form, e.g. marketing research, in which hypotheses of consumer buying behaviour are developed and tested in order to assess market demand. The process may also be a non-linear one: i.e. a *hermeneutic learning process*. Such a process is associated with a pre-understanding of the current situation and adding knowledge by recognising patterns that yield new insights. Knowledge is fallible and "breakdown" in relation to the design is an essential aspect of the learning process. Actually, breakdown is a requirement in order to see problems and new needs. The organisation selects projects by various methods. Formal criteria and screening are used by some firms, but the most important aspect of selection is embedded in the organisation's structure. A product or communication concept is positioned against the target group's perception of cognitive space. Implementation of solution is concerned with co-ordination and control of the process. This is a management task, but design also contributes by its use of visual aids for corporate visual identity. Business provides the means of project management, but clever use of identity programmes may serve as "constitutions". They are means of controlling norms by appealing to people's emotions and feelings. Corporate identity programmes can be regarded as deliberate manipulations of organisational culture. In this, design services underpin the expressive aspects of the corporation, underlining the corporate strategy by providing symbols and visual cues (Olins 1986).

So far, this chapter has been concerned with tools for business and design – something that people can use to achieve business goals by deliberate actions. But one of the most important attributes of the business of design is the systemic, hidden and embedded characteristics of the firm's core competencies that may let design give the firm a sustainable competitive position (Jevnaker, see Chapter 1).

DESIGN COMPETENT FIRMS

Typically, design is often represented by a professional designer, but even though it may not always be a professional designer at work, design can be present in the organisation as a competence (Leonard-Barton 1992). It can be present in the form of values, norms and routines in the company (Selznick 1957). The values, norms and routines reveal themselves in the form of the company's artefacts. These are the visualisations of the firm itself or its products and communication. Typically, design competent firms have a

---

Braun's 10 Principles of Good Design

1. Good design is innovative
2. Good design enhances the usefulness of a product
3. Good design is aesthetic
4. Good design displays the logical structure of a product; its form follows its function
5. Good design is unobtrusive
6. Good design is honest
7. Good design is enduring
8. Good design is consistent right down to details
9. Good design is ecologically conscious
10. Good design is minimal design

Figure 10.1   Braun's mission statement

consistent and coherent programme for their corporate identity, communication, branding (where relevant) and products. An example is Braun, the German producer of audio, electric household appliances, personal hygiene etc. Braun has a long tradition and reputation for being design oriented and competent, and design is represented at the highest management level. Dieter Rams was Braun's chief designer for many years, reporting directly to the chairman of the company. He has a background from the Ulm school of design[6] and many of Braun's classic designs were made in cooperation with the Ulm design school (see Dormer 1993; Rams 1996). Braun has a mission statement that focuses on design and which is deep-rooted in the firm's core values and corporate communication. This is stated in Figure 10.1.

Such formulae may sound like advertising slogans (Rams 1996), but if they are embedded in the firm's routines and judgements, they then form an integral part of the core of the firm's values, routines and procedures. According to Leonard-Barton (1992, pp. 11–12) competencies are considered "core" if they differentiate a company strategically. That is, if the competencies are concerned with specific diversification strategies, yield absolute cost advantages, serve particular rich markets and in so doing lead to sustainable competitive advantage. These are all characteristics of Braun.

Being design competent does not necessarily imply that professional designers are at work all the time, but that a design competent firm has established work relations with one or more designers. Braun is characterised by having a large in-house design department; however, not all design competent firms have such a facility e.g. in some large furniture firms. (See Chapter 2 for discussion of in-house and out-sourced design studies.)

It has been estimated that 70% of all design is "silent design", that is not undertaken by a *professional* designer (Gorb and Dumas 1987). In other cases third parties may be involved, e.g. advertising which in many cases works closely with design. The boundaries between design and advertising are transparent, which means a complicated division of labour and potential conflicts. Another boundary line exists between industrial designers and product engineering. Here also, the collaboration may be of mutual benefit or conflict.

Design competent firms are characterised by the embeddedness of design expertise, and design norms are an integrated part of all decisions. In doing so, they form part of the firm's culture, i.e. they become institutionalised. Design management competence is the competence to make judgements; about the selection of professional designers, briefing them, taking suggestions and proposals made by professionals and making decisions about such proposals. Such communication is expressed in a "design-brief" (Walsh et al 1991 and 1981) which is a tool for describing the task in the form of a contract with expected results, resources, budget, schedule, etc. (Walsh et al 1991). Often the design brief is verbal. Even this, together with the fact that design artefacts often have symbolic and emotional qualities, visual and tactile elements, the brief is a vehicle of tacit knowledge. If the parties understand each other well, then discussion of the brief serves to stimulate ideas and imagination. However, when problems occur with the design outcome, then conflicts can be problematic, since conflict resolution (e.g. litigation) requires complete descriptions of the relevant knowledge. Obviously, the meaning of a verbal design-brief may be problematic, particularly when the design and client parties shaping the brief disagree.

The term "design-oriented" means that the firm's core values are infused by design ideas and design is institutionalised into the firm's strategic orientations. A *design-oriented firm* has a top level manager responsible for design. If not, design projects may be vulnerable and prone to failure. When new ventures are planned, the person responsible engages in formulation and planning of projects, very much as a meta-routine (Nelson and Winter 1982). Whether that person is a designer is not important because in most circumstances professional designers will be contracted to undertake specific assignments. Then design competence also means being able to select, work with and "cultivate" relations with design suppliers that are effective for the particular firm.

The electronics company Philips leads the field in many of its products, but most of their advanced products serve an industrial purpose and are designed mostly by engineers. In these products industrial designers work on re-interfaces, design of cabinets etc. Philips' consumer products design, its corporate communication, is led by a vice-president who has industrial design as primary responsibility and who is a designer. Philips former design manager, Robert Blaich, explains that design is a core competence – after technology, but more important than other competencies such as marketing and service (Blaich and Blaich 1993, p. 93). Evidence of this is the use of design for getting a foothold in the upper end of the market for kitchen products. While most Philips products are rather discrete products, the Philips–Alessi line represents a complete new orientation. The product line was established by Blaich's successor, Stephano Marzano, an Italian with long-standing personal contacts with Alessi. The alliance led to completely new product design, pricing, distribution and market focus. The experiment was a great success, but one should ask what would happen if it had not been so? The result could have been a vicious circle with design reducing its influence relative to other competencies. In the present case, the new product design necessarily puts design in a highly visible position where its success is transparent. The new products are not technologically superior. They are marketed in much the same way as other products, although through other channels than the main line Philips products.

A *non-design-oriented firm* is one where the boundaries do not reveal such qualities as coherent signals, a portfolio of products that are well designed, user-friendly, functional etc. But a firm may well have a sustainable competitive position without ever dealing with design. Other "isolating mechanisms" (Rumelt 1987) may serve the same purpose, e.g. soliciting a "monopolistic" practice. This is advanced by real monopoly status, by effective patent protection, by trade secrets, lead-times etc. In such a firm, there may be a drive to enter into design for other reasons, e.g. aesthetic qualities, customer satisfaction or corporate communication.

HOW DESIGN CAN CONTRIBUTE TO SUSTAINABLE COMPETITIVE ADVANTAGE

Design is a competence which at least is partly traded in the market. Design consultants offer their skills for a fee, which is typically below that of management consultants.[7] Quality of competence and service varies and can lead to different expectations about what design can achieve in particular cases (Barney 1986, p. 1233). The combination of a firm "placing its bet" on design and on a particular designer may account for idiosyncratic insights or even "luck", thus creating a unique combination of resources for a strategy to be built (Barney 1986, p. 1236). If a more integrated/personal relationship between designer and client is found which is perceived to be prospectively long term, then competitive advantage in the long run may be achieved by establishing a design-based competence (Jevnaker 1996).

The accumulation of the knowledge of design is a different matter. Raymond Loewy was working with Coca-Cola in a period with only incremental changes in the design for a very long period.[8] An anecdote notes that Loewy was asked why Coca-Cola paid him so much, whilst his designs changed so little. Loewy responded: "that's why". Creating and sustaining a strong identity may mean *not* changing it, when persistence over a long period is the best strategy. In this way, long-term engagements can give sustained competitive advantage, if the designer and the firm understand the particular context in which they are working. Designs sometimes are a result of a long-term relationship between designer and consultant and so involve time compression diseconomies (Dierickx and Cool 1989, p. 150). Engagements can last for maybe 20–30 years in which both parties accumulate a considerable stock of knowledge about each other's idiosyncrasies. It may not matter that the firm in question has a high turnover of executives, if the designer has multiple connections with the functions of the firm, its customers and suppliers. (See Jevnaker in Chapter 5 for an example of Peter Opsvik's relation to Norwegian producers.)

In these cases, design competence may become endemic to the operations that are performed and development occurs. A routine that implies better understanding of consumer needs, of effective cross-functional co-ordination might happen – even as a coincidence. Since design is not completely articulated or codified, the knowledge can be kept in-house for a long period. Experiences from large companies, for example, Philips, Corning Glass, 3M and Sony, all point in this direction, particularly when the group of designers consists of a combination of in-house staff with high reputation and external designers who constantly bring new inspiration for the technological and manufactured solutions, on the one hand, and consumer taste and problems on the other. These examples indicate that design at a high level reinforces effective communication between engineering and marketing because design is a composite of visual symbolic, emotional, olfactory and tactile knowledge. Thus it facilitates cross-functional communication in a way that would not be easily transferred by formal networks alone. For the same reasons, these communication links may be idiosyncratic to the firm, and even designers (or other professionals) can have problems transferring their part of the total knowledge to other firms who may offer them a new job. Their knowledge is a form of tacit knowledge that has been generated in the firm and cannot be duplicated easily.

To a large degree the long-term perspective is concerned with organisational culture (Barney 1986b, p. 660). Often, design is indistinguishable from organisational culture – especially those dimensions that concern the firm's identity and image – as the knowledge is partly skills-based and tacit (Reed and DeFillippi 1990, p. 93) and partly because it is infused into the firm's norms and values (Mintzberg and Dumas 1990).

Design serves as a linkage between other functions, for example, Marketing, R&D and Production. When successful, it can catalyse imagination and motivation, thereby increasing the value of other assets, e.g. marketing and production. This catalysing function is complex and ambiguous and may not be susceptible to imitation.

Design affects the operations of the firm in many ways. It influences the way products are produced and marketed daily. The production process is independent on the quality criteria set by design, for example in the furniture industry. Toolmakers, cabinet makers, production engineers collectively draw up the manufacturing plan. Quality standards affect directly which processes are used, which machines will be applied, how machinery is adjusted, the measurement tolerances for details, etc. Much of this is routine work and much of it depends on the craft-based skills of the work. Even when craft work essentially is reduced to the management of machines, the skills and expertise that enter into the process comes from negotiations between those involved, including the designers. The American furniture maker Herman Miller wanted to produce a chair by the Danish designer Paul Kærholm. The chair was produced in Denmark, but transportation costs prevented importation, so Herman Miller wanted to produce on license. In the planning process they found that satisfying the quality standards set by the designer Paul Kærholm meant that the production costs were higher than in Denmark, where collaboration between Kærholm and Fritz Hansen, a Danish manufacturer, had been going on for years.[9] The chair could not be sold at a competitive price and it was decided that the chair should not be produced in the US.

Linkages come from long-term personal relations that bring marketing, sales and production closer, particularly in the early phases of product development that are concerned with creating product and user concepts. The process entails a continual "to'ing and fro'ing" between product functionality and user needs (Hauser and Clausing 1990). But contrary to the somewhat static image given by Hauser and Clausing, it is a matter of many interactions until a concept is created. In addition, the concept is holistic, so there is another "shuttle" between the whole (*gestalt*) and constituent parts. In this process, long-term engagement of the industrial design enables Production to accommodate user needs and enhances Marketing's understanding of production and product technologies.

Design has also been subject to "agglomeration effects" and design movements. The Bauhaus School (1919–1933), Danish design in its peak period between the 1930s and 1950s, Italian design (Memphis School) around Milan in the 1980s, and Catalonian design today are all examples of this. Some leading performers in the field were able to set the standards, attract talent and make good connections with their clients. It has been regarded as surprising that the Danish furniture makers who benefited from the Danish design "movement" were not enamoured when some of the subsequently famous designers presented their work for the first time. This pressed the designers to improve their designs and perceptions of the market for their products. In a number of anecdotes, the designers had to find the customers for their end products, which must have implied thorough knowledge of their clients' (the manufacturers/retailers) customers.

One may postulate that there exists a relationship between sustainable competitive advantage and degree of integration of design in the firm. The use of pure "in-house" design should account for the strongest degree of embeddedness of design knowledge and may therefore (all else being constant) give the best protection for the firm's competitive position. It should be so because in-house means creating the best conditions for mixing design with other functions, letting design enter into the deeper structure of the routines (culture) and it is the best way of avoiding imitators' insights. Such insights are prevented because of complexity and ambiguity. This is a long-term strategy, but is certainly not the only one available. A study of design consultants in the UK, Denmark and Sweden (Bruce et al 1996) reveals that in-house design is rapidly declining as a *modus operandi*. The use of designers at an arm's-length basis, as more typically found in the UK, may actually serve the same purpose, as long as the firms have the necessary competence as regards routines in the firm, regardless of which designer is actually operating at a particular time. The use of serial contracts may facilitate "a need to know" basis where no single design consultant gets to know more about the firm's routines than is required for a particular assignment. Such a way of dealing with design contradicts some of the maxims of good design; e.g. long-term commitments and personal trust as a major building block for a design–client alliance. Another possibility is spatial definition, such as proximity to the firm's core operations, deciding whether designers are in-house or contracted. A question would be whether long-time profitable firms use in-house design but contract external designers for smaller tasks. In such a situation, one of the primary tasks of the design manager would be to decide the design strategy, what could be contracted and how the bits of the puzzle should be cut and reassembled. Such a view would be consistent with protecting the core business/core know-how, but contracting the co-specialised and complementary assets such as distribution and packaging, depending on the specific requirements. There seems to be no simple strategy that serves both the purposes of creative novelty and a protection at the same time. There is a trade-off concerning which parts to protect as core and which parts to contract out of the firm.

CONCLUSION

This chapter has been concerned with the business of design. It has dealt with various facets of designers' individual expertise and how that expertise links up with the expertise of business people. It has also described how design and business expertise mix in the process of exploration, development and implementation of projects. In order to understand how design may serve as a means of realising sustainable competitive advantage, the systemic, tacit and embedded knowledge of design may be placed in the firm.

The claim is that only when design is ambiguous, systemic, and hidden from imitators, may it serve as a means for sustainable competitive advantage. But this is problematic. Design is about the visible side of business and just as the process leading to a product may be unclear, so also the competency that creates visible artefacts may be hidden.

If design remains within the penumbra of the articulate/tacit, intuitive/formal domain, constantly transforming the process of change into novelty and innovations, both in products, communication and other artefacts, then it may well continue to form a basis for firms' attempts to achieve sustained competitive advantage. However, if, on the other hand, design becomes a formula to produce "ready-made solutions", its contributions to sustainable competitive advantage will decrease. Managers in design-oriented firms may talk easily about their design decisions, but the organisation and communication of design is a complex issue. Design is not yet well understood and, in a business setting, it appears exotic, artistic and intangible.

Further research will provide an enhanced conceptual understanding of its nature and provide empirical support for the theoretical arguments and postulations discussed here.

NOTES

1. I am indebted to Sara Little Turnbull for sharing her knowledge and views with me. While I have benefited immensely from that, Sara is totally without any responsibility for the errors and shortcomings of the article. Margaret Bruce undertook the tedious work of detailed comments and suggestions for the present publication. I also wish to thank Dave Smith, Geir Gripsrud and Kjell Grønhaug for their valuable comments.
2. "Expertise" refers to the knowledge possessed by highly qualified individuals and "competence" refers to knowledge embedded in the company organisation. But the use of competence and expertise are used interchangeably.
3. That is a major theme in many books on modern product development (Wheelwright and Clark 1992, 158 ff).
4. Presentation at design conference in Louisiana Museum, April 1996.
5. National Academy of Science quoted by Barabba and Zaltman 1990, p. 47.
6. Some regard the Ulm School as a successor of the Bauhaus School (1919–1933) because of its focus on durability, timelessness, simplicity, etc. The ideological underpinning of this school was simple forms, the idea that beauty was an outcome of functionality and a responsible view towards the customer. The "mechanistic-metaphor" served as a guidepost for almost all design, whether architecture, product design or art (Heskett 1980, pp. 85–103). The Bauhaus school was put down by the Nazis in 1933 (Westphal 1991). It was in a way recreated as the Ulm school in 1946 as the *Hochschule für Gestaltung*. Here, Rams was among the first students. Dieter Rams and Hans Gugelot's radios, record-players and shaving machines from the 1950s all count as major contributions to design. The two were working on a scientific method for design (Dormer 1993, p. 17). Among the early contributions, subsequently followed by others, was miniaturisation, e.g. the slimming down of radio-cabinets, which was made possible by the introduction of semi-conductors.
7. Bruce, M. et al (1996). Report on Design Consultants in the UK, Denmark and Sweden.
8. Some of these changes were so miniscule that they are hardly a matter of design, rather of smart marketing and styling (see Heskett 1980).
9. I owe this example to Robert Blaich (personal communication).

REFERENCES

Agger, S. (1992). *Kompendium i Skitsering og Programmering for design og arkitektur*, Bygningsteknisk Studiearkiv.
Akerlof, G. (1970). The Market for Lemons: Quality Uncertainty and the Market Mechanism, *Quarterly Journal of Economics*, (84) 488–500.
Alexander, C. (1964). *Notes on the Synthesis of Form*, Harvard University Press, Cambridge, MA, (13th edition 1994).
Alchian, A. and Demsetz, H. (1972). Production, Information Costs and Economic Organization, *American Economic Review*, (62), 777–795.
Barabba, V. P. and Zaltman, G. (1990). *Hearing the Voice of the Market: Competitive Advantage through Creative Use of Market Information*, Harvard Business School Press.

Barney, J.B. (1986). Strategic Factor Markets: Expectations, Luck and Business Strategy, *Management Science*, (32), 1231–1241.

Barney, J.B. (1986b). Organizational Culture: Can It Be A Source of Sustained Competitive Advantage?, *Academy of Management Review*, (11), 656–665.

Brennan, G. and Buchanan, J. (1985). *The Reason of Rules Constitutional Political Economy*, Cambridge University Press, Cambridge.

Berg, P.O. and Kreiner, K. (1990). Corporate Architecture: Turning Physical Settings into Symbolic Resources, in Gagliardi (ed.) (1990). *Symbol and Organisation: Views on the corporate landscape*, DeGruyter, New York.

Blaich, R. and Blaich, J. (1993). *Product Design and Corporate Strategy*, McGraw-Hill, New York.

Bruce, M. et al (1996). Report on Design Consultants in the UK, Denmark and Sweden.

Bruce, M. and Roy, R. (1991). Integrating Marketing and Design for Commercial Benefit, *Marketing Intelligence and Planning*, **9**(5).

Clark, A. (1997). *Being There Putting Brain, Body, and the World Together Again*. MIT Press, Cambridge, MA.

Clark, K. and Fujimata, T. (1992). *Product Development and Performance*, Harvard University Press.

Collingwood, C. (1938). *A Theory of Art*, OUP, Oxford.

Collins, J.C. and Porras, J.I. (1994). *Built to Last*, Random House, London.

Cyert, R.M. and March, J.G. (1963). *A Behavioural Theory of the Firm*, Prentice-Hall, Englewood Cliffs, N.J.

Damasio, A. (1994). *Descartes Error Emotion, Reason and the Human Brain*, version Papermac, London 1996.

Dierickx, M. and Cool, C. (1986). Causal Ambiguity and Uncertain Imitability, *Management Science*, (32), 867–882.

Dierickx, M. and Cool, C. (1989). Asset Stock Accumulation and Sustainability of Competitive Advantage, *Management Science*, **35**(12), December, 1504–1513.

Dormer, P. (1993). *Design After 1995*, Thames and Hudson, London.

Eco, U. (1976). *A Theory of Semiotics*, Indiana University Press, Indiana.

Ghemawat, P. (1991). *Commitment: The Dynamics of Strategy*, Free Press, N.Y.

Gorb, P. and Dumas, A. (1987). Silent Design, *Design Studies*, **8**(3).

Hauser, J. and Clausing, D. (1992). House of Quality, *Harvard Business Review*, March–April.

Hayes, R. and Wheelwright, S. (1987). *Manufacturing*, The Free Press, N.Y.

Hein, L. and Myrup Andreasen, M. (1985). *Integneret Produktudvikling*, Copenhagen.

Herbert, S. (1976). *Sciences of the Artificial*, 2nd edition, MIT Press, Cambridge, MA.

Heskett, J. (1980). *Industrial Design*, Thames and Hudson.

Holt, K. (1972). *Product Innovation Management*, 3rd edn 1988, Butterworth-Heinemann, Oxford.

Holt, K. (1989). Does the Engineer Forget the User?, *Design Studies*, **10**(3).

Jevnaker, B. (1996). *Industrial Design as Creative Competitive Factor* (in Norwegian), SNP report 54/96.

Jones, C. (1970). *Design Methods*, John Wiley, Chichester.

Krippendorf, K. (1991). Imaging, Computing and Designing Minds, *Design Management Journal*, (2), Winter.

Krippendorf, K. and Butter, R. (1993). Where the Meanings Escape Function, *Design Management Journal*, (Summer), 27–30.

Kristensen, T. (1990a). Organisering af produktudvikling under usikkerhed i Davis, L. et al (eds) (1990), *Økonomisk Organisering*, Samfundslitteratur København.

Kristensen, T. (1990b. Global Decision Making and Narrow Strategy Windows, *Design Management Journal*, (1), Winter.

Kristensen, T. (1992). User-Interfaces and Metaphor: An Essay on Design Management, in Geschka, G. and Hübner, H. (eds) *Theories of Innovation*, Elsevier, Amsterdam.

Kristensen, T. (1994). The Virtues of Crafts: A Key to a Rejuvenation of Scandinavian Design? *Scandinavian Journal of Design History*, (4), 7–14.

Lakoff, G. and Johnson, M. (1980). *Metaphors We Live By*, Chicago University Press, Chicago.

Landis, G.H. (1984). The Micro Foundations of Competitive Strategy, *INSEAD*, Fontainbleu, France.

Leonard-Barton, D. (1991). Inanimate Integrators: A Block of Wood Speaks, *Design Management Journal*, (2), 61–67.

Leonard-Barton, D. (1992). Core Capabilities and Core Rigidities: A Paradox in Managing New Product Development, *Strategic Management Review*, (13), 111–135.

McGrath, M.E., Antony, M.T. and Shapiro, A.R. (1992). *Product Development Success Through Product and Cycle-Time Excellence*. Ballinger, Boston.

Miller, G.J. (1990). Managerial Dilemmas: Political Leadership in Hierarchies, in Cook, K.S. and Levi, M. (eds), *Limits of Rationality*, Oxford University Press, Oxford.

Mintzberg, H. and Dumas, A. (1989). Designing Design Management, *Design Management Journal*, **1**(1).

Nelson, R. and Winter, S. (1982). *An Evolutionary Theory of Economic Change*, Belknap Press, Cambridge, MA.

Norman, D. (1987). *Psychology of Everyday Things*, Addison-Wesley, Reading, MA.

Olins, W. (1989). *Corporate Identity*, Thames and Hudson.

Polenyi, M. (1958). *Personal Knowledge – Towards a Post Critical Philosophy*, London.

Rams, D. (1996). *Less But Better: Weriger Aba Besser*, Joklatt Design and Design Verlag, Hamberg.

Piore, M. et al (1994). Product Innovation, *Research Policy*.

Reed, R. and DeFillippi, R. (1990). Causal Ambiguity, Barriers to Imitation and Sustainable Competitive Advantage, *Academy of Management Review*, (15), 88–102.

Rumelt, R. (1987). Theory, Strategy and Entrepreneurship, in Teece, D. (ed.) (1986). *The Competitive Challenge*, Ballinger Publishing Company, Cambridge, MA.

Selznick, P. (1957). *Leadership in Administration*, John Wiley & Sons, New York.

Steadman, P. (1979). *The Evolution of Designs*, Cambridge University Press, Cambridge.

Svengren, L. (1995). *Industriell Design – En Strategisk Resurs*, PhD Dissertation, Lund.

Teece, D. (1987). Profiting from Technological Innovation: Implications for Integration, Collaboration, Licensing, and Public Policy, In Teece, D. (ed.). *The Competitive Challenge: Strategies for Industrial Innovation and Renewal*, Ballinger Publishing Company, Cambridge, MA.

Teece, D. (1990). Contributions and Impediments of Economic Analysis to the Study of Strategic Management, in Frederickson, J.W. (ed.), *Perspectives on Strategic Management*, Free Press, New York.

Tversky, A. and Kahneman, D. (1981). The Framing of Decisions and the Psychology of Choice, *Science*, (211), 453–458.

Urban, F. and Hauser, J. (1993). *Design and Marketing of New Products*, 2nd edition, Prentice-Hall, Englewood Cliffs, New Jersey.

Von Hippel, E. (1988). *Sources of Innovation*, Cambridge University Press, Cambridge.

Wallheim, R. (1978). *Art and Its Problems*, 2nd edn, Cambridge University Press, Cambridge.

Walsh, V. (1991). *Design, Innovation and the Boundaries of the Firm: Implications for Management*, paper presented at the Colloquium on Management of Technology, Berkeley, May.

Walsh, V. et al (1991). *Winning by Design*, Blackwells, Oxford.

Watson, T. Jr (1990). *Father and Son, Inc.*, Bantam, New York.

Westphal, V. (1991). *The Bauhaus*, Gallery Books, New York.

Wheelwright, S. and Clark, K. (1992). *Revolutionizing Product Development Quantum Leaps in Speed, Efficiency and quality*, Free Press, New York.

Wildhagen, F. (1991). *Technologica e Internazionalizzione come Aspetta della Storia del Design*, Politecnico di Milano, 15–16 April.

Winograd, T. and Flores, F. (1986). *Understanding Computers and Cognition*, Ablex Publishing Corporation, Norwood, N.J.

CHAPTER ELEVEN

CHALLENGE OF DESIGN RELATIONSHIPS: THE CONVERGING PARADIGM

Brigitte Borja de Mozota

INTRODUCTION

Design is a necessary aspect of business, offering a source of creative inspiration for product innovation as well as corporate communications. However, design expertise is not always effectively managed and integrated into business processes. Research in the area of design management has focused on the economic contribution of design (Walsh et al 1992) and the interface between design and marketing and production activities. This research has not addressed a number of issues that are of fundamental importance for, on the one hand, understanding the barriers to design and management integration and on the other, the opportunities that may arise by doing so. This chapter identifies the cognitive structures that design managers consider often to separate them, and then explores ways of building bridges between these. Distinctions are made between "design" organisations that are treated as revolutionary in their approach to the integration of design thinking throughout their systems, whereas "evolutionary" organisations treat design as "bolted" on to their existing practices.

Management of Design Alliances. Edited by M. Bruce and B. H. Jevnaker.
© 1998 John Wiley & Sons Ltd.

DESIGN AND THE VALUE CHAIN CONCEPT

A frequently cited tool for strategic analysis – or for analysing the different operations involved in an organisation – is the concept of Porter's (1985) *Value Chain*. Porter distinguishes between two types of value-creating functions in an organisation:

1. *Basic activities*: internal logistics, production, external logistics, sales and distribution, services; and
2. *Support functions*: governance and administrative infrastructure, human resources management, technological development.

What is missing in this conceptualisation is the integration of design, both as a value-creating basic activity and as a potentially strategic resource in need of governance and co-ordination. Yet is it not difficult to relate design to this strategy model and to this emphasis on value-creating activities as a foundation for corporate performance. For an organisation to build a sustainable *competitive advantage* using the architecture of the value chain. three possible directions for differentiation exist:

1. *The optimisation of elementary functions*: analysing each basic activity in term of its contribution to building a competitive advantage and choosing one or two functions that will be recognised as strategic.
2. *Interfunctional co-ordination*: competitive advantage is provided by improving the co-ordination within the value chain, that is concentrating on the links between functions. This may imply a reorganisation of the management style and company structure.
3. *External co-ordination*: the value chain of any organisation cannot be isolated from its context, but is linked with the various value chains of all the organisations involved in the activity. Competitive advantage is built by better co-ordination with suppliers, sub-contractors and distributors.

The value chain concept may provide a framework for explaining how design creates value within an organisation. Design management requires various competencies that are value creating at three different levels:

1. *Operational Design Management – managing a design project*: Select and programme design resources in the organisation's basic activities.
2. *Functional Design Management – managing the design function*: Integrate the design expertise into all management processes such as production, innovation communications, strategy, human resources and so "infuse" design in the support functions of the organisation.

Table II.I How design creates values

Level I – Design action	Level 2 – Design function	Level 3 – Design vision
Design as an economic competence	Design as a management competence	Design as a psychological competence
VALUE	VALUE	VALUE
to principal activities Marketing, Production Corporate Communications	to support activities organisation structure Technological Development Human Resources purchasing	to understanding the organisation environment Prospective and History Time Management

3. *Strategic Design Management – managing the design vision*: Integrate and control the coherence of design methods and decisions with the company's mission and strategy.

These three levels of design management can be regarded as akin to the "value chain", as shown in Table 11.1. From this illustration we also see that essential aspects of design management are related to the governance and weaving together across principal or basic activities. From the previous empirical chapters of this book, it emerges that this weaving across internal functions and organisational borders may be difficult, yet possible (see Part II of this book).

evolutionary_____ revolutionary

Integrating design within business processes entails an evolution of the role of design management from an economic perspective to a managerial approach. In other words, a shift from design valued as a *tool*, to design valued as a *process* for creating customer value and competitive advantage. This shift from an evolutionary to a revolutionary organisation entails the convergence of design cognitive structure with managerial cognitive structure, discussed later in the chapter. Each of the three levels of design action, design function and design vision are explained in the following sections.

DESIGN ACTION

At this level, design is acknowledged as having economic value. The demand for design competence is driven by such economic trends as:

■ The significance of *quality versus price*. Design was a source of differentiation because of its proven impact on quality, service, product performance, technology and innovation.

■ *The globalisation of branding*, the 'dictatorship' of market positioning and segmentation. Design for consumer goods became the driving force of the design profession in the 1980s, leading to design consultancies specialising, for example, in zinc packaging design.

■ *The multiplication of management alliances and strategic changes* stimulated a demand for corporate graphic design in order to create new corporate identities that merge organisational cultures and help the assimilation of the different partners to the alliance.

■ The growth of *services industries* – banks and insurance companies, leisure, tourism and distribution. Nowhere is the design slogan "make our strategy visible" more significant than for these economic sectors where services have to be given a tangible form and differentiated.

■ *The new consumer's needs and desires.* Consumers tend not to buy products but rather a "life experience" or *des lieux de lien* (Cova 1995). Mitchell (1993) argues that the design process is moving away from a producer orientation to a consumer orientation, that is with a concern to build in an emotional appeal.

■ *The latest consumption mode of the nineties* – directed towards a consumption of "reassurance" (Rochefort 1995), or needs for assurance against societal harm has developed a demand for social and philosophical design, more in tune with its humanist side, such as design for a sustainable economy, ecology and "green design", "transgenerational design" or "design for all". A new design consciousness for an "ecology of the artificial environment" (Manzini 1991) is emerging.

DESIGN FUNCTION

An economic approach to design management tends to consider design from the "outisde", evaluating the quality of forms created by designers by their impact on sales, profit, image and market share for the organisation.

By contrast, the managerial approach to design management tends to understand design from the "inside" (Borja de Mozota 1995). It starts from the design process, analyses the reasons for the difficulties of design integration and considers the management problems that design can resolve.

The demand for this approach to design is driven by new management concepts. The organisation understands that design constitutes a new knowledge – a specific "know-how" in idea and concept generation, in creativity and analysis methods, in innovation and project management, that may create a distinctive competence and a competitive advantage. In other words this level is concerned with connecting the value of the design process with the support activities and processes of organisations and is concerned with design potential for improving R&D management, organisational structure and interfunctional communications (Design Management Institute 1995). The demand for design competence is driven by managerial trends such as:

■ *Communications in product development*: In the management of product development, a central issue is the linking of knowledge and information held in different departments and functions (Clark and Fujimoto 1991). The visual language of design can help to improve communication and interfunctional co-ordination in product development (Leonard-Barton 1995).
■ *Market/Customer orientation*: The "new management" model of horizontal, flat structures with a focus on consumer needs. Design is by essence a customer-oriented profession that can help to foster this new management approach.
■ *Total Quality Management* (TQM): most organisations have developed a system of total quality management, which embraces products, processes, policies, services, programmes and human resources. TQM focuses mainly on tangible and measurable aspects of customer value. Design fits naturally with a TQM perspective, but goes beyond this since it focuses on quality perceived and measured.

The above trends may be closely related to design management, although these connections are often not drawn, in practice, by managers and staff unfamiliar with design. Furthermore, effective design management is about vision, conceptual and systemic thinking, and creativity whose objective is satisfying users' latent needs or desires.

Design management is concerned to foster, integrate and govern design in the organisation and reflect this systemic and process-oriented management thinking.

DESIGN VISION

Table 11.2 illustrates the change in design management that has occurred, and arguably should occur to bring about the design vision. This entails a conscious integrative process whereby managers use design as a tool to change

Table II.2   The changing nature of design management

Levels of design management	Role
Operational design management	Building a competitive advantage by improving a function; Engineering, Marketing, Communications. Design managed by another activity.
Functional design management	Building a competitive advantage by focusing on the relations in the value chain. Design as a co-ordinating technique. Design as an independent function.
Strategic design management	Building a competitive advantage by changing the company's vision. Design at Board level.

behaviours and methods in the organisation from design at a functional and strategic level. This entails a convergence of cognitive structures of design and management.

To achieve strategic design management, that is a shift from treating design simply as a tool to create products to design for systems and ideas, requires a thorough knowledge of the activity of design. Also, it entails an understanding of design thinking in terms of its cognitive structure.

COGNITIVE STRUCTURES

Design has been recognised as a management technique or a function-creating value for the organisation. Design management is about the co-ordination of design-related resources and activities (Gorb 1990). Design has to interface with other processes and activities, notably marketing and production, R&D, corporate communications. Why, therefore, is its implementation and development so difficult in most organisations?

The cognitive assumption explains these difficulties by the perceived differences of the cognitive approaches of designers: most managers and designers think that significant differences exist in their cognitive structures. But are they so different? Perhaps management and design are more *con*verging than *di*verging activities.

Design is a managerial activity that can be described in different ways. Design is a problem-solving activity, a creativity activity, a systemic activity

Table 11.3   Design and management: comparative cognitive structure

Design concept	Management concepts
Design is a problem-solving activity	Process − problem
Design is a creative activity	Idea − Innovation
Design is a systemic activity	Systems
Design is a co-ordinating activity	Communications
Design is a cultural activity	Organisational culture: rites, leadership style, symbols

and a co-ordinating activity. Management is also a problem-oriented activity, an innovation activity, a systemic activity and a co-ordinating activity. But design is also a cultural activity which brings arts, aesthetics and culture to an organisation – there is no corresponding management concept for this. Table 11.3 compares design and management concepts and their overlaps.

In terms of design's search for originality, novelty and creativity and its methods of doing so, design can clash with an organisation's conservative attitude and reluctance to change, with its prevailing "classic" management styles and approaches. Traditionally, management has been regarded as rational and focused more on control and strategic planning rather than creativity and this is where differences between design and management can arise. However, more recent management authors, such as Mintzberg (1994) refer to strategic thinking developed by members of the organisation and they recognise the role of intuition and an "artistic" managerial framework. From this perspective, both design and management are regarded as inquisitive and experimental in the activity of decision making, and may be convergent in their cognitive structures.

This fact has been acknowledged by some intellectuals. Simon (in Buchanan 1995) refers to the thought processes of creating, judging, deciding and choosing as the real subjects of the new intellectual free trade among cultures and disciplines. Perhaps one of his greatest insights was not to reduce design to any one of the theoretical sciences:

> "Engineering, medicine, business, architecture and painting are concerned not with the necessary but with the contingent – not with how things are but with how they might be – in short with design. The possibility of creating a science or sciences of design is exactly as great as the possibility if creating any science of the artificial."

> (Simon 1969)

However, these similarities between design and management do not explain the problems that designers face when entering an organisation with a poor understanding of the design process. They do not explain why companies that have been able to implement design effectively regard this knowledge as a core competency that has to be protected (Kristensen in Chapter 10). The ability to integrate design into business processes is of benefit in a competitive sense. The capability to source, integrate and diffuse design in an organisation is a source of strategic advantage and tacit knowledge, which forms part of a company's assets. This is developed by the resource-based perspective of management (see Jevnaker, Chapter 1).

Rather, the difficulties for integrating design arise because designers and managers have their own visions of reality and their own "organisational paradigms". They tend to perpetuate the decision processes they used in the past and the knowledge patterns they are familiar with (Borja de Mozota 1992). Understanding the nature of these visions and how they are built up habitually can give a framework for improving design management research and practice.

The cognitive approach of management (Laroche and Nioche, 1994) develops a model for the decision-making process: the strategic model of contingent reality. This model explains the impact of memory and observation on our understanding of the environment and also how our logical decision process is balanced by our beliefs and desires. The cognitive concept suggests that facts recurrently prove that the decision-making process does not follow a rational model, for example, managers do not perceive change easily – they tend to favour already acquired information and to ignore signs of imminent upheavals (Kiesler and Sproull, 1982).

Thus, managers investigate the implementation of design from the perspective of their past decisions. Cognitive maps show that when making a decision, managers are not immersed in the reality of objective facts, but that they are immersed in a "creation of reality" and tend to protect their beliefs. Designers also create their own visions of reality and this constitutes a source of "unknown information" for managers. Thus, the integration of design is not likely to happen unless the company is going through a crisis where past beliefs and mechanisms have proved inefficient and there is a willingness to be receptive to new kinds of information. Integrating design and management cognitive structures raises questions: How much do designers know of managers' cognitive maps when starting on a project? How much do managers know of designers' perceptions of reality?

Given these deep-seated cognitive differences between management and design, which are rooted in experience and perception, it is argued here that design managers, designers and managers should start from their conceptual structure to improve design integration into business processes.

TOWARDS A CONVERGENT APPROACH

Building design relationships with management traditionally can follow different approaches, either "evolutionary" or "revolutionary" (Borja de Mozota 1992). The evolutionary approach is concerned with integrating design expertise into existing processes and to discover methods for a more efficient design process and design management process.

The "revolutionary" approach of design management tries to capture the ways that designers work in order to discover new ideas and methods for a more efficient management process, so that an understanding of how designers perceive reality allows managers to anticipate problems and opens up new creative routes for management. The converging approach of integration design and management tries to integrate both management and design paradigms to build an integrative model for design management. These approaches are discussed in the rest of this chapter.

THE EVOLUTIONARY APPROACH

From this perspective, design management starts from management paradigms to learn from management. Managers, marketers, engineers and communicators all have cognitive structures different from one another, and different from that of designers. Consequently, their interest in design will be aspects that perpetuate their mode of knowledge and their own expertise. If designers and educators are to expand the scope of design, they have to admit this cognitive process as a fact and use it as a starting-off point. This means assuming that design could be used either to reinforce management theories or to develop management paradigms. The present areas of design constitute a limited territory in management practice and thinking, in which design management is related to operational management, and more particularly to management functions such as marketing, production, and communication. If design is to be a useful management tool, it has to structure its development in terms of different approaches to management, in other words design management should duplicate management structures. Since management is both a practical field of knowledge and a variety of theories, design management should develop its territory by investigating new management problems in the practical operational field, and by absorbing related theoretical approaches to enhance its effectiveness.

DEVELOPING OPERATIONAL DESIGN MANAGEMENT

Whole areas of managerial activities do not deal with design. Developing operational design management – design management applied to management operations – requires the identification of these areas. At present design projects are restricted to areas like R&D, production, purchasing, marketing and communications departments, and project management. However, new territory for design management might be the finance and personnel departments, as well as designing standard procedures for planning, organising, co-ordinating, and controlling.

IMPROVING DESIGN MANAGEMENT EFFICIENCY

Operational design management is worthless if it is not related to the schools of thought that explain management paradigms. Design managers have to influence this thinking process in order to develop more efficient design management decisions. These schools of thought can provide material to explain the value of design to managers. Design management, like manage-ment, should be scientific (modelise processes), behavioural, decisional, systemic and situational.

BEHAVIOURAL DESIGN: GETTING DESIGN DONE THROUGH PEOPLE

Management entails getting things done through people. How much of design management has studied interpersonal relationships through all the phases of a project – creative implementation and so on. How much emphasis has been given to well-organised teamwork? What are the rewards, the motivational and training tools used in human resources management that designers could utilise?

DECISIONAL DESIGN: STUDYING THE DECISION PROCESS

What information is necessary to making decisions about design projects? Deciding is selecting among alternative courses of action. How much do design managers know about managers' approaches to this selection process? Managers working at or coming from design-oriented companies such as Novo, Sony or Braun are very likely to have different decision-making processes than managers from other companies. But managers with no design experience are more numerous, so it is a good idea to study managers' current decision-making processes in order to convince them of the need for good design, using arguments already familiar and credible to them.

SYSTEMIC DESIGN: ORGANISING SYSTEMS AND INTERACTIVE SUBSYSTEMS

A systemic approach to design often is key to its success. But design management should also be systemic, that is, the different subsystems of the organisation should be considered throughout the design process. For example, in a corporate communication these should all be considered in parallel. A good example of the lack of systemic process is the incoherence of graphics and text in many documents such as users manuals, brochures or annual reports. The information subsystem should be related to the corporate graphic subsystem which should be related to the corporate organising system of communications, as seen from a co-ordinated or systemic perspective.

SITUATIONAL DESIGN: STUDYING THE PSYCHO-SOCIOLOGY OF THE ORGANISATION

Managers' roles are varied. They depend on experience, interpersonal situations, psycho-sociological circumstances. Corporate cultures have their routines, rites and heroes. How much does a designer know of these sociological contexts and rituals when working with a company? How much does he or she understand of the psycho-sociology and power structure of an organisation.

Concurrent engineering is a good example of a management theory that is creating a demand for design in a company (Borja de Mozota 1995).

THE REVOLUTIONARY COGNITIVE SOLUTION: DESIGN AS A NEW PARADIGM

In this section, the path for the future of design management education and research is different. The starting point is not management paradigms that can be improved through design, but design as a new paradigm and the possibilities that design provides to enrich management.

According to Thomas Kuhn, the concept of a paradigm can be used in three broad senses:

- as a complete view of reality, or way of seeing;
- as relating to the social organisation of science in terms of schools of thought connected with particular scientific achievements; and
- as relating to the concrete use of specific tools and texts for the process of scientific problem solving.

Could design be used as a paradigm? This might require more research, but design certainly can be used in the senses that follow.

DESIGN AS AN IDENTIFICATION OF ALTERNATIVE REALITY

Designers have their own way of seeing reality that can apply to management issues. Their expertise in seeing, even their specific competence in viewing, artifacts are valuable assets to managers' views of reality. A designer's view of reality is an organised system, which therefore tends to protect itself using a sort of immunological organisation, forcing back data or issues dangerous to its integrity. For example, designers accept innovation – a concept reinforcing their vision – but will resist sociological facts like other people's resistance to change. Just as managers tend to accept design solutions that reinforce their paradigms, designers tend to search all the other visions of reality for that which reinforces their own vision. Literature, science, art, philosophy – all these disciplines become tools to develop design, or ideas dangerous to its development. Design develops artifacts: it is an activity in which ideas and concepts are given physical form, initially as solution concepts and then as a specific arrangements of elements, materials and components. In management, this means identifying the reality of the organisation in terms of shapes and forms. These shapes and forms of documents, buildings, products, uniforms – become a system of design outputs of artifacts.

HOW DESIGN CREATES VALUE

The world's largest electricity producer had to face a change in the perception of its pylons in the minds of its publics. The high pylons were not signs of progress and modernity. The general public thinks electricity useful but that lines and pylons deteriorate the landscape, i.e. the public wants the service (electricity) but not the nuisance (the pylon). Finding harmony between the landscape and the pylon design became a strategic issue for a public utility company that is conscious of its responsibility in terms of consensus and solidarity. Having signed a protocol with the French government, EDF Electricité de France (EDF) defined its service-oriented mission as "We owe you more than light" and devised a design strategy named "From a new ethics to a new aesthetics".

A European product design competition was launched in 1995 for the Very High Voltage Pylon – the highways for electricity that technically could not be hidden in the ground. The design should reinforce concentration with all publics, bring to the population a tangible proof of this new ethics and anticipate future users' needs. After a very thorough briefing and selection system, eight design teams were chosen to work on a concept. The solutions were then tested by a technical commission and a corporate image commission (the latter measuring their perceived value among the public). The final jury chose two solutions – both complementary to the landscape. What is exemplary in this project is that EDF had only one vote in the final jury. The other members of the jury were experts in arts, design and architecture. What a perfect example of aesthetics-driven product development, aesthetics driven by experts, including also users' needs.

DESIGN AND MANAGEMENT OF CREATIVITY

Design is a creative technique, consequently it is related to the methods the organisation implements in order to manage ideas and creativity. How are a designer's ideas integrated with the flow of ideas in the company? Managers can broaden creative management by integrating the information systems and methodology used for building consensus with the ideas that designers have, in particular their ability to be visionary and future-oriented.

The car industry is currently using "concept cars" to foster creativity, and helping customers to get used to new forms. This model is also being used in the textiles industry with "haute couture" in fashion design. Now "dream products" are developed in many industries, setting the trends and offering other choices for consumers.

DESIGN-ENRICHING MARKET RESEARCH

Managers face the problems of anticipating consumers' latent needs and hyper-changing behaviours, as well as consumers looking for authenticity in search of new meaning in their consumption practices. Designing a product becomes more and more akin to inventing a story and a "life experience" for a specific user. Designers are sociologists of objects, they enrich market research by exploring the various logics of users' perception (S. Dubuisson, A. Hennion 1995):

■ The logic of the object: a product should have sense in itself (Is it beautiful, functional, coherent?).
■ The logic of its use: a product should give sense to the relation the consumer has with the product.
■ The logic of the user: a product should given sense to the relation the user is having with other people (Why is she/he buying? What does she/he want from objects?).

Tension exists between these three logics and designers grapple with them when designing artifacts. They conceptualise the object according to the logics that have priority for a specific user and so they need ethno-cultural market research in the analysis phase of any design project.

The research techniques, based on user observation, that designers have used often in the first stages of the creative process to help them understand the problem, have made them able to interact, anticipate and develop user-interface and new concepts. These more or less ethnographic-associated methods are useful for market research. Moreover, designers also need to improve in their observational abilities to avoid disastrous designs of "the everyday things" (see Norman for examples).

DESIGN RESEARCH ENRICHING INNOVATION

Interesting studies have been conducted which measure the quality of form or a design preference and which associate a measure of words to qualitative visual sensations. Two examples follow.

The sensorial profile (Jean François Bassereau at ENSAM 1995)

The idea was to invent tools capable of specifying the future sensations perceived by users. The researchers focused on tactile sensations and established a sensorial profile for materials combining a list of "descripteurs" (words said by users in coherence with the material) and a numerical scale for users' preferences. They developed a graph – similar to marketers' "consumers" scale preferences profiles – but based on tactile perceptions of materials that are impossible to measure with traditional technology tools. Applications for industry are in progress: car keys, kitchen appliances.

Verbal language versus visual language (P. Babayou, J.L. Volatier 1995)

What information of the product culture do designers need in order to improve their relation with marketing? One answer has been software that visualises users' "representations" of different objects with words, images and even the sound of users' reactions to different objects.

A CONVERGENT APPROACH: "DESIGNENCE"

Instead of regarding "design" and "management" as different entities, there are grounds for focusing on the similarities between the two and to examine the learning that could occur between design and management. The model of convergence may help in this as it starts from their common ground. Design and management are both activities of "making and doing", and share concepts and thinking processes. The convergence model would try to widen the relevance of the management theories for designing and/or design theories for managing. Therefore, any concept from either of these cognitive worlds of design management can be explored in terms of their capacity to improve design integration or design management practice. Total Quality Management (TQM) is a good example of this converging model (Borja de Mozota 1993). Designers can learn from qualiticians by using quality tools for measuring the performance of the design process: impact of design on lowering production defects, errors, delays, just-in-time (JIT), value engineering and by integrating TQM users' satisfaction ratios as a tool for measuring design management performance.

But qualiticians can learn from designers. Design process and designers' creativity can help the diffusion of the Quality model through the organisation and develop its basic concepts: concentration on action, continuous improvement and total company improvement. So far, there is not a complete model of convergence to draw on, but this chapter has sketched some potential links between evolutionary and revolutionary design management dynamics. In particular, the design collaborators' strategic conceptual perspective has been highlighted as anchored in path-dependent mentalities. This cognitive approach stresses the thought process of designing. Thus, following Simon (in

Buchanan 1995) the future of design management research may be to build "a science of design". Indeed, design's future in organisation requires developing design territory in management. To do this requires designers to move from the mere technique of designing outputs to the new challenge of designing design processes and methods.

This science of design, which may be called *Designence*, links Design and Science in a new idea which considers that the proper study of design is not limited to the profesionally educated designer but that it is a core discipline for business.

REFERENCES

Amit, R. and Schoemaker, P. (1993). Strategic assets and organizational rent, *Strategic Management Journal*, **14**, 33–46.

Babayou, P. and Volatier, J.L. (1995). *Design et forme naturelle de l'objet CREDOC Cahier de recherche*, no. 72 Juin 1995, Paris.

Bassereau, J.F. (1995). Metrologie Sensorielle, Comment Mesurer la Perception de L'objet? Laboratoire de Conception de Produits Nouveaux ENSAM Paris, Actes du 3éme Colloque A2RP Ministére de la Recherche (pp. 605–620).

Borja de Mozota, B. (1992). Design education and research: A theoretical model for the future, *Design Management Journal*, Fall, **3**(4), 19–25.

Borja de Mozota, B. (1993). Total Quality Management and Design Management excellence. Proceedings of the Fifth International Forum on Design Management Research and Education, Massachusetts Institute of Technology, Boston, USA, 18–22.

Borja de Mozota, B. (1995). Giving sense to objects and the design management: can the design Process be conceptualized? Proceedings of the Seventh International Forum on Design Management Research and Education, University of Stanford, USA, 12.

Borja de Mozota, B. (1995). La Gestion Stratégique de design: Design et Systéme d'information. Actes des léres rencontres du Design Prospectif, Janvier 1995, Institut Supérleur de Design Valenciennes, France, 6–12.

Bruce, M. and Biemans, W. (1995). *Product Developments: Meeting the Challenge of the Design–Marketing Interface*, John Wiley & Sons, Chichester.

Buchanan, R. (1995). *Rhetoric, Humanism and Design: Discovering Design*, University of Chicago Press, Chicago, 12.

Clarke, K.B. and Takahoto Fujimoto (1991). *Product Development Performance*, Harvard Business Press, 291.

Cooper, R. and Press, M. (1995). *The Design Agenda: A Guide to Successful Design Management*, J. Wiley & Sons, Chichester.

Cova, B. (1995). Au-delà du Marché: Quand le Lien Importe Plus Que le Bien, editors L'harmattan Paris (19, 62, 79). *The Design Management Institute* (1995), Cross Functional Design, **5**(4), Fall.

Dubuisson, S. and Hennion, A. (1995). Qualité Mesurée, Qualité Perçue: du Produit à l'usager Centre de Sociologie de L'innovation, Actes du 3ème Colloque A2RP, Ministère de la Recherche, 591–601.

Gorb, P. (1990). Design Management et Question des Organisations Revue Française de Gestion, (80), Sept–Oct, 67.

Hanna, J. (1995). Communication Design Management in the Digital Environment, 20th International Design Management Conference, The Design Management Institute, Cape Cod.

Hetzel, P. (1993). Design Management et Constitution de l'offre Thèse de Doctorat de Sciences de Gestion, Université de Jean Moulin, Lyon 3.

Hollins, B. and Hollins, G. (1995). The Management of Concurrent Engineering and Total Design, Co-Design (04.05.06 1995), 22–27.

Jevnaker, B.H. (1995). Interview quoted during the Workshop on Design Alliances, SNF/NHH, Bergen, Norway, June 7–10.

Kiesler, S. and Sproull, L. (1982). Managerial Response to Changing Environments, *Administrative Science Quarter*ly, (4), 548–570.

Laroche, H. and Nioche, J.P. (1994). L'approche Cognitive de la Stratégie d'entreprise, *Revue Française de Gestion*, Juin/Juillet/Aout, 65–78.

Lebahar, J.C. (1994). Le Design Industriel: Semiologie de la Séduction et code de la Matiére, Editions Parenthéses, Marseille, 25–26.

Leonard-Barton, D. (1991). Inanimate Integrators: A Block of Wood Speaks. *Design, Management Journal*, **2**(3), 61–67, Summer.

Mahoney, J. and Rapendran Pandian, J. (1992). The resource-based view within the conversation of strategic management, *Strategic Management Journal*, **13**, 363–380.

Manzini, E. (1991). Artefacts: Vers une Nouvelle écologie de l'environment Artificiel, Les Essais Centre Georges Pompidou, Paris, 17.

Mitchell, C.T. (1993). *Redefining Designing from Form to Experience*, Van Nostrand Reinhold, N.Y.

Mintzberg, H. et al (1994) *The Strategy Process*, Prentice Hall, 104.

Montfort, B. (1994). Infostyle: Vers une Nouvelle Culture d'entreprise (Technal) ESCP Paris Actes du Colloque: Sixth International Forum on Design Management Research and Education (Annexe 3).

Norman, D. (1987). *Psychology of Everyday Things*, Addison-Wesley, Reading, MA.

Nonaka, I. and Takeuchi, H. (1995). *The Knowledge Creating Company*, Oxford University Press, Oxford.

Oakley, M. (1990). *The Handbook of Design Management*, Basil Blackwell, Oxford, UK.

Porter, M.E. (1985). *Competitive Advantage Creating and Sustaining Superior Performance*, The Free Press/Macmillan NY, Traduction Française: L'avantage Concurrentiel: Interéditions, Paris, 53.

Rochefort, R. (1995). La Société des Consommateurs, Editions Odile Jacob, Paris, 121.

Sethia, N. (1995). Shaping the New Corporate Voice: The Challenge of Heeding Customer Voice, *Design Management Journal*, **6**(1), 34–39, Winter.

Simon, H. (1969). *The Sciences of the Artificial*, MIT Press, Cambridge, reprinted 1981.

Topalian (1979). *The Management of Design Projects*, Associated Business Press, London.

Walsh, V. et al (1992). *Winning by Design*, Basil Blackwell, Oxford.

CHAPTER TWELVE

A COMPARATIVE STUDY OF DESIGN PROFESSIONALS

Margaret Bruce and Barny Morris

In the 1990s, design is becoming a public policy issue, with the UK government's latest White Paper on Competitiveness (HMSO 1995) referring to the need to bolster design expertise and its utilisation by British firms, especially small and medium-sized enterprises. Given that design expertise is increasingly outsourced (Westamocott 1992), then the structure and organisation of the design profession is important to consider, and yet surprisingly little is known about the nature of the design consultancy profession itself. There is little cross-country comparative information about the structure and organisation of the design profession and about different approaches to managing design-client relationships.

One aspect of design management is explored in detail in this chapter; that is the design–client relationship, where design is provided by an external supplier to the client company. This is a sensitive relationship for various reasons. Perhaps most significantly, the relationship has to facilitate creativity, as the outcome of the interface between design and other functions in the client company is expected to be something that is distinctive and fulfils marketing needs. Central to the relationship is a tension between, on the one hand, a need for the free-flow of ideas and openness and, on the other, a fear that proprietary information and company confidences are given away to a design supplier who may (perhaps unwittingly) reveal this information to another of the design company's clients. This dilemma is not present when all the competencies are within the boundaries of the firm, even though other

Management of Design Alliances. Edited by M. Bruce and B. H. Jevnaker.
© 1998 John Wiley & Sons Ltd.

problems of communication may exist between design and its interface with other areas, such as marketing (Davies-Cooper and Jones 1995). One approach to dealing with this tension is to build up long-term relationships with design suppliers to instil a sense of loyalty and trust. Another is to integrate the external designers and treat them as "part of the family" and akin to an in-house design capability.

The overall aim of the research reported here was to compare the client–design relationship between UK and Nordic companies to see if differences between the nature and management of this relationship were evident.

From company interviews conducted in each of the three countries studied, it was clear that for UK companies short-term and arm's length client–design relationships were quite common, whereas for the Nordic companies longer-term and close, "family-like" relationships were more typical. The findings of the comparisons between UK, Swedish and Danish practices will be presented and major differences will be highlighted.

COMPARATIVE STUDIES

- The British design profession has been influenced by the decline in manufacturing and the growth in service industries throughout the past two decades, so that the profession is dominated by graphic companies rather than product. In Denmark and Sweden the reverse is the case.
- Independent graphic design companies in the UK offer a range of design services, including corporate identity, brochures and leaflets, as well as interior and product design. In Sweden, graphic design is closely linked with advertising and graphic design firms are rare. This is a major source of difference between the British and the Danish and Swedish professions.
- The British design profession has small, medium and large design companies and staff to help manage the company. Danish and Swedish companies are small and owned and managed by designers.

These are the major differences in organisations and structure between the British on the one hand, and Danish and Swedish firms, on the other. The survey findings reflect these differences.

AIMS

The purpose of this comparative survey of design consultancy firms was to:

- examine the organisation and structure of the design professions in Britain, Denmark and Sweden;
- document approaches to strategic management;
- identify different types of client relationship;
- allow some comparisons to be made of the design professions in Denmark, Sweden and the UK.

The first section of this chapter gives demographic details of the design companies and assesses performance in terms of profit, turnover and exports and identifies industry trends.

The next section appraises strategic management approaches. Finally, management of client–design relationships is discussed. In each section, the company information is presented and key issues are summarised.

UK DESIGN PROFESSION

Design consultancies experienced significant growth during the 1980s and it was one of the fastest growing service sectors (*Business Ratio* 1991). The UK design consultancy profession has been heralded as the strongest in the world in terms of numbers of companies – estimated as up to 3000, employing 40,000–50,000 designers and with 7000 graduates coming into the profession each year (Hancock 1992) – and seven of the eight largest design consultants in the world are British companies (Rawsthorne 1989). Turnovers of design companies were growing at an average rate of 30% per annum between 1986 to 1989 (*Keynote* 1989).

However, the onset of the recession in 1990 brought about a sharp deterioration in trading conditions for most UK consultants. A 1991 *Business Ratio* report stated that "Average rate of return on capital fell from the very high level of 8.1% in 1989 to the much more modest 2.1% in 1990/1, whilst average profit margins almost halved from 8.4% to 4.7%".

The main reason for such a sharp decline in the profession is attributed to its parasitic nature relative to other industries, and when those industries began to cut back, this naturally had an effect on design consultants. Leisure industries, consumer products, publishing and broadcasting, some of the main buyers of design expertise, have all contracted.

The external factors affecting design consultants have brought about some management changes. Firms have slimmed down and become specialised by building on their core design skills, or they have become multi-functional in terms of design, or have added other services, such as management consultancy. Technology has had a major impact, allegedly speeding up and changing the design process, as well as automating jobs.

It is clear that a number of factors were creating a situation of continuous change and uncertainty, perhaps the main ones being change in demand, adoption of technology in the design process, and lowering barriers to entry for new start-ups.

COMPANY PROFILES AND TRENDS

In Denmark a large number of the middle ground companies (between 11% and 25% profit on turnover) have seen a sharp fall in profits leading to a dramatic increase in the number of companies earning less than 10% profit on turnover in 1991, and a rise in the number of companies making a loss in the same time period (Figure 12.1). In Sweden (Figure 12.2), the 1991 figures suggest a sharp contraction in the number of companies earning greater than

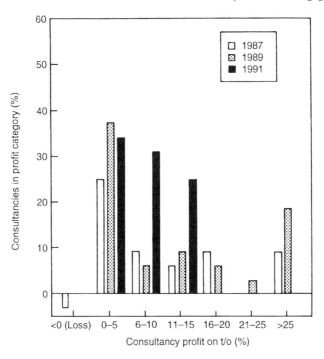

Figure 12.1   Consultancy profit, Denmark

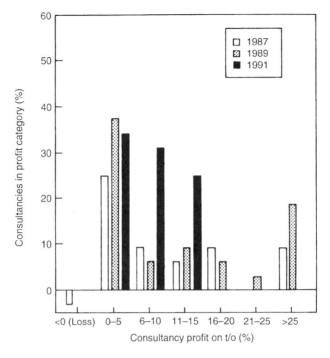

Figure 12.2   Consultancy profit, Sweden

16% profit on turnover. The overall trend for companies is to have declining profitability in this period, with Swedish companies coping with the recession slightly better than Danish firms.

It can be seen that profitability has fallen starkly between 1987 and 1991. Companies which were in the higher profit categories in 1987 and 1989 are now in the lower categories in 1991. 1987 was the heyday and a successful period for design companies. A leaner and tougher environment is evident by 1991 (Figure 12.3).

The size of consultancies was compared with level of profit (Table 12.1). Medium- and large-sized consultancies have been excluded from the comparison as the numbers are too small to be of significance. It is evident that in this small consultancy category that there is a greater proportion of Danish medium profit level consultancies (68%) than their Swedish counterparts (32%). Also, there are a greater percentage of low profit Swedish consultancies operating (41%) compared with Danish consultancies (9%). For British companies, it can be seen that larger companies are more likely to have

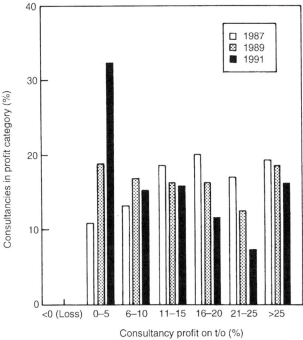

Figure 12.3   Consultancy profit, UK

low to medium levels of profit and smaller companies are more likely to have medium to high levels of profit.

Starting-up in Business

In Britain and Sweden, the majority of the consultancies surveyed were established in the 1980s, lending support to the view that the 1980s was the "designer decade". In Denmark, an increase in new entrants occurred in the

Table 12.1   Profit and size in consultancy

Profit 1991 (%)	Consultancy size (small category only)		
	UK	Sweden	Denmark
Low	16	41	9
Medium	40	32	68
High	44	27	23

Table 12.2   Year of company set-up

| | % of companies setting up | | |
	UK	Sweden	Denmark
Pre-1970	10	6	22
1970–79	19	26	20
1980–89	62	62.5	37
1990 or later	9	6	22

Note: n is 74, 31 and 43 respectively

1980s but was less marked by comparison with Britain and Sweden. A downturn in the rate of growth of the industry is indicated by the small numbers of companies setting up in the early 1990s (Table 12.2).

Turnover Accounted for by Repeat Business

A general increase in the proportion of repeat business is shown in Figures 12.4, 12.5 and 12.6. This may indicate a fostering of close relationships with clients to encourage repeat business.

Clients' Contribution to Turnover

The majority of companies are reliant on a small number of clients who comprise at least 10% of their annual turnover (Table 12.3). Hence the demise or loss of these clients can seriously affect the performance of the design company leading to, for example, staff cuts, wage cuts and threaten ultimately the survival of the firm.

Turnover Accounted for by Foreign Clients

Overall, both Sweden and Denmark consultancies are very reliant on their domestic market. This is particularly true for Danish consultancies where the proportion of consultancies which have no foreign clients has increased year by year. By comparison with Sweden, whose proportion of consultancies with no foreign clients actually decreased in 1991 (Figures 12.7, 12.8 and 12.9).

The UK design consultancies are even more successful than the Swedish at exporting their design services. This may be due in part to their more aggressive

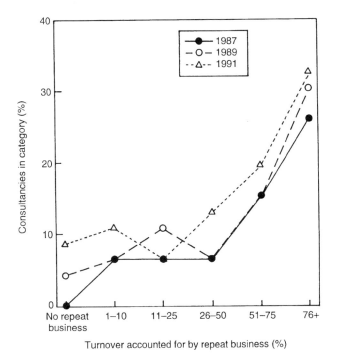

Figure 12.4   Turnover accounted for by repeat business, Denmark

marketing, their flexibility in meeting customer requirements, and their reputation for commercial "international design".

On the other hand, Denmark and Sweden focus on quality and functional design, with less emphasis on price and their own sales activities.

Reasons for Setting up

As Table 12.4 indicates, by far the most frequently stated motive for setting up a new design company was the opportunity for founders to "use their own design skills". "Redundancy" and in "response to a client", were more significant motives for Danish companies than companies from Sweden and Britain. "Apply their own business philosophy" was also cited as a reason for setting up. The categories in Table 12.4 are not mutually exclusive (e.g. respondents were able to pick more than one category as part of their answer), suggesting that design consultants were motivated to set up a consultancy for a number of different reasons. Nonetheless, individualism and creativity are core

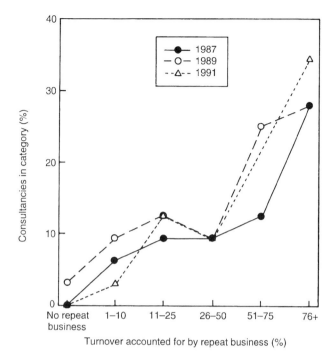

Figure 12.5   Turnover accounted for by repeat business, Sweden

values running through the design profession and the motives for setting up one's own design company reflect this.

Background of Partners

Overwhelmingly the background and training of the major partners in design firms was that of art school, with the remainder having a background in marketing/sales and a background in economics and business studies. By marked contrast, a background in business was relatively uncommon, in spite of a recognised need to encourage designers to take on board business and management skills themselves, or to work closely with those who have such skills. The engineering bias of Swedish consultancies is reflected by the fact that a quarter of all company founders have an engineering background.

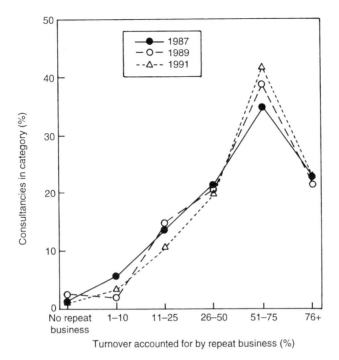

Figure 12.6   Turnover accounted for by repeat business, UK

Approaches to Strategic Management

Respondents were asked to rank in order of importance the main strategic aims of their company and the mean score for each of these was then calculated, as shown in Table 12.5. A lower mean score indicates a more important strategic aim. "Company expansion" and "investment in new technology" were the least important strategic aims. Overall, "providing clients with effective solutions" and "enhancing company reputation" were important goals. Emphasis on the design competence and quality of service were regarded more highly than factors that would affect long-term business performance,

Table 12.3   Clients' contributions to turnover (%)

Number of clients	UK	Sweden	Denmark
1. Yes, only	28	19	28
2. Yes more than 1	64	72	59
3. None	8	6	6.5

Note: n=74, 31 and 43 respectively.

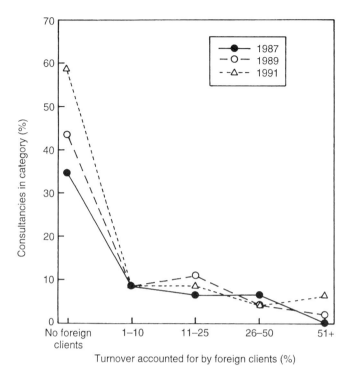

Figure 12.7 Turnover accounted for by foreign clients, Denmark

namely adding value to the service offered and differentiation from competitors and company expansion. Hence, it appears that short-termism and satisfying current customer needs is a prevalent aspect of strategic management for design firms. It is worth noting that British and Swedish companies are more concerned about investment in technology than are Danish design firms. This may be due to either a late adoption of technology in the design process, or to more intense competitive pressures, such that efficiency gains are of uppermost concern.

Approaches to Business Planning

The majority of Danish and Swedish respondents indicated that their approach to business planning was informal, describing it as "in the hands of partners" and more "a sense of direction".

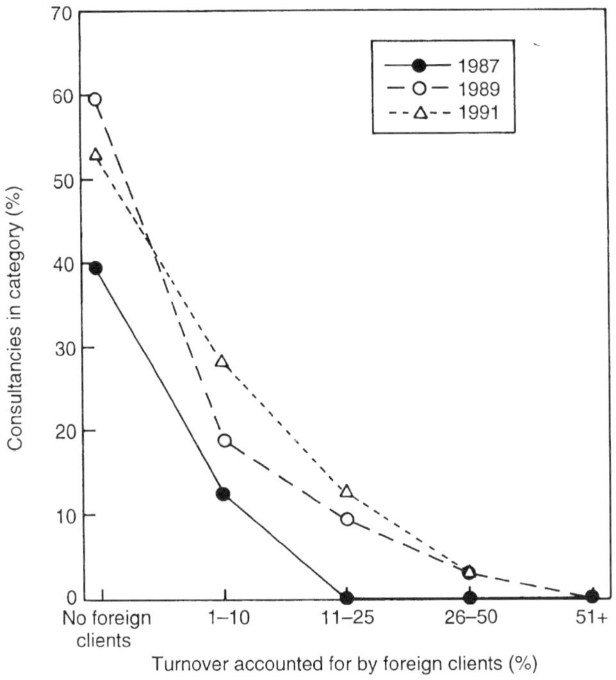

Figure 12.8   Turnover accounted for by foreign clients, Sweden

For UK companies, just over one-third had "formally written plans that were regularly reviewed", with about a quarter adopting an informal approach and the remainder of companies having a "sense of direction to guide them along". Whilst a more informal approach may assist flexibility and increase the ability to be more opportunistic in the face of changing market circumstances, it may also result from a *laissez-faire* attitude with little attention being given to long-term planning (Table 12.6).

Nature of Business Plans

Table 12.7 indicates that targeting clients to help grow or to move into new areas tends to lie at the heart of the business plans of Danish and Swedish design companies, followed by profit targets and flow of business (both 22%). Financial issues are uppermost for UK firms with 64% of firms having set profit targets. Cash flow is a top priority, whereas reinvestment for future

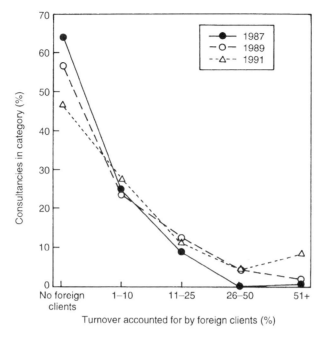

Figure 12.9   Turnover accounted for by foreign clients, UK

expansion is a lower priority, as indicated by staff expansion, growth of disciplines and office expansion.

Environmental Changes

Respondents were asked to indicate the relative significance of a number of external changes affecting the design industry and the effects of these on their

Table 12.4   Reasons for setting up (%)

	UK	Sweden	Denmark
Apply own business philosophy	56	9	15
To allow our founder members to use their own design skills	51	59	30
Always wanted own business	50	0	13
Spin-off from another company	21	9	13
In response to a client	10	9	24
Redundancy	5	9	28
Few job opportunities	5	3	17
Other	4	9	11

Table 12.5   Strategic aims

	UK mean	Sweden mean	Denmark mean
To make a lot of money	3.42	6.68	8.66
To contain company growth	5.72	8.22	8.26
Company expansion	4.40	9.84	9.93
Provide clients with effective solutions	2.23	2.56	4.93
Differentiation from competitors	3.90	8.38	7.59
Add value to our service	3.96	6.56	8.66
To reduce fees	8.02	10.52	9.76
Choose clients we wish to work with	4.11	5.58	6.80
Enhance reputation	3.04	5.74	6.67
Invest in new technology	4.90	5.97	9.06
Other	2.00	10.68	10.78

Table 12.6   Approach to business planning

	UK	Sweden	Denmark
Formally written regularly reviewed	36	12.5	9
Formally written, not reviewed	30	–	13
Not formally written, but in the mind of partners	25	62.5	54
Sense of direction	9	22	–

Table 12.7   Nature of business plans

	UK	Sweden	Denmark
Profit targets	64	31	26
Budgets	69	19	26
Balance of clients	28	34	17
Target clients	62	44	37
Expand staff	43	3	13
Expand disciplines	28	25	6.5
Expand offices	20	9	4
Flow of business	70	37.5	22
Other	12	9	4

Table 12.8   Environmental changes

Respondents ranked the following statements:	UK mean	Sweden mean	Denmark mean
Increase in pitching	3.92	5.86	7.30
Designers more professional at running their business	4.39	5.80	10.55
Designers more professional at managing their clients		5.43	6.07
Increased competition between design companies	3.96	5.88	6.67
Increased investment in new technology	3.56	*	7.41
Increased use of new technology	3.42	5.86	6.15
Clients are more adept at commissioning design consultants	5.30	5.07	6.10
Clients have increased their use of in-house designers	5.50	6.81	7.98
Introduction of ISO 9000/British Standard (BS) 5750	6.24	8.18	7.22
Other		9.27	9.96

*This suggests that the Swedish respondents misunderstood/misinterpreted the statement (so gave no value), rather than representing a significant answer.

companies, as shown in Table 12.8. The total mean scores displayed in this Table are a measure of the significance of the changes, as assessed by the respondents, a lower mean score indicating a change regarded as more significant.

The most significant change is that clients have become more adept at commissioning work, followed by increasing competition in the industry and the increased use of new technology.

DESIGN – CLIENT RELATIONSHIPS

From the interviews in all three countries, it was clear that personal relationships between the actors from the client and design firms were central to the design process. The three most important choice criteria used by clients to select design firms were personality, competence and reputation. Designers themselves referred to "giving something of themselves to the project", that is they totally immerse themselves in the project and draw on their senses to gain a deep understanding of the problem and work intuitively, visually and sensually to create the design solution. From the client's perspective, the opportunity to work with someone who understands their problem and who has the skills to achieve their business aims is reassuring, so it was not surprising that these three criteria were stated by clients.

Different practices were evident, so that some clients preferred to buy in design expertise as and when they needed it and had not any expectation of the contact lasting beyond the project's duration. Other companies had a rosta of design suppliers (i.e. multiple sourcing) that they would use depending on the skills needed, and others built up long-term relationships with their design suppliers, even though the design firm was only needed on a sporadic basis.

In addition, some companies kept their design suppliers at arm's length, whilst others embraced the design firm and closely integrated it with their own in-house team. In the UK, a range of design management practices were evident but the rationale for these appeared to be experiential and *ad hoc*, based on the personal preference of the managers involved. The decisions regarding the design supplier and management of this relationship were not taken as strategic decisions, nor were they based on a systematic body of knowledge about "best practices". In Denmark and Sweden, however, the marketing–design relationship tended to be enduring, single-sourcing was typical and the design firm was usually a close relationship. The participants of the research had little experience of an arm's length relationship with their design suppliers.

From the design professional's perspective, it was expressed from all three countries that long-term relationships were desirable because they allowed the design firm to gain a better insight into the needs of the client and thereby produce better quality solutions. The degree of empathy or compatibility established between the client and external design company appeared to be dependent upon such social elements as personal chemistry, the ability to speak the same language (i.e. in the sense of effective transfer of knowledge), and mutual trust. Financial stability and the ability to offer a better design solution were regarded as the basis for long-term relationships from the consultant's point of view. One of the designer's interviewed by Bruce and Docherty (1993) emphasised the role of long-term relationships:

"... we try to help people understand what they really want by giving shape to their ideas and needs. To do this, the designer becomes very close to those people ... you have to know what the clients' likes and dislikes are. It is a very private and intimate relationship. It is the intimacy of the relationship that determines the success of the design."

Where trust is established, the client can place confidence in the designer and sensitive information is more likely to be revealed that may result in a better design solution. The analogy of the doctor and patient relationship was made by some of the participants. Also the trust and openness can facilitate creativity, so that the designer is given enough information to be creative but is not inhibited by the client being overly directive.

The major factors positively affecting the relationship between client and design firms were "client evaluation", "increase in budget", a good "design brief" and the production of "information on request". An understanding of what the designer does and the possession by the client of visual skills and design management skills were also seen as important.

The major factors cited as negatively affecting client relationships were when "clients, withheld information" and became "too involved" and "tried to take over the design work".

Long-term Relationships (LTRs)

Long-term relationships were perceived as "very important" and "important" to the success of the design firm by about 90% of survey respondents. Only 7% of all consultancies did not actively seek long-term relationships with their clients. Just over half of all relationships that respondents had with clients became long-term and the main factor leading to this development was "initial project success". Respondents were then asked what was uppermost in their minds when defining long-term relationships (Table 12.9).

Quality was a key feature of long-term relationships and this was understood in terms of trust, respect, honesty and mutual understanding. Quality is more important than other factors in influencing long-term relationships, such as frequency or duration of contact, or the financial security of such a relationship.

Table 12.9   Long-term relationships (% respondents' definitions)

	UK	Sweden	Denmark
1. Quality	69	72	74
2. Frequency of contact	9	12.5	2
3. Duration of relationship	7	12.5	4
4. Financial security	11	3	6.5

DEVELOPING LONG-TERM RELATIONSHIPS

Respondents were given a list of methods for establishing long-term relationships with clients, and asked to rank the top five methods that they most commonly used themselves. Table 12.10 lists these methods, where the lowest mean score indicates the most commonly used method by consultants.

Triggers cited as leading to the development of long-term relationships were "personal rapport" and "regular contact with the client". For LTK companies, "involvement of a partner" was particularly important, given that the client contact could be managed by others in the firm, such as marketing personnel. For Danish and Swedish firms, "involvement of a partner" was virtually common practice. Using the designer in a "fire-fighting role" was important and was likely to trigger a long-term relationship. The next most important factors were "investment of personal time and money", "educating the client" and "visiting the client". Sending mailers and having the client visit the design firm were less important. Clearly, it is the personal aspect of the relationship that is the key to selective long-term relationships.

CONCLUSIONS

For Scandinavian design companies, the competition for work in the domestic market was intense. Repeat business had become more important than new business and attempts by companies to seek opportunities overseas in the face of a decline in demand from the home market had been unsuccessful, particularly by Danish companies. Design companies in these countries were small and dominated by product design.

Table 12.10   Ways of establishing long-term relationships

	UK (% mean)	Sweden (% mean)	Denmark (% mean)
Regular contact with client	2.91	5.00	6.80
Mailers	3.42	11.88	12.50
Invest personal time, money	3.26	8.25	9.72
Educate the client	3.18	9.69	9.63
Visit the client	3.33	8.97	10.54
Invite client to design firm	3.84	12.22	12.63
Personal rapport	2.58	6.03	8.30
Extra resources to client	3.52	13.78	13.50
Partner	2.70	14.00	13.26
Dedicated team	3.09	12.81	12.48

The British design profession had undergone immense change, from a period of rapid growth and high profitability to sharp decline. A period of consolidation characterised the profession at the beginning of the 1990s. Fewer new companies were being set up, profits had fallen and were harder to achieve. Repeat business was the financial basis of the larger companies and these were looking overseas to sustain their growth, given the decline in demand from the home market. Companies ranged in size from small to large global firms and product design was not the dominant expertise offered. An independent graphic design sector existed and the skills offered by the graphic companies sometimes overlapped those of the product firms, for example, graphic firms undertook three-dimensional design and used similar technological systems to realise their designs as did product design firms. Companies of different sizes were facing distinct challenges, for example, larger companies were finding it harder to meet all their overheads and smaller companies were experiencing problems with generating and sustaining clients.

The larger British companies were aiming to expand by moving into foreign markets and were being successful at this, whereas Danish and Swedish companies were reliant on their home markets. The small size of the Danish and Swedish design companies prohibited their ability to trade internationally.

Core values running through the profession are those of "effective design", "creativity" and "equality services". Company mission statements reflect these core values and commercial success is perceived as being dependent on achieving these goals. Design companies are set up, managed and owned by designers who show not only a lack in business management skills but also a lack of foresight in investing for future expansion. However, "effective design" and "quality service" may be attained without due regard to changing market needs and commercial goals. Excelling at design matters, but so does an ability to think ahead and be aware of market changes and to be proactive in the approach to these changes. The structure of UK companies, particularly the medium-sized and larger companies, used marketing and administrative personnel to help manage their design companies as profitable concerns. This management structure and approach was influencing the commercialisation of the wider design community, so that smaller British design companies with simple structures were becoming more professionally run and managed.

Business planning is undertaken mainly by owners and senior managers; it is more likely to be informal and in the heads of those who have created the plans. Continual evaluation of plans to assess the company's performance and

Table 12.11   Strategic archetypes

Dynamic (Effective strategic practice)	Stuck in a rut (Less effective strategic practice)
Build up a balanced portfolio of longer-term and shorter-term client relationships.	Over-dependency on large client accounts. This may aid turnover growth but is not necessarily profitable.
Identifying new market opportunities, preferably in expanding and robust markets.	"We know what market we are in."
Knowing what adds value to your existing and potential clients' business development.	"The client will brief us."
Developing skills in new business development.	Designers chase up business when they can. *Ad hoc* and irregular approach to new business development.
Being aware of major factors affecting your market environment and that of your clients.	"We sell good design."
Having longer-term perspective, being visionary and be prepared to be flexible and ready to work in newer, expanding markets.	Short-termism and meeting the needs of current clients only.
Focusing on the companies' core strengths and continually developing these.	Too many/confused design and management offerings. What is your main business?
Protecting creativity in larger companies by devising a structure that permits creativity for designers at all levels.	Too large and controlling. Creativity is stifled.
Investing in state of the art technology and continually developing the competence to fully exploit this.	Reactive to technological trends in the design process.

make adjustments is not a typical part of the strategic process, with very few firms actually having company mission statements. This was less evident for British companies, a high proportion of which did evaluate their financial plans regularly, again indicating the relative commercialisation of these firms. It may be argued that this approach to planning allows for flexibility but it can also lead to a poorly-managed business that does not have a clear vision of what it is striving for. Two strategic archetypes were identified: "dynamic" refers to a more effective strategic practice and "stuck in a rut" implies a less effective strategic practice. These are shown in Table 12.11. Examples of both types could be found in all three countries, but more of the "dynamic" type was found in the UK overall. This can be explained, in part, by the intensely competitive environment in which design firms are trading in the UK and the shift towards design expertise being regarded increasingly as a commodity and where the best price, not necessarily the best design, was becoming the basis of choice of design supplier.

Client relationships were important, given the high degree of repeat business. However, companies were over-dependent upon clients. Clients have a part to play in the process of strategic decision-making and "if they went bust" then they could have a devastating effect on the design as business. Designers in all three countries wanted to establish long-term relationships with their clients because they believed that this affected the understanding they had of the client's needs and hence the effectiveness of the design solution. It was clear that the relationship was not purely economic. It is a social relationship with personal factors, trust and understanding playing a critical part in the relationship. Buying design and building up longer-term relationships is heavily influenced by "personal chemistry". Buying design expertise is not buying "nuts and bolts", it is about buying creativity and people's skills. As the client is also involved in the creative process, the quality of the client–design relationship is crucial.

However, differences in the nature of relationships were observed. In Denmark and Sweden, relationships tended to be enduring and single-sourcing of design firms by clients was typical. High switching costs were perceived because of the value they placed on the design competence that had evolved in the long-term relationship. In Britain, multiple sourcing of design firms was commonplace, with clients having a rosta of approved design suppliers they could use and with whom they may establish long-term relationships. Clients would switch from one design supplier to another on a regular basis and the selection of design firms was increasingly made on price. Loyalty to a single design company would not prevent a client from seeking a new design supplier. Whilst close and friendly relationships with clients existed in the UK the designers always recognised the professional basis of these and relationships were always seen as ultimately tenuous. The danger with this approach is that the more intangible elements of the client–design relationship were less and less valued, with the implication that buying design expertise would be regarded as akin to buying a commodity – with the risk that poor quality and standardised design may well ensue.

This comparative study has revealed fundamental differences in attitude to the client–design relationship and to the nature of design competence. In Nordic companies, design is recognised as a competence that is a worthwhile investment. In the UK, design may be regarded as being of commercial value but is treated as a dispensable commodity and as an "add-on" component, rather than as a long-term investment.

REFERENCES

Business Ratio Report (1991). *UK Design Consultancies*, ICG Group Publication.

Bruce, M. and Docherty, C. (1993). It's All in a Relationship: A Comparative Study of Client–Design Relationships, *Design Studies*, **14**, 402–422.

HMSO (1995) *White Paper on Competitiveness*. HMSO London.

Davies-Cooper, R. and Jones, T. (1995). The interfaces between design and other key functions in product development, in Bruce, M. and Biemens, W. (eds) *Product Development: Meeting the challenge of the design–marketing interface*, John Wiley & Sons, Chichester.

Keynote (1989). *An Industry Sector Overview: Design Consultancies*, Keynote Publications Ltd, London.

Westamocott, T. (1992). Decentralised design market: Where the trends are leading us, *Design Management Journal*, **3**(2), Spring.

PART FOUR

LESSONS FOR THE FUTURE

CONCLUSION
Margaret Bruce and Birgit H. Jevnaker

Throughout this book, the value of design skills in creating novel and distinctive products has been stressed. Design's direct impact on business performance has been emphasised also. Whilst many companies would recognise the importance of design, others only pay "lip service" to it and so fail to establish a design competence as a strategic resource. The central theme of the book has been to argue that design is a strategic asset that has to be nourished and protected in order to attain a sustainable competitive advantage. The case of Marimekko (Chapter 8) provides a telling example where ultimately the failure to integrate design into business processes resulted in commercial difficulties.

One of the main problems that affects design being regarded as a strategic asset is the acknowledgement of design as a distinctive competence, which Jevnaker notes in Chapters 1 and 5. This reluctance may be deeply rooted in the different cognitive structures of design and management that Borja de Mozota refers to in Chapter 11. However, it is only when design has become part of the norms and values of the company and institutionalised in such a way that design influences the strategic orientation that design can become a core competence (see Chapter 10).

In the company case studies, the various approaches that companies have adopted to utilise design skills are described. All share problems of resourcing and utilising design competence but deal with these in different ways. What is refreshing is the recognition of the importance of design and the learning between the design and client companies that can occur when new and

Management of Design Alliances. Edited by M. Bruce and B. H. Jevnaker.
© 1998 John Wiley & Sons Ltd.

successful designs emerge. This is particularly true for Ingersoll-Rand (Chapter 3) and the Norwegian companies documented in Chapter 5.

Design competence may reside in the company, as an in-house activity, or be engaged from a design firm, or be a blend of these two. Examples of all of these can be seen in the company cases in Part Two, although most of these illuminate differences in managing design relationships, or design alliances.

The remainder of this section deals with issues relating to the management of design alliances.

ADVANTAGES OF DESIGN ALLIANCES

Mutual benefits accrue to both design firms and their clients from design partnerships. For the client, the design firm can provide fresh insights and bring new knowledge and skills, which have to be combined with the company's own skills and processes. For the design firm, there are novel problems to work on, which may involve the design firm acquiring and developing new expertise. So, both the design and client may undergo a learning process to achieve the final result.

If the alliance is successful, then there may be an overspill of design know-how into other projects, both for the design firm to use for other clients and for the company to discover new applications. A successful design outcome can strengthen the alliance.

In some cases, clients are moving into the designer's company, or co-locating to be closer to their external design resource, such as Korean Samsung with the British American design consultancy IDEO (Chapter 1). Another solution is long-term collaboration and reciprocal mobility. For example HAG and Stokke with the Norwegian designer, Peter Opsvik (Chapter 5). Cost savings may be made, particularly by the client, where information and development costs can be shared by parties of the alliance, rather than being borne totally by the client.

However, some companies are reluctant to foster such close ties with their design suppliers, preferring a more "arm's length" relationship and cultural differences may account, to some extent, for differences in approaches to the management of design alliances (see Chapter 12). Nonetheless the design alliance could be the company's major source of creativity and push the firm ahead of its competition. Such personalised sources of creative know-how are difficult to imitate and special relationships and personalities are visible in the design alliances discussed in this book. The evolution of skilled teams can occur across geographic and cultural borders, as in the global development of IBM's Notebook computers (Chapter 4). Obviously Information Technology facilitates "virtual" design alliances, but face-to-face interactions may be needed also. The Dutch design consultancy Ninaber/Peters/Krouwel had to have discussions with the Norwegian manufacturer Hamax to facilitate the design of a new and complex children's bicycle seat (Chapter 5).

PROBLEMS

However, the external designers may receive some hostility from internal staff and have problems in becoming acknowledged as the idea source for the product. This was true for Ericsson (Chapter 7) where product development was decentralised and controlled by engineers, and where the industrial design consultants experienced difficulties in being recognised at a more senior level in the company. As a consequence, the design activities were not co-ordinated at a corporate level.

Top level commitment is required if design is to be taken seriously as a strategic resource. In the cases of HAG (Chapter 5) and Novo Nordisk (Chapter 6), top level support was given to the design partnerships and to the importance of design, more generally, in the company. Also, in these cases, senior management recognised that the designers could communicate with other managers, marketers, dealers, etc. to convey more effectively the values of the product's design.

STRATEGY AND DESIGN

The cases in the book reinforce the view that designers seldom are directly involved in the formulation of their clients' strategic plans (Dreyfuss, Chapter 9 was an exception), even though their designs may influence the company's strategic direction, for example Stokke (Chapter 5) and Ingersoll-Rand (Chapter 3). Indeed, the product can become the most powerful symbol for the company. Through its philosophy of ergonomical and environmental designs, the chairmaker HAG attempted to refurnish the world. Design can build a distinctive and attractive profile by continually improving product lines.

INVESTMENT IN DESIGN RELATIONSHIPS

The six cases highlight the effort needed to develop and capitalise on design relationships. The ambitions and needs of the firms vary, but a long-term investment (at least 10 years) appears necessary if the design is to take on a strategic role to differentiate the company. For instance Richard Sapper was given the title of industrial design consultant for IBM in 1980, but the development of distinctive Notebook computers only "took off" in the 1990s. Peter Opsvik's relationships with HAG and Stokke started in 1974 and 1967 respectively, but the strategic significance of the innovative product lines did not occur before the 1980s.

The initial contact between the designers and companies appears as more or less random, but the contact of key managers and the designers is critical, for example between IBM's corporate design manager and the industrial design consultant (Chapter 4). What is important, in addition to the access to talented designers, are the continued efforts and sustained investments made in the design competence.

Design knowledge is not simply a commodity that can be easily replaced or treated as an economic exchange. Design alliances encompass a social dimension and relational dynamics, for example as in the global development of IBM's Notebook computers which involved partners from three continents (Chapter 4).

FUNDAMENTALS OF DESIGN RELATIONSHIPS

Recipes for success do not exist because they relate to the individuals concerned and the context in which they operate. Design–client relationships are, in essence, tailor-made. Nonetheless, some fundamental rules for effective partnering of client and design companies can be stated. Perhaps the most important is that of *courage* to allow for openness and the frank exchange of ideas. *Acknowledgement of design* as a valuable, or equal, partner in the development of projects is a fundamental aspect of creative relationships. *Learning from experience* is another significant feature. Companies may utilise design in an *ad hoc* manner and repeat the same mistakes and encounter the same types of problems, rather than continually improving and learning from these. Establishing long-term relationhips between client and design experts can foster trust, acknowledgement and learning, although this may not happen always, as shown by the long-term (but arm's-length) design relationships that can exist (see Chapter 11). By contrast, some of the design relationships portrayed in the cases show how design can produce substantive competitive advantages. Developing capabilities in design is a continuous process, but can reap rewards.

Unless these fundamentals of design relationships are heeded, then design will continue to have an uneasy relationship with business. Design alliances are fragile and intangible. Once destroyed, they may never be rekindled and the company will have recognised, but too late, that it has lost its creative and competitive edge.

INDEX